CAPTIVE TO THE WORD

Martin Luther: Doctor of Sacred Scripture

CAPTIVE TO THE WORD

Martin Luther: Doctor of Sacred Scripture

by

A. SKEVINGTON WOOD

B.A., Ph.D., F.R.Hist.S.

10821

*"I am bound by the Scriptures . . .
and my conscience is captive
to the Word of God".*
Martin Luther

THE PATERNOSTER PRESS

SBN: 85364 087 4

Copyright © 1969 The Paternoster Press

AUSTRALIA:
Emu Book Agencies Pty., Ltd.,
511, Kent Street, Sydney, N.S.W.

CANADA:
Home Evangel Books Ltd.,
25, Hobson Avenue, Toronto, 16

NEW ZEALAND:
G. W. Moore, Ltd.,
3, Campbell Road, P.O. Box 24053,
Royal Oak, Auckland, 6

SOUTH AFRICA:
Oxford University Press,
P.O. Box 1141, Thibault House,
Thibault Square, Cape Town

Made and Printed in Great Britain for
The Paternoster Press Paternoster House
3 Mount Radford Crescent Exeter Devon
by Cox & Wyman Limited Fakenham

CONTENTS

CONTENTS

PREFACE

"LUTHER LIVED IN THE CLIMATE OF THE BIBLE, NOT as if in the sunlit archipelago of a few chosen books; rather he was at home in the whole continent of Holy Writ, and was the first biblical cosmopolitan for over a millennium." So writes Bertram Lee Woolf, and the correctness of his estimate is being increasingly recognized today. Luther is indeed one of the pivotal figures in current dialogue, and the whole question of his relationship to Scripture is of major significance. If we are to reach a right judgment on the theological issues which now confront us, we cannot afford to ignore the contribution of the pioneer reformer. He represents something more than merely an echo of the past. Because his supreme concern was to transmit the Word of God, his is still a living and therefore a relevant voice.

The full measure of Luther's stature is presently emerging into view. "Even if Christianity disappeared so that he survived only as a maker of myths," Sir Herbert Butterfield has declared, "he would still be a colossal figure – almost the greatest of the giants in modern times." But, of course, Luther's essential contribution lay in the realm of faith. He was the instrument of God in recalling the Church to the truth of the gospel. It is as the progenitor of the Protestant Reformation that he is to be assessed today. And it is recognized that the renewal he initiated was in the first instance theological rather than either ecclesiastical or political. It arose, moreover, from his own encounter with God in the Scriptures. It was because he thus experienced divine grace in Christ, through the medium of the written Word, that henceforward the Bible was to be central in the Reformation. Throughout his career as a remodeller of the Church, Luther occupied the chair of biblical exegesis at the University of Wittenberg. As he himself often explained, it was simply as he fulfilled his academic function of expounding the Word of God that the Reformation was effected. The title he most cherished was "Doctor of Sacred Scripture".

Our approach to Luther in these ecumenical times is immeasurably facilitated by the virtual disappearance of previous caricatures. There was a Roman Catholic distortion which presented Luther as a renegade monk whose revolt against the papacy was motivated largely by pique. There was a Protestant legend which deprived him of all the temperamental traits that make him seem so human, and blew him up into a king-size

Gothic hero figure who put to flight the armies of the alien. Happily, each of these caricatures is now emphatically repudiated by responsible historians, whether Protestant or Roman. More recently, a psychological reinterpretation of Luther has been attempted by scholars like J. Paul Reiter and Erik Erikson, which might unfortunately encourage the perpetuation of a further misunderstanding. It is to be hoped that this pseudo-Freudian mock-up of a Luther whom the historians find hard to recognize will be discarded as resolutely as the two former misrepresentations, and that we may be left free to meet him as he really was, untrammelled by preconceptions. This man and his Bible provide the theme for the present study.

No claim is made to originality, except in the organization and projection of the material. The footnotes sufficiently indicate the range of my indebtedness. The only justification for such an undertaking as this is that comparatively little has been written on the subject in English. My aim has been to put the general reader in the picture: there is scant likelihood that the specialist will come across much that he has not seen somewhere before. But in this country such specialists are rare, and the need to know more about Luther is great. It is this consideration that has prompted me to rush in, no doubt foolishly, where angels fear to tread! Wherever possible I have tried to let Luther speak for himself, making use of the latest English translations as these are available. A historian's passion for accuracy has compelled me to provide references to a considerable number of German sources, but it would be misleading to imply from these a general familiarity on my part with such literature.

In addition to recording my gratitude to the publishers and printers, along with a list of libraries too lengthy to itemize, it is a particular pleasure to mention two teachers without whose help and inspiration such a work as this would hardly have been possible. The project was first discussed more than twenty years ago with my former Principal at New College, Edinburgh, the Very Reverend Doctor Hugh Watt, under whose aegis I pursued post-graduate studies. The counsel of this distinguished Church historian, who in 1967 celebrated the sixtieth anniversary of his ordination, proved invaluable. My first serious introduction to Luther research, however, dates back to my days as a theological student at Wesley College, Headingley. It was then that the Assistant Tutor succeeded in communicating to me some of his own enthusiasm for the subject. He is now Professor Philip S. Watson of Garrett Theological Seminary, Evanston, Illinois, and belongs to a select band of British-born Luther experts. To these men, and others like them who have influenced my thinking, must be attributed any merits this book may possess: its shortcomings are all my own.

York, September, 1968   A. SKEVINGTON WOOD

PART I

The Bible and Luther

LUTHER'S INTRODUCTION TO THE SCRIPTURES

IT WAS AS HE OPENED THE PAGES OF CHAPMAN'S
Homer, and feasted on the riches he found there, that John Keats became
aware of his poetic vocation. The experience gave birth to the now
familiar sonnet in which his genius first revealed itself. Previously Keats
had read Homer only in Alexander Pope's rather formal translation.
When he was introduced to the more exciting version of George Chapman
and heard him "speak out loud and bold", he tells us that he felt

> . . . like some watcher of the skies
> When a new planet swims into his ken;
> Or like stout Cortez when with eagle eyes
> He star'd at the Pacific – and all his men
> Look'd at each other with a wild surmise –
> Silent, upon a peak in Darien.[1]

Such was Martin Luther's reaction to the Word of God. His discovery
of the Scriptures marked the decisive turning-point in his career, and
destined him to be a reformer. Before he began to use the Bible to such
good effect as he set about his task of calling the Church to renewal, the
Bible had already transformed him. This, indeed, is the key to Luther's
ministry and mission.

But we cannot be sure just when it was that Luther first held a copy of
the Scriptures in his hands. The precise facts which lay behind Keats'
discovery of Chapman's Homer have been laid bare by the literary
historians.[2] It was on a summer evening in the year 1817 that his friend
Charles Cowden Clarke, son of his former schoolmaster, brought him
the precious volume. We even know that it was the folio edition of 1616,
loaned to Clarke by Alsager of *The Times*. The two young enthusiasts
were intoxicated by what they read. Keats more than once shouted aloud
in the intensity of his delight. All through the night they pored over the
pages, and the grey light of dawn found them still engrossed. That very
day Keats penned the sonnet which launched him as one of the immortals.

Luther's first acquaintance with the Bible was similarly determinative

---

[1] *The Poetical Works of John Keats*, ed. H. W. Garrod (1939), p. 45.

[2] Cf. Albert Erlande, *The Life of John Keats* (E.T. 1929), pp. 60–61; *The Cambridge History of English Literature*, ed. Sir A. W. Ward and A. R. Waller, Vol. XII, *The Nineteenth Century*, Pt. I (1915), Chap. IV "Keats" (C. H. Herford), p. 79.

for him, and of considerably greater consequence to the world. But the recorded details are much less exact. We cannot name the day, nor can we be altogether certain about the circumstances. According to a traditional story, Luther was astonished to find a copy of the Scriptures in a library whilst he was at Erfurt. One version identifies this with the University library and places the incident in the period when he was a student prior to his entry into the monastery, that is to say sometime between May 1501 and July 1505.[1] Here is how the event was described by Johann Mathesius of Joachimstal, who helped to compile the *Table Talk*. He also published the first extended biography of Luther, based on a series of sermons, from which this is an extract.

"When there were no public lectures he spent his time in the University library. On one occasion when he was carefully examining the volumes one after another, so that he might learn to know the best among them, he happened on a copy of the Latin Bible, which he had never in his life seen up to this time. Then he noticed with great amazement that it contained many more texts than those that were in the ordinary postils or were ordinarily explained from the pulpits of the churches. As he was looking through the Old Testament, he chanced to see the story of Samuel and his mother, Hannah, which he rapidly read through with great enjoyment and delight, and, because it was all new to him, he began to wish from the bottom of his heart that our good Lord would at some time bestow on him such a book as his own."[2]

Alongside this must be set a report in the *Table Talk* during the summer of 1540. "In my youth I saw a Bible in the University library and I read part of the story of Samuel, but then it was time to attend a lecture. I would very gladly have read the whole book, but at that time I had no opportunity to do so. But when I had forsaken everything to go into the cloister I once again asked for a Bible, since I had lost hope in myself."[3]

A variant of the tale appears to transfer the location from the University library to that of the Augustinian monastery at Erfurt, which would demand a date after Luther was received as a novice on the 17th July 1505. In the *Table Talk* for the 22nd February 1538, Luther is reputed to have made the following statement: "When I was twenty years old I had not yet seen a Bible. I thought that there were no Gospels and Epistles

[1] Willem Jan Kooiman, *Luther and the Bible* (E. T. 1961), p. 1.
[2] Johann Mathesius, *Historien von des ehrwirdigen Manns Gottes, Doctoris Martini Luthers, Anfang, Lehr, Leben und Sterben* (1566), p. 20; cf. J. Michael Reu, *Luther's German Bible* (1934), pp. 79–80.
[3] WATR. 5. 75. No. 5346. References to Luther's own writings are supplied throughout in abbreviated form, the first number indicating the volume and the second the page. In the case of the *Table Talk*, as here, the number of the extract is cited also. Wherever possible English translations of Luther are used, principally the new American Edition: the standard Weimar Edition, or other German collections, are only annexed where an English translation is not readily available. For a list of abbreviations see pp. 179–80.

except those which were written in the Sunday postils. Finally I found a Bible in the library and forthwith I took it with me into the monastery. I began to read, to reread, and to read it over again, to the great astonishment of Dr. Staupitz."[1] The reference to the monastery seems to be sufficiently explicit, although at the age of twenty Luther was still pursuing his preparatory studies at the University. He did not come into contact with Johann Staupitz, the vicar-general of the reformed order of Augustinian *Observantists* until later.

These discrepancies indicate that the narrative rests on an insecure historical foundation. It has, moreover, acquired a number of purely fictitious accretions, designed to underline the alleged neglect of the Scriptures during the Middle Ages. The Bible which Luther discovered was said to be chained up, hidden away, enveloped in dust, or altogether overlooked. Legendary details of this kind appear as soon as the end of the sixteenth century, as, for instance, in the editions of Luther's German translation of the Bible, which contain a brief biography of the reformer as an introduction. Most of them are hardly probable. One, however, was no doubt accurate – namely, that such a Bible would be chained. But the implication that this precaution was taken in order to prevent it being examined is the reverse of the truth. It was the valued books of constant reference which were thus permanently fastened to a reading desk.[2]

The story was further embellished with the even more unlikely suggestion that Luther's monastic superiors were displeased with his eagerness to consult the Word of God, and burdened him with extra chores in order to prevent him from fulfilling his desire. In the end it was only when his professors intervened that he was allowed to study it without interruption.

Much of this clearly belongs to Protestant legend of Luther. Some of the suspicious features were noticed by Charles Beard as far back as 1889, although he did not entirely dismiss the account.[3] Julius Köstlin and Georg Kawerau corrected several errors in 1903.[4] In point of fact, the Bible was not so seriously ignored in the Middle Ages as had been formerly imagined, and certainly not in the monasteries where its reading figured prominently in the discipline. The Augustinian Eremites in particular, like their patron, greatly reverenced the Scriptures. When Luther was admitted to the novitiate, he was presented with his own Latin Bible, with the accompanying injunction "industriously to read, thoughtfully to hear, and carefully to study" God's holy Word.[5]

[1] WATR. 3. 598. No. 3767.
[2] Kooiman, op. cit., p. 1. Ernest G. Schwiebert, *Luther and His Times: The Reformation from a New Perspective* (1950), p. 122.
[3] Charles Beard, *Martin Luther and the Reformation in Germany* (1889), p. 143.
[4] Cf. Schwiebert, op. cit., p. 122.
[5] Kooiman, op. cit., p. 2. Cf. Georg Oergel, *Vom jungen Luther* (1899), p. 82.

There are comparable difficulties involved in accepting the earlier date during Luther's University days. The regulations governing the Erfurt library did not permit undergraduates to wander in at will. They could only make use of it if escorted by a member of the teaching faculty, and in order to consult or withdraw a book they would have to enjoy a special privilege and pay a deposit.[1] It is possible, as Heinrich Boehmer hints, that a professor might have taken young Luther in with him and thus introduced him to the Bible.[2]

The majority of scholars today, however, having re-examined the Erfurt story, are extremely dubious about its authenticity as it stands. The *Table Talk* is a far from reliable source, composed as it was in a somewhat haphazard fashion by "a motley club of inferior Boswells", as Gordon Rupp has characterized them.[3] Admittedly the manuscripts which came to light at the turn of the present century have provided a much more trustworthy text than Aurifaber's original edition of 1566. But even these do not offer us verbatim reports and need to be treated with considerable caution. A careful comparison of the *Table Talk* extracts with other evidence both from Luther's own writings and elsewhere leads to the conclusion that the best-informed account of the reformer's introduction to the Bible is that supplied by Veit Dietrich who acted as Luther's amanuensis for some time, before returning to his native Nürnberg as preacher in St. Sebald's Church.

This is his version of what occurred. "Once when he was a boy he happened upon a Bible. In it he read by chance the story about Samuel's mother in the Books of the Kings. The book pleased him immensely, and he thought that he would be happy if he could ever possess such a book. Shortly thereafter he bought a postil; it also pleased him greatly, for it contained more Gospels than it was customary to preach on in the course of a year.

"When he became a monk he gave up all his books. Shortly before this he had bought a copy of the *Corpus iuris* and I do not know what else. He returned these to the bookseller. Besides Plautus and Vergil he took nothing with him into the monastery. There the monks gave him a Bible bound in red leather. He made himself so familiar with it that he knew what was on every page, and when some passage was mentioned he knew at once just where it was to be found.

"'If I had kept at it,' he said, 'I would have become exceedingly good at locating things in the Bible. At that time no other study pleased me so much as sacred literature. With great loathing I read physics, and my heart was aglow when the time came to return to the Bible. I made use of the

[1] Schwiebert, op cit, p 121
[2] Heinrich Boehmer, *Road to Reformation: Martin Luther to the Year 1521* (E.T. 1946), p. 30.
[3] E. Gordon Rupp, *The Righteousness of God: Luther Studies* (1953), p. 6.

glossa ordinaria. I despised Lyra, although I recognized later on that he had a contribution to make to history. I read the Bible diligently. Sometimes one important statement occupied all my thoughts for a whole day. Such statements appeared especially in the weightier prophets, and (although I could not grasp their meaning) they have stuck in my memory to this day. Such is the assertion in Ezekiel, "I have no pleasure in the death of the wicked," etc. (Ezek. 33: 11).'"[1]

This account by Veit Dietrich would seem to place Luther's first contact with the Scriptures in his boyhood, and yet to allow a ripening of interest during his term as a monk. Schwiebert is justified in assuming that such a sequence is most consistent with other known facts.[2] However, a technical question of textual criticism is involved. It is only in the earliest texts that Luther is referred to as a boy (*puer*) when he "happened on a Bible". Soon it was altered to *adolescens* or *baccalaureus*, presumably to fit in with the later tradition that he was already a young man or had taken his bachelor's degree.[3] But both Otto Scheel and Henri Strohl, amongst others, insist that the original reading is the most probable, and thus conclude that Luther's encounter with the Scriptures occurred neither in the Erfurt cloister nor during his University career.[4]

On the face of it, the likelihood that he should never have set eyes on a complete Bible until so late seems small. The facts of circulation militate against such a circumstance. It has been estimated that between twenty and twenty-seven thousand copies of the Vulgate were printed in Germany alone before 1520.[5] In addition to these, many thousands of handwritten facsimiles must have been available. Furthermore, the German translation of the Bible printed by Johann Mentelin of Strasburg in 1466 ran into fourteen editions in fifty years. With such an abundance, it is difficult to believe that Luther did not even catch a glimpse of one until he was out of his 'teens.

If we accept the reading of *puer* in the Veit Dietrich narrative, then we are compelled to conclude that it was whilst he was still at school that Luther made his initial acquaintance with the Scriptures. Schwiebert takes the view that it was probably whilst he was at Magdeburg that Luther was introduced to the Bible at first hand.[6] But even before this he must have had some knowledge of it. What we now know about medieval schooling dispels the impression that he could have been completely unaware of God's Word.

Until he was fourteen young Martin attended the *Ratschule*, or City School, at Mansfeld, next to St. George's Church in the central square.

[1] LW. 54. 13–14. No. 116.   [2] Schwiebert, op. cit., p. 121.   [3] Ibid.
[4] Otto Scheel, *Martin Luther, Vom Katholizismus zur Reformation* (1917), Bd. I, pp. 91–92; Henri Strohl, *L'Évolution religieuse de Luther jusqu'en 1515* (1922), pp. 47–49.
[5] Reu, op. cit., pp. 10–11.   [6] Schwiebert, op. cit., p. 119.

The school was later named after the reformer. He was probably under
five years of age when he enrolled. Here he would be drilled in the *Trivium*
of grammar, logic and rhetoric. The school was divided into three *Haufen*,
or groups. In each the lad would come to know something about the Bible
and its contents. The *Tabulisten*, or beginners, learned the rudiments of
Latin from a primer called the *Fibel*. But they also learned the Benedicite
(the prayer before meals) and the *Gratias* (the thanksgiving after meals),
the Lord's Prayer, the Ten Commandments, the Creed, the Confession of
sins, and the Hail Mary. Three times a day they went through their
recitations. The second group was composed of *Donatisten*, so named after
the Latin textbook, the *Donat*, published with a German interlinear.[1] The
pupils soon began to construe whole passages, and these were invariably
taken from Scripture – either a Psalm or some other selection from the
Vulgate. "Doubtless, Luther's later mastery of the Latin Bible, his ability
to quote verbatim almost at will even late in life," comments Schwiebert,
"dates back to the Mansfeld days."[2] Luther often complained afterwards
about the harsh discipline, but there can be little doubt that he gained
much. The upper division was known as the *Alexandristen*, from the
Doctrinale by Alexander de Villedieu, which contained more advanced
Latin grammar and syntax. These pupils also served as choirboys at matins
and vespers each day, and in the Sunday services. In order that they might
sing praises with understanding, they were taught the hymns, versicles,
responses and Psalms along with an explanation of the Scripture lections.
The impression left by some of Luther's biographers that there was little
or no biblical instruction during his schooldays obviously needs modifying.

Luther may not have reached the third stage before he was moved from
Mansfeld to Magdeburg. Historians have tried to establish what school it
was that Luther attended. It was once thought to be the celebrated
Stadtschule, but this did not exist before the Reformation. Amongst the
parochial schools of Magdeburg, that of St. John's was the most outstanding, but it seems doubtful whether Luther was ever a pupil. Luther
himself supplies a clue, for he once disclosed the fact that he had gone to
school with the *Nullbrüder*, or Brethren of the Common Life. Their nick-
name was derived from their self-abnegation – making themselves null
and void.[3] These Zerobrothers, as we might now call them, did not have
a school of their own in Magdeburg, but it has been established that three

[1] LW. 41. 350; 54. 235. No. 3566a. It was named after Aelius Donatus who lived in the
fourth century. Luther described him as "the best grammarian" (LW. 54. 211. No. 3490).
[2] Schwiebert, op. cit., pp. 111–12.
[3] Schwiebert (op. cit., p. 119) thinks that the name *Nullbrüder* was connected with their low
singing or "lollen" in their devotions. He quotes EA. 29. 370; End. 3. 402. n. 3 and Scheel,
op. cit., Bd. I, pp. 78–82. The names of Lollards or Nollards seem to have been supplied by
their enemies, cf. NSH. 3. 174; 7. 69. For the contribution of the *Nullbrüder* to education, *vide*
Kenneth S. Latourette, *A History of the Expansion of Christianity*, Vol. II, *The Thousand Years of
Uncertainty A.D. 500–A.D. 1500* (1959), p. 393; CE. 4. 167.

or four of their community taught at the *Domschule*, or Cathedral School. It would look as if this was where Luther was registered.

If so, he could hardly have escaped the strongly biblical influence of the *Nullbrüder*. The Brethren of the Common Life had their rise in Holland, The principal figures in their foundation were Geerte de Groote, a Canon of Utrecht, and his friend Florentius Radewijns. Their aim was to foster a higher level of Christian life and devotion in the Church. Thomas à Kempis was of their company. They laid unusual emphasis on the Scriptures and were active in the distribution of Bibles in the language of the people. It would appear that whilst at the *Domschule* Luther not only gained his first sight of a complete volume of Scripture, but also through the Brethren came to know more of its content and significance. It is understandable that he had not actually seen a Bible for himself before this, for his instruction at Mansfeld would be by the blackboard and wax tablets. The boys did not use many books themselves.

According to Veit Dietrich, Luther bought a postil very soon after he had come across the Bible. This would be a collection of Scripture passages used in the liturgy of the Church (later termed pericopes), together with glosses or abbreviated expositions of them. The official title was the *Plenarium*. Luther must have heard about it at Mansfeld, but now he managed to get one for himself. It would contain considerably more selections from Scripture than the Epistles and Gospels for each Sunday. There were about five times the number of those used at the normal weekly service, including many from the Old Testament. In the first German *Plenarium* to be printed there were no less than two hundred and forty extracts. In addition there were another two hundred and seventy related to saint's days. When he got hold of his postil, Luther was able to read a great deal of the Bible as often as he wished.

We know that dozens of such books were printed in German from 1743 onwards. They were a help to those who had to preach, as well as to worshippers who would prepare themselves for divine service in this way and to others who, like the youthful Luther, wanted to brood on the Word of God. There were so many of the postils available that the cost was not exceptionally high. Five were sold in Leipzig in 1510 for a gulden: a fatted ox fetched three gulden in the market.[1] Nevertheless, it was quite a sum for a schoolboy. It is a mark of his keenness that he was ready to save his pocket money and maybe take on some jobs so as to be able to buy one.

After only a year at Magdeburg, Luther's parents transferred him, for some reason still not clear, to the parish school of St. George's at Eisenach in Thuringia. Later he always thought of Eisenach as "his beloved town".[2] The *Georgenschule* had not been particularly distinguished in the fifteenth

[1] Kooiman, op. cit., p. 9   [2] WA. 30. ii. 576.

century, but just about the time when Luther went there the standard had been raised by the advent of several notable new teachers. Two of them made a marked impression on the boy. One was the rector, Johann Trebonius, who was rather extravagantly praised by Melanchthon. Matthäus Ratzeberger, court physician to the Count of Mansfeld, who later acted as guardian for Luther's children, spoke of Trebonius as a highly respected man of learning. The tale of his raising his hat in front of his scholars since he did not know what any one of them might eventually become, bears the stamp of *post factum* fabrication. The other teacher of calibre was Wigand Gueldenkampf of Fritzlar, who was to serve afterwards as a pastor at Waltershausen. Luther recalled his indebtedness to him and endeavoured to secure a pension for him from the Elector in 1526. The curriculum was that of the typical *Trivialschule* and Luther would be classed amongst the *Alexandristen* at this period. Some have wondered whether it was at Eisenach that he came into touch with the humanism of the renascence, but this is improbable. He was, however, influenced by Johann Braun, the vicar of St. Mary's and superior of the Franciscan monastery at the foot of the Wartburg. It may well have been that Braun noted the youth's zeal and devotion, together with his love for the Bible, and planted a seed in his mind which led to his entry into the cloister at Erfurt.

Luther went to Erfurt from school, but not to go into the religious community immediately. He matriculated from the University in May 1501, and occupied a hall of residence, the *Georgenburse*. There he would hear a chapter from the Bible each day at table, and he himself would take his turn in reading the lessons. His studies for the law included logic which, as in the case of John Wesley, equipped him for his future ministry and made him one of the most acute controversialists of his time. When in 1505 Luther fulfilled his vow and entered the Augustinian monastery, he was presented, as he himself tells us, with his own copy of the Bible in Latin, bound in red leather.[1] The rules of his order required him to devote himself to the mastering of its contents. This stipulation had been re-emphasized by the vicar-general in 1504 with respect to the German communities. The master of novices had the responsibility of seeing that it was observed. In view of these facts, we cannot accept the truth of the tradition that Luther as a newly-fledged monk fell foul of his superiors through his longing to search the Scriptures.

When he was ordained to the priesthood in 1507, Luther was enrolled in the theological school of his order where he embarked on a course of study which included exegesis as well as dogmatics. This was no doubt the time to which he referred when he gained such an intimate knowledge of the Bible, and when no other pursuit was so pleasing to him as sacred

[1] LW. 54. 14. No. 116.

literature. When he moved over to Wittenburg in 1508, he had to leave his beloved leather-bound copy in the cloister, much to his sorrow. But he found others in the monastery in Wittenberg, and was thus able to continue his daily reading of the Word.[1] In 1509 as a *baccalaureus ad Biblia* he began to lecture in biblical subjects, and in 1512 he was appointed for life to the *lectura in Biblia*. His doctorate in sacred Scripture equipped him to take up the post from which he launched the Reformation – the chair of biblical exegesis at the University of Wittenberg.

A collateral question to the one we have been seeking to answer about Luther's introduction to the Scriptures concerns the time when he first began to use the original text of the Old and New Testaments. The Vulgate, of course, was the accepted version in the Church of his day. Luther began to learn Hebrew soon after the publication of Johann Reuchlin's *De Rudimentis Hebraicis* in 1506. This combined grammar and dictionary heralded a new era in the acquisition of the language, and Luther was quick to take advantage of it. By 1509 it was evident that he had made good progress and had profited from his application, for in the marginal notes to the *Sentences* of Peter Lombard, on which he lectured, he began to show the signs of his skill.[2] When he referred in his *Dictata Super Psalterium* (1513–1515) to the "Hebraeus", he meant simply Jerome's Latin translation of the Psalms, and not the Hebrew text itself. But it is equally clear that very soon he used Reuchlin's *Septem Psalmi Poenitentes* (1512), with its setting out of the original Hebrew along with a Latin translation and short expository notes. By the time he came in 1517 to compose his own exposition of the Penitential Psalms designed for laymen, he no longer adhered to the Vulgate as authoritative, but turned to the Hebrew in Reuchlin's edition instead. In his *Operationes in Psalmos* (1518 to 1520) Luther was completely emancipated from the Vulgate and worked on the Hebrew text as the basis of his comments. He had received the edition of the entire Psalter in Hebrew, published in 1516, as a gift from his friend Johann Lang, prior of the Erfurt cloister. Luther had evidently mastered the language sufficiently to start out from the original. From this point on, as Michael Reu brings out, it was decisive for him.[3]

Luther took up the study of Greek at a later date than his wrestling with Hebrew. First Johann Lang, who had taught at Wittenberg, and then Philip Melanchthon, who became Professor of Greek there in 1518 acted as his tutors. In February 1516, Erasmus' edition of the Greek New Testament appeared: when it came to Wittenberg in August of the same year, Luther made use of it right away in preparing his course on Romans. Henceforward he always worked from the original text. His Bible translation bears ample testimony to his familiarity both with Hebrew and

---

[1] J. Michael Reu, *Luther and the Scriptures* (1944), pp. 7–8.
[2] Ibid., p. 8.　　　　　　　　　　[3] Ibid., p. 9.

Greek.[1] Luther was a man of one book, the best of books, and he knew it through and through in the languages in which it was written. The Church was to be reformed according to the Word of God. Providence saw to it that the one who was chosen to lead that Reformation was himself steeped in the Scriptures.

CHAPTER II

LUTHER'S STRUGGLE FOR FAITH

T HE BIOGRAPHERS OF LUTHER – ESPECIALLY THE MORE
recent ones – have devoted many pages and even chapters to his agonizing
search for peace of soul. Some have been mainly concerned to sift the
factual evidence, and there is a measure of confusion in the sources. Some
have sought to relate Luther's spiritual awakening to his theological
development, and this connexion must never be overlooked. Some have
probed deep into Luther's complex personality with the aid of psychological criteria and have exposed hitherto unrecognized factors, not all of
which bear the stamp of verisimilitude.[1]

Yet the abiding fascination of Luther's struggle for faith does not reside
in any of these more theoretical aspects. What holds our interest is the
realization that all of us share to some degree in the great reformer's
experiences. Luther was no mystical figure, removed from the sin and
strife of life as we know it, but a man of like passions with ourselves. His
is the quest of everyman for a valid and satisfying form of belief. Our
concern, as Roland Bainton suggests, is not so much with the disease as
with the cure. "How was it that Luther, despite his travailing of spirit,
could be so tremendous in his faith, so incredible in his courage, so
astounding in his output?"[1] Those who are involved in Luther's battle
long to taste his victory.

It is our purpose in this chapter to trace Luther's conflict of soul before
his crucial encounter with a gracious God at Wittenberg, and to show
how it was only as he came to a fuller understanding of the Scriptures that
he was led out of the darkness of doubt and frustration into the light of
assurance and fulfilment. But it would be unrealistic to imply that
Luther's struggle was confined to the period prior to his illumination.
This would be an oversimplification, as well as a distortion of the facts.
Luther never altogether ceased to struggle. The Christian life for him
was always a warfare. Faith was not passive acquiescence, but "a living
busy, active mighty thing".[2] No longer, of course, did he have to agonize
for faith, but he continually agonized *in* faith. And on occasions the contest
was fierce indeed.

It was not until he entered the monastery that Luther became aware of

[1] Roland H. Bainton, *Studies on the Reformation* (1964), p. 13.
[2] LW. 35. 370.

spiritual tensions in an acute form. There had indeed been some hints in his childhood and youth which presaged the impending onslaught, but he had supposed that when he became a monk his problems would be resolved. Just the reverse proved to be the case, for he found that the medieval prescription for anxiety failed to meet his need. It was as a result of his dissatisfaction with the traditional remedy that he was compelled to seek for another, and was ultimately enabled to find it through the guidance of God's Word. Luther's struggle for faith took place, then, during his years between his reception into the Augustinian cloister at Erfurt in 1505 and his *Türmerlebnis*, or tower experience, which probably occurred in 1514.[1]

Before we deal with that critical period, a word must be said about what preceded it. We cannot altogether set aside the influence of Luther's upbringing. The child is father to the man. As Vivian Green reminds us, "he imbibed and never lost the religious mythology of his peasant background."[2] There was a curious mixture of the Gothic and the Christian in what he had been taught to believe. It left him with a sharpened awareness of the supernatural, and in particular of the antipathy between the forces of good and evil. The universe was a stage on which was acted out the drama of redemption. The devil and all his satellites were locked in unending conflict with the armies of our God and of His Christ. No doubt the victory would be won – indeed it had been won at the cross and the empty tomb – but the assurance of final triumph did not altogether relieve the intensity of the contemporary contest.

This sense of strain was accentuated by the conception of God which had been engendered by Luther's environment and early training. It would not be true to say that he had never heard of God as Father, but that aspect of His character was nevertheless obscured by a much more vivid emphasis on His anger. He was a wielder of thunderbolts who might at any moment strike down those who displeased Him, and who at the close of life would consign to unspeakable tortures those who had failed to reach the required standard of behaviour in His sight. This frightening portrait of a God whose wrath was untempered with mercy even cast its shadow on the face of his Son, the Saviour. Luther found no more comfort in Christ than he had in the Father. "From childhood on I knew I had to turn pale and be terror-stricken when I heard the name of Christ; for I was taught only to see him as a strict and wrathful judge."[3] Little wonder, then, that throughout his adolescence Luther was subject to moods of depression, and that in the six months before he decided to take the monastic vow he was in a veritable agony.

[1] Cf. below, p. 57.
[2] Vivian H. H. Green, *Luther and the Reformation* (1964), p. 28; cf. Robert H. Fife, *The Revolt of Martin Luther* (1957), pp. 12–14.
[3] EA. 1.261. Cf. Scheel, op. cit., Bd. I, p. 20.

Luther's struggle for faith, falling as it does in the period when he was a monk first in Erfurt and then in Wittenberg, is flanked by two decisive experiences. At the farthest extreme stands his encounter with God in the tower. This we might well regard as his evangelical conversion, although we must not press the parallel too hard. But at the outset there is his call to the cloister, and this carries with it some of the features of a crisis experience. Certainly it was in the providence of God that Luther was brought into the Augustinian community, for it was here that he came to recognize his need of grace, and here too that he was able to look into the Word and find out how he could get right with God. To be sure, there was much anguish of spirit and many sore buffetings to be endured, but we cannot dismiss Luther's entry into the monastery as a mere accident.

Crotus Rubeanus, who had been a room-mate of Luther in his hall of residence at Erfurt, and who blossomed forth as one of the leading humanists of the age, wrote to the reformer in 1519 to encourage him in his task. He reminded Luther that God himself had destined him for his mission when he was flung to the ground outside the town of Erfurt by a stab of lightning. This was what drove Luther into the monastery, and Crotus Rubeanus did not hesitate to compare what happened to the experience of Saul of Tarsus on the Damascus road.[1] Luther himself has left a statement in an open letter to his father which was prefixed to his tract *Monastic vows* (1521). In it he reveals that he did not become a monk by his own choice, but was "called by terrors from heaven,".... "walled in by the terror and the agony of sudden death and forced by necessity to take the vow."[2]

According to the *Table Talk*, Luther recalled in 1539 that the 2nd of July was the anniversary of the momentous day when he entered the priory.[3] He identified the spot as Stotternheim, about a mile north from Erfurt. He was so frightened by the thunderstorm that when he was thrown down he invoked the aid of St. Anne, the mother of the Virgin Mary, and there and then pledged himself to become a religious. It may well have been, as Boehmer suggests, that the lightning was merely the catalyst of a decision which had been building up in Luther's mind over many months or even years.[4] He himself informs us that the melancholia which overtook him in the spring of 1505 arose from a spiritual source. It has been thought by some that the sudden death of a fellow-student of whom he had been particularly fond was the occasion of Luther's depression, but there was more to it than that. It was, so he says, *tentatio tristitiae*, anxiety over his sins and fear of judgment to come.[5]

Luther's decision to enter the monastery, then, was not the result of un-

[1] WAB. 1. 543.
[2] LW 48. 332; WATR. 4. 440. No. 4707; cf. Oergel, op. cit., p. 27.
[3] WATR. 4. 440. No. 4707.   [4] Boehmer, op. cit., p. 34.   [5] Ibid., p. 33.

premeditated impulse. It is more likely that, as Boehmer puts it, "a resolution which had long been prepared for in the inner struggles of the last month, but which had been repressed until now by doubts and scruples of one kind or another, suddenly came to expression in that moment of extreme nervous tension. For Luther was one of those men who make decisions only after long and tenacious struggles, but whose decisions are crystallized abruptly in a moment of tempestuous activity. We may even conclude that, inwardly, he was already on the way to the monastery before the lightning flashed down on him at Stotternheim. The convulsive fear which seized him in that moment only hastened the decision but did not call forth the mood from which it sprang."[1] Strohl comes to a similar conclusion: "The stroke of lightning merely made him aware of what was already in his soul."[2]

Whatever may have led up to Luther's vow, the consequences which flowed from it were considerable. Although it was to point him down a road which did not bring him to his desired destination, it nevertheless marks the beginning of his preparation as a reformer. He now advertised the fact that he wanted to give his life to God. Although not at all in the way which he himself envisaged, God took him at his word. In one sense, everything that Luther eventually became stems from this decision. "The kept vow," declares John M. Todd, "is a pivot from which in general proceed all the later developments."[3] Luther had a profound impression which never left him, that somehow his life had been overruled from above. It was not so much that he had made a vow, but that a vow had been made for him.[4]

There were no less than six monasteries in Erfurt at this time. There was the Benedictine abbey on Peter's Hill, the Carthusian in the southern area, the Dominican convent on the left bank of the river, the Franciscan on the right, and the little cloister of the Servites, or servants of the Virgin, at the Krämpfer Gate, in addition to the Augustinian chapter-house. Why, asks Boehmer, did Luther choose the latter? There is no specific clue in Luther's writings, but the supposition is that he opted for the Black Cloister, as it was commonly known, because here "he could hope soonest to reach the goal of 'evangelical perfection' toward which he was striving".[5] The Erfurt chapter was attached to the stricter Observantist wing of the Eremites, originally founded in Italy but later introduced into Germany with a reformed constitution. It had a reputation as being the foremost centre of spiritual life. No doubt this was what prompted Luther to apply for admission. He was concerned to save his soul, and this seemed the likeliest place to help him. He was to be disappointed in the guidance he

[1] Ibid., p. 34.   [2] Strohl, op. cit., p. 59.
[3] John M. Todd, Martin Luther: A Biographical Study (1964), p. 25.
[4] LW. 54. 109. No. 623, 338. No. 4414.   [5] Boehmer, op. cit., p. 36.

got, but the very failure of even the best in monasticism drove him to the Word and to the feet of God alone.

Until September 1505 Luther was on probation, so that the state of his soul might be observed and it could be made clear that his call was indeed of God. At his reception as a novice, the first question put to him by the prior, Winand von Diedenhofen, was one which went to the heart of the matter as far as Luther was concerned. "What do you desire?" he was asked. And his reply, according to the rubric, was equally significant: "God's grace and mercy." After he was invested with his habit – a white house-dress over which a black mantle was worn, with a leather sash – the prior closed the ceremony with these words: "The Lord clothe you with the new man, according to which you were created in righteousness and true holiness." At his profession for the priesthood in September 1506, the prior admonished him in the customary fashion: "Keep this rule, and I promise you eternal life."[1] This, of course, was the disciplinary code of his order. Luther was determined at all costs to be obedient. "I had no other thoughts, but to keep my rule."[2]

How diligent he was in this respect is indicated by independent evidence. In 1543 the Jena theologian, Matthias Flacius, met a friar who had been with Luther at Erfurt, and who readily conceded that he "lived a holy life among them, kept the rule most exactly, and studied diligently."[3] This was Luther's own testimony. "For I was a good monk, and kept strictly to my order, so that I could say that if the monastic life could get a man to heaven, I should have entered: all my companions who knew me would bear witness to that."[4] Attempts have been made in the past to cast doubts on the integrity of Luther in this respect. It used to be part of the stock-in-trade of Roman Catholic denigrators like Denifle and Grisar to make out that he was irresponsible and undisciplined, if not also morally depraved.[5] Joseph Lortz has repudiated this misrepresentation on the part of his biased predecessors in the line of anti-Protestant polemic, and another son of Rome, Thomas M. McDonough, can rejoice to report that "all historians of our age agree that the material evidence portrays Luther as a zealous and exemplary Augustinian, obedient to his superiors and faithful to the monastic rule".[6]

In all this, his aim was solely to please God and not man. Luther did not have it in him to be double-minded. "I myself was a monk for twenty years. I tortured myself with prayers, fasting, vigils, and freezing: the frost alone might have killed me. It caused me pain such as I will never

[1] WA. 51. 83; 40. i. 244.   [2] WA. 47. 92; 40 ii. 15.   [3] Scheel, op. cit., Bd I, p. 10 n. i.
[4] WA. 38. 143. Cf. WA. 40. i. 685 – "ego war ein rechter fromer Monch"; LW. 26. 458.
[5] Heinrich Denifle, *Luther und Lutherthum*, Bd. I (1904), pp. 215-18, 245-51; Hartmann Grisar, *Luther*, Vol. I (E.T. 1913), pp. 26, 79, 110-12.
[6] Joseph Lortz, *Die Reformation in Deutschland* (1941), Bd. I, p. 159; Thomas M. McDonough, *The Law and the Gospel in Luther* (1963), p. 31.

inflict on myself again, even if I could. What else did I seek by doing this but God, who was supposed to note my strict observance of the monastic order and my austere life? . . . . . . I did all this for the sake of God, not for money or goods."[1] His self-inflicted privations were harsh indeed. Luther was not the man to do things by halves. If there was anything in asceticism, then he must go all the way with it. "I vexed myself with fasts and prayers beyond what was common," he admitted.[2] And later he declared: "If I could have got to heaven by fasting, I would have merited that twenty years ago."[3]

But all his fierce self-punishment did not bring him peace. How could it? He was seeking to appease an angry God by the sacrifice of himself. But he had no personal knowledge of the One he was serving. This he could only find in Christ, and as yet Luther had not come to know Him. "For I did not believe in Christ: I regarded Him only as a severe and terrible judge, portrayed as seated on a rainbow. Therefore I cast about for other intercessors, Mary and various other saints, also my own works and the merits of my order. . . . Nevertheless this was heresy and idolatry, since I did not know Christ and did not seek in and through Him what I wanted."[4] And again: "In the monastery I lost my soul's welfare and salvation and my body's health, while I imagined that I knew God the Father intimately, and that it was God's will that I keep the monastic rule and obey the abbot. This, I assumed, would please God and was a knowledge of the Father and of the Father's will."[5] But since Luther had no knowledge of Christ, he could not possibly be in conscious communion with God, for no one comes to the Father but by the Son. Luther was to learn and confess that "God has ordained that He would not communicate with man through any other medium than Christ alone".[6]

Yet before he gained deliverance, Luther went through untold agonies not only of physical mortification but also of mental uncertainty. He piled confession on confession, penance on penance, denial on denial. It was all to no avail. When he had done all, he knew himself to be an unprofitable servant. He would chastise himself with the fear of insufficiency: "You did not do that properly. You were **not** contrite enough. You left this out of your confession." "The more I tried to remedy an uncertain, weak, and afflicted conscience with the traditions of men, the more each day I found it more uncertain, weaker, and more troubled."[7] So he stepped up the frequency and intensity of his self-discipline, yet still without achieving ease. "The more I sweated it out like this, the less peace and tranquillity I knew."[8] After a welter of flagellation, he would find himself asking: "Who knows whether such things are pleasing to God?"[9]

[1] LW. 24. 23–24.   [2] WA. 40. ii. 574.   [3] Ibid., 453.
[4] LW. 24. 24.   [5] WA. 33. 561.   [6] Ibid.
[7] WA. 40. ii. 15.   [8] WA. 44. 819.   [9] WA. 40. ii. 414.

Commenting later on Galatians 5:17, which epitomized the struggle in his soul, Luther reminisced: "When I was a monk, I used to think that my salvation was undone when I felt any desires of the flesh, that is any malice or sexual desire or anger or envy against any of my brothers. I tried many methods. I made confession every day, etc. But none of this did any good, because the desires of the flesh kept coming back. Therefore I could not find peace, but I was constantly crucified by such thoughts as these: 'You have committed this or that sin; you are guilty of envy, impatience, etc. Therefore it was useless for you to enter this holy order, and all your good works are to no avail.'"[1]

It is fashionable nowadays to dismiss all this as the outcome of a too tender conscience. Luther is classified as a scrupulant. It is said that undue perfectionism is "one of the occupational diseases of the religious."[2] Certainly it was on this score that Luther's spiritual advisers in the priory eventually lost patience with him, although Staupitz never abandoned him.[3] But even allowing for such a factor, Luther's malaise cannot be diagnosed only in this way. There was an underlying reason for his distress. Although, to quote McDonough, "he worked, worked, worked to do *quod in se est*," he still did not feel in his heart the perfect love of God which was demanded of him by the ascetic ideal, nor did he find deliverance from his bondage.[4] In his own words: "though I lived as a monk beyond reproach, I felt that I was a sinner before God, with an extremely disturbed conscience. . . ."[5] It was not that his disturbed conscience made him a sinner: it was rather that because he was a sinner his conscience was disturbed.

It must not be forgotten that all this time Luther was more and more under the scrutiny of God's Word. We have seen how even before he entered the monastery he had been delving into his postil. On his reception into the community he was presented with his red leather-bound Bible. It was then that he soaked himself in it so thoroughly that he could turn up any text he wanted. It was not to be expected perhaps that, with so much medieval lee-way to make up, he should all at once get to the heart of the saving message. It would seem that the strange work of the law (*opus alienum*) paved the way for the proper work of the gospel (*opus proprium*). The aroma of Christ was a fragrance of death to death before it became a fragrance from life to life (II Cor. 2:16). The depth of self-despair into which Luther was plunged may have been induced to some extent by the reading of the Scriptures, which kill before they quicken.

Those who have looked for a psychological explanation of Luther's vicissitudes as a monk have interpreted his faltering at his first celebration

[1] LW. 27. 73.   [2] Todd, op. cit., p. 50.
[3] WATR. 1. 125. No. 302; WA. 26. 55.
[4] McDonough, op. cit., p. 37.   [5] LW. 34. 336.

of the mass in terms of a father-complex. Hans Luther was present, and afterwards at the festive meal which followed, rather crudely queried his son's call to the priesthood. But it is much more probable that what brought the young celebrant to a temporary halt was an overwhelming sense of his own sinfulness in the sight of a holy God. This, moreover, had been stimulated by the words of Scripture in the Sanctus, which immediately preceded: "Holy, Holy, Holy, Lord God of Hosts, heaven and earth are full of thy glory. Hosanna in the highest. Blessed is he who comes in the name of the Lord. Hosanna in the highest." It was as he reached the prayer beginning: "Therefore, O most merciful Father. . . ." that Luther was so overcome as to be unable to continue for a few moments. He was so stupefied that he might have fled, had he not been under the eye of the prior.[1]

Many years later Luther recalled the incident in conversation with his friends. "For when I read the words, 'Thee, therefore, most merciful Father,' etc., and thought I had to speak to God without a Mediator, I felt like fleeing from the world like Judas. Who can bear the majesty of God without Christ as Mediator?"[2] And on another occasion he gave this account: "At these words I was utterly stupefied and terror-stricken. I thought to myself, 'With what tongue shall I address such majesty, seeing that all men ought to tremble in the presence even of an earthly prince? Who am I, that I should lift up mine eyes or raise my hands to the divine majesty? The angels surround Him. At His nod the earth trembles. And shall I, a miserable little pigmy, say, 'I want this, I ask for that?' For I am dust and ashes and full of sin and I am speaking to the living, the eternal and the true God."[3]

It is Lortz who draws attention to the fact that it was something from the Word of God which arrested Luther.[4] Nothing was more typical of the reformer than that he should react like this to a phrase from Scripture, detached as it was from its context. With the hindsight we now possess, it is not difficult to discern the voice of God Himself speaking through His appointed medium of the Word. There is no evidence to indicate that Luther really tried to run away from the altar. The pause was only momentary. But, as Todd remarks, "it remained for Luther a milestone in the building of his own spiritual outlook, his religious life."[5]

Whilst inclining to the view that Luther derived more help than he realized from his study of the Scriptures, we must not depreciate the assistance he received from his superiors. In the end, they felt powerless to speak to his condition, and, with the exception of Staupitz, evidently wrote him off as a hopeless case. But this is not to say that they failed to

---

[1] LW. 54. 234. No. 3556a; cf. 325. No. 4174.   [2] Ibid., 234. No. 3556a.

[3] WA. 43. 382; cf. LW. 4. 340. Luther linked *Te igitur* with a quotation garbled from the offertory (cf. Fife, op. cit., p. 100 n. 49).

[4] Lortz, op. cit., Bd. I., p. 161.   [5] Todd, op. cit., p. 40.

do their best, according to their lights. Several of them Luther remembered with gratitude in later years. There was Johann von Grefenstein, the "fine old man" who had charge of Luther as a novice.[1] There was the prior himself, Winand von Diedenhofen. There was Johann Nathin who super-intended Luther's theological studies after his ordination, and referred to his pupil as a "new St. Paul converted by Christ himself".[2]

But Luther owed most of all to Johann Staupitz, the vicar-general of the order. It was he who held the chair of biblical exegesis at Wittenberg before Luther was appointed to it. Staupitz took a kindly interest in Luther from his first meeting with him and later wrote about his affection as "passing the love of women".[3] Luther reciprocated the friendship and cherished a high regard for Staupitz. But it is clear that he was indebted to his preceptor for something more than a tender concern for his welfare. Luther's tribute is crisp but touching. "He bore me to Christ."[4] That is the most any man can do for another. "If Dr. Staupitz had not helped me out," he confessed, "I should have been swallowed up and left in hell."[5] And what he admitted to others, Luther did not withhold from Staupitz himself. "I cannot forget or be ungrateful, for it was through you that the light of the gospel began first to shine out of the darkness of my heart."[6] The core of his counsel was this, as Luther recalled in 1542: "Why do you trouble yourself with these speculations of yours? Accept the wounds of Christ and contemplate the blood which poured forth from His most holy body for our sins — for mine, for yours, for those of all men. 'My sheep hear My voice.'"[7] No wonder Luther referred to him as "my spiritual father in Christ" and "the man who first suggested to me the teachings I now embrace".[8]

These, however, were but men. At most they could put Luther on the right way, as they spoke of Christ and sent him back to the Word. But Luther's struggle for faith would not end until, without any human intermediary, he stood before God to plead no merits of his own but only those of the Redeemer. "I was often frightened by the name of Christ," he confessed, "and when I looked upon Him and the cross, He seemed to me like a flash of lightning. When His name was mentioned, I would rather have heard the devil mentioned, for I believed that I would have

[1] Boehmer, op. cit., p. 40.
[2] Schwiebert, op. cit., p. 151. Cf. R. Kohlschmidt, "Luther im Kloster der Augustiner-Eremiten zu Erfurt 1505–1511" Luther, Vierteljahrsschrift, Bd. XIII (1931), p. 45.
[3] Rupp. op. cit., p. 117. On the indebtedness of Luther to his vicar-general vide Ernst Wolf, "Staupitz und Luther", Quellen und Forschungen zur Reformationsgeschichte, Bd. IX (1927).
[4] Dok., 512.   [5] WA. 58. i. 28.   [6] End. 4. 231; cf. 5. 122.
[7] LCC. 18. 134. Cf. LW. 54. 97. No. 526 – "My good Staupitz said, 'One must keep one's eyes fixed on that man who is called Christ.'"
[8] LCC. 18. 189. Cf. LW. 54. 97. No. 526 – "Staupitz is the one who started the teaching of the gospel in our time." Boehmer (op. cit., p. 107) contends that Staupitz was nevertheless still very far from the gospel.

to do good works until Christ was made gracious to me through them[1]."
That was Luther's pitiable state as he sought some solid ground to rest
upon and could not find it. But soon he could rejoice in discovery: "Thank
God we again have his Word, which pictures and portrays Christ as our
righteousness."[2] It was as he kept at his scanning of the Scriptures that at
last the light of hope dawned. For as Boehmer underlines, "from the very
beginning his struggle for a gracious God was at the same time a struggle
for a right understanding of the Bible".[3]

[1] WA. 47. 590.
[2] Ibid.
[3] Boehmer, op. cit., p. 91.

CHAPTER III

LUTHER'S DEBT TO THE PAST

T HE ATTEMPT TO RECOUNT THE SPIRITUAL SAGA OF
Martin Luther from the angle of his biblical motivation must be broken
off for the meantime in order that consideration may be given to his
theological development. The pilgrim's progress cannot be divorced from
the battle for the mind. Whilst Luther struggled to find a faith for living,
he also strove to grasp the key which unlocks the treasury of the revealed
Word, on which all authentically Christian doctrine must needs be based.
Any adequate account of Luther's growth in theological understanding
has to include an assessment of his indebtedness to Christian thinkers who
preceded him and whose works he consulted. Increasingly he learned to
look to the Scriptures alone for guidance: at this stage, however, he did
so partly as he copied his predecessors. Those to whom he expressed his
deepest gratitude for the way in which they had come to his aid, were
themselves men who took the Bible seriously. They taught Luther to do
the same, although later he used the yardstick with which they had
supplied him to measure their own teaching, and in some instances to
expose its insufficiency. But he was candid enough to acknowledge how
much he owed to those from whom he ultimately differed in important
respects.

This linkage between Luther and the tradition of the Church would
have surprised many of his contemporary opponents, who regarded him
as a dangerous innovator and a deviationist from accepted doctrines. If it
were to be conceded that he was in any way related to the historical past,
it would have been alleged that he was a reviver of ancient heresies. When
Luther's Ninety-Five Theses were scrutinized by the University of Paris,
this was the line of attack. The resultant publication, the *Determinatio*
(1521), deplored the fact that throughout the Christian centuries the threat
to orthodoxy involved in the perversion of truth had assailed the body of
the Church like a malignant growth. Amongst the heresiarchs explicitly
named were Marcion, Sabellius, Mani, Arius, and, more recently, Waldo,
Wyclif and Hus. "Alas, in our times new members have been added to
this family of vipers. . . . The most important among them is a certain
Martin Luther who tries to reinstate the teachings of the aforementioned
heretics."[1] The document comes to the conclusion that on free will and

---

[1] *Collectio Judiciorum de Novis Erroribus*, ed. Charles du Plessis d'Argentré (1724), Vol. I.,
p. 365. Cf. Heiko A. Oberman, *Forerunners of the Reformation: The Shape of Late Medieval
Thought* (1967), p. 27.

grace Luther was Manichean; on contrition, Hussite; on confession, a
Wyclifite; on the precepts of Christ, akin to the Brethren of the Free
Spirit; on the punishment of heretics, a Cathar; on the authority of
councils, a Waldensian; and on the observance of laws, a near Ebionite.
A formidable indictment indeed!

The rejoinder to the *Determinatio* was entrusted to Melanchthon, who
penned a spirited *Apologia*. He had little difficulty in demonstrating the
injustice of the charges laid against Luther as a perpetrator of heresies.
Whilst Scripture was recognized as the sole source of revelation, Luther
repeatedly appealed to the fathers of the Church for corroboration of his
views – Augustine, Ambrose, Hilary, Cyprian, John Chrysostom,
amongst others. Luther's doctrine, asserted Melanchthon, agreed for the
most part with that of the older theologians.[1] It was with them that his
name should be associated, and not with the notorious heretics.

Now it is obvious that Melanchthon could hardly have made such
claims so early as 1521 unless Luther had already disclosed in his lectures,
sermons and treatises the extent to which he was dependent on the past.
For all his sharp criticisms on occasion, Luther had clearly derived more
benefit than perhaps he realized from his extensive patristic reading, as
well as from his examination of the medieval writers. Of course, this
indebtedness must not be exaggerated, as is sometimes the tendency today
by way of reaction from earlier distortions. As Jaroslav Pelikan observes:
"One could ask whether some of the interpreters of Luther's early development adequately considered the possibility that he derived some of his
ideas from the Scriptures rather than from Augustine, Occam, Lyra,
Hugo Cardinal, or his own virtuosity."[2]

Robert H. Murray was thus justified in insisting that Luther was "no
intellectual Melchizedek".[3] His thought had a pedigree. That ancestry can
be traced through Occam and the Nominalists to Augustine and the early
fathers. Luther's own summary of his programme was: "Back to the
Bible, to Augustine, and to the Church fathers!"[4] It was in fact largely
through Augustine and the fathers that he was forced back to the Bible as
alone possessing final and exclusive authority.

But first we must indicate Luther's debt to the more immediate past in
the Middle Ages. This has tended to be the missing factor in any estimate
of the reformer's derivations. One of the problems formerly lay in the
lack of clear evidence about this enigmatic era. This handicap has been
virtually removed. for there has been a notable revival of medieval
research in recent years. In consequence, a revised version, as it were, of
the Middle Ages is emerging, in which the contrast between pre- and

[1] CR. I. 405.
[2] LW. Companion Volume, 'Luther the Expositor', p. 42.
[3] Robert H. Murray, *Erasmus and Luther: Their Attitude to Toleration* (1920), p. 39.
[4] Cf. LW. 31. 75.

post-reformation conditions is not so universally stark as it was once supposed to be. Adolf Harnack went so far as to define the medieval Church as a middle stage – a "fore-reformation" – between the early Church and the Church of Protestantism, and enquiries since his day partly substantiate his claim.[1]

As Brian A. Gerrish rightly recognizes, in his study of Luther's theology entitled *Grace and Reason*, the whole question of the reformer's relation to Occamism is highly controversial.[2] The difficulty is that not only are we uncertain about the extent to which Luther drew on the thought of the Nominalists: we are still not altogether sure about what the Nominalists themselves were driving at, despite a good deal of research into their works. It is therefore essential to proceed with some caution, and to avoid misleading generalizations or pronouncements which go beyond the present evidence.

William of Occam (c. 1280–1349), the reviver of Nominalism and nicknamed "the invincible doctor", was an Englishman from Surrey. He entered a Franciscan order and first studied and then taught at the University of Oxford. One of his leading tenets was that beings should not be multiplied unnecessarily. By the application of this principle – usually known as "Occam's razor" – he denied all reality to universals. Hence it was impossible to provide logical proof either of the existence or attributes of God. The distinction between the latter was held by him to be merely nominal. It was the essence of Nominalist philosophy, which had its origins in the eleventh century, that universals are simply names (hence the title) invented to indicate the qualities of particular things. The Realists, against whom Nominalism was a protest, regarded universals as possessing substantial reality existing *ante res*.

As Warren Quanbeck points out, in a perceptive treatment, Occam's philosophy "developed in a time of corroding scepticism".[3] The Thomists tried to counter the critical spirit of the period with a theology of repristination. The mystic turned inwards and concentrated on spiritual experience. Occam preferred to meet the situation by developing a new epistemology and establishing the realities of faith on the basis it supplied. At the same time, however, Occam sought to reinstate the supremacy of Scripture as the fountain of revelation, and to expose the incapacity of human reason to rise to a knowledge of God without such aid. It can readily be seen how significant for Luther was Occam's emphasis on the place of the Word.

---

[1] Adolf Harnack, *Lehrbuch der Dogmengeschichte*, Bd. III, *Die Entwicklung des Kirchliken Dogmas* (5th edn. 1932), pp. 374–6.
[2] Brian A. Gerrish, *Grace and Reason: A Study in the Theology of Luther* (1962), p. 5. On Nominalism, *vide* DTC. 11. 718–83.
[3] Warren A. Quanbeck, "Luther's Early Exegesis", *Luther Today. Martin Luther Lectures*, Ed. Gerhard L. Belgum, Vol. I (1957) p. 42.

Luther frequently referred to Occam as his "beloved master".[1] He had the highest respect for his abilities. He spoke of him as *summus dialecticus*.[2] He affirmed that Occam was "without doubt the most eminent and the most brilliant of the Scholastic doctors".[3] He even claimed that he himself belonged to Occam's party.[4] These tributes offset the rather harsher things that Luther also had to say about the Nominalists generally as "hog theologians".[5] Much of Luther's invective arose no doubt from his disappointment that the philosophy in which he had placed his confidence failed in the end to bring him to Christ. But even though he later repudiated much that he had learned from the Occamists, and often with characteristic vehemence, in more sober moments he realized that he had found at least some wheat amongst the chaff.

As soon as Luther started on his courses at the University of Erfurt in 1502 he would be introduced to the prevailing Nominalist influence. Two of his teachers – Jodocus Trutvetter and Bartholomeus Arnoldi from Usingen – were notable enthusiasts for Occam, and when Luther started his theological studies in the monastery his instructor was Johann Nathin, who had been a personal disciple of Gabriel Biel, as had Johann Jeuses von Paltz, who had also had a hand in training Luther. As he prepared himself for ordination, Luther read "with a bleeding heart" Biel's *Exposition of the Canon of the Mass* (1499).[6] During the academic year of 1508–1509 in addition to lecturing in ethics at Wittenberg he helped Trutvetter (who had moved there by then) with his course on Occamist theology. When Luther returned to Erfurt he set about paraphrasing the *Sentences* of Peter Lombard with the help of commentaries written by Occam, Biel and Pierre d'Ailly. It would thus appear that Luther was introduced to Occam both by his own teachers and through the writings of Biel and d'Ailly. We must deal with Luther's debt to the latter after looking more closely at what he gained from Occam himself.

In his *Dialogus*, Occam laid the utmost stress on the infallibility of the Bible. Hence he argued that a Christian is bound to accept what is written in it or what follows from it as a logical consequence. On the other hand, "what is not contained in the Scriptures, or cannot with necessary and obvious consistency be deduced from the contents of the same, no Christian needs to believe".[7] The authority of Scripture rests, according

---

[1] WA. 30. ii. 300; cf. 39. i. 420, 38. 160. Rupp notes that many of Luther's deferential remarks about Occam turn out to be ironical (E. Gordon Rupp, *Luther's Progress to the Diet of Worms* (1951), p. 17).

[2] WATR. 5. 516. No. 2544a; cf. 4. 679. No. 5135.   [3] WA. 6. 183.

[4] Ibid., 600; cf. 195; also WATR. 5. 653. No. 6419. *Vide* Gerrish, op. cit., pp. 44–45.

[5] WA. 56. 274.

[6] LW. 54. 264. No. 3722. Luther said he still had the work in his library in 1538.

[7] William of Occam, *Dialogus*, I. 2. i, in Melchior Goldast, *Monarchia Sancti Romani Imperii*, Vol II (1614), p. 411; cf. II. 2. x, in Goldast, Vol II, pp. 769–70; Reu, *Luther and the Scriptures*, p. 134.

to Occam, on its divine inspiration. The Bible is instinct with the Holy Spirit.[1] Nevertheless, the foundation of Christian truth is not the Bible alone, but also the apostolic tradition and the continuing disclosures of the Holy Spirit.[2] No doubt each of the additional items was regarded as springing from the first, yet the door was left open to allow the entrance of all sorts of unscriptural extras, as Luther was quick to realize.

As Boehmer shrewdly remarks, Occam's attitude to Scripture could only have helped Luther to find a resolution both of his spiritual and theological dilemmas if he had been able at the same time to have furnished the key to a true understanding of the biblical message.[3] This Occam was quite incapable of doing, for "highly as he thought of the Bible in theory, he actually saw nothing more in it than a fortuitously assembled *omnium gatherum* of divine oracles which are contrary to reason, and the meaning of which can only be ascertained with the help of Catholic dogma.... If Luther had simply followed in Occam's footsteps, the Bible would have remained for him a book with seven seals, and it would never have occurred to him, even remotely, to try impartially to find out what the Book actually contains."[4] Reinhold Seeberg made a similar observation: "In spite of the fact that in principle the Scriptures are acknowledged as the sole authority, positive interest in discovering Bible truth is almost entirely absent. In the last analysis, the real interest of Occam as well as of many of his contemporaries, in stressing the authority of the Bible, was to secure a means of criticism by which the authority of the Church's dogmas could be shaken, or the dialectics with which they were upheld at least be made more complicated. By stressing the sole authority of the Bible the Nominalists also helped to prepare the way for the coming of the Reformation. By this ecclesiastical positivism, however, they impeded its progress mightily and contributed very little toward the work of rediscovering fundamental Bible truth."[5]

Two other elements in Occam's teaching, not directly related to his attitude to Scripture, nevertheless proved decisive in shaping Luther's thought. One was the conviction that unaided human reason is incapable of arriving at a sure knowledge of God. The methods and approach of philosophy, though valid in their own sphere, possess no value or relevance when applied to that which can be apprehended only through revelation. The truths of such revelation, conversely, are absolutely certain and sure, and must be accepted on the authority of Scripture, even if they seem contradictory to reason. Although recent research suggests that this presentation of Occam's teaching may require modification, it will be

[1] Occam, op. cit., II. 3. iv (Goldast, Vol. II, p. 822).
[2] Occam, op. cit., I. 2. v (Goldast, Vol. II, pl 416).
[3] Boehmer, op. cit., p. 142.   [4] Ibid., pp. 142–3.
[5] Reinhold Seeberg, *Lehrbuch der Dogmengeschichte* (4th ed. 1930) Bd. III, p. 724. Cf. Reu, *Luther and the Scriptures*, pp. 135–6.

apparent that Luther was strongly influenced in the direction of exalting the efficacy of Scripture over that of man's unenlightened reason. Occam's critique of Aristotelian presuppositions necessarily threw faith back on biblical revelation for its basis.

The other feature of Occam's outlook which affected Luther was his stress on the sovereignty of God. This he derived largely from Augustine. In essence, God is absolute, even arbitrary, will. The plan of redemption is an expression of His nature. The method of incarnation and atonement is the choice of the divine will which reflects the character of the divine being. Occam's view of God involves "unconditioned and unforeseen predestination", as Febvre recognizes.[1] All this clearly had its impact on Luther, and came out in his controversy with Erasmus on free will. But it also had its bearing on Luther's struggle for faith and an understanding of the Bible. This overwhelming emphasis on the ineluctable sovereignty of God – carried to an extreme which ignores the scriptural balance between wrath and mercy – contributed to Luther's difficulties in realizing that God is indeed gracious. Much of his *tristitia* may have been due to the pressure of such a one-sided conception of God. "Perhaps, more than any other human factor, Nominalism may have been decisive in intensifying his sense of sinfulness and unworthiness before God (*coram deo*)," explains McDonough.[2] This, of course, was to lead him in the end to a full trust in Christ, but we cannot help feeling that he lingered rather longer than was needful in the Slough of Despond.

As we have seen, Luther probably reached Occam indirectly through his disciples. Of these, Biel and d'Ailly were the most influential. Gabriel Biel (c. 1420–1495) who has been dubbed the last of the Scholastics, was himself educated at Erfurt after leaving Heidelberg. He later joined the Brethren of the Common Life and was instrumental with Count Eberland of Würtemburg in founding the University of Tübingen, where he held the chair of theology. We have seen how Luther read his *Exposition of the Canon of the Mass* as he prepared himself for the priesthood. He also knew Biel's *Collectorium*, which was a commentary on the *Sentences* of Peter Lombard, on which Luther lectured at Erfurt. Biel modified Occam's dichotomy between faith and reason, allowing that although the Word of God alone conveys the whole of revelatory truth, reason may legitimately be employed to interpret and confirm it. He acknowledged the Bible as the unique source of revelation, and held all canonical books as inspired. Yet he also found a place for the apostolic tradition, on the strength of what he had read in the writing of Basil the Great. The Church and the pope can transmit the knowledge received through the Scriptures, but they cannot add to it. They are to be obeyed only in so far as they do not violate the integrity of the Word.

[1] Lucien Febvre, *Martin Luther: a Destiny* (E.T. 1930), p. 33.   [2] McDonough, op. cit., p. 32.

It is not hard to see how all this appealed to Luther, and became part
of his own thinking. When he was expounding the *Sentences* with the
assistance of Biel he would sometimes call his pupils Gabrielists. "I know
what Gabriel says," he told Johann Lang in a letter written in October
1516, "and it is all very good, except when he talks about grace, love,
hope, faith and the virtues. Then he is a Pelagian."[1] Later, however, in
his *Disputation against Scholastic Theology*, he made Biel his main target of
attack.[2]

The other outstanding Occamist known to Luther was Pierre d'Ailly
(1350–1420), a French Cardinal and Chancellor of the University in Paris.
Along with Biel, he is regarded as one of the chief exponents of the new
way (*via moderna*) as over against the old way (*via antiqua*) represented by
Thomas Aquinas. The Thomists kept a place for reason in reaching the
knowledge of God, but the advocates of the new way, following Duns
Scotus, taught that in matters of faith the Bible was the sole guide. As
we have noted, this was also a Nominalist axiom. Pierre d'Ailly spoke in
the most explicit terms about the supremacy of Scripture, alluding to its
"infallible author"; and to the apostle Paul as a "celestial secretary".[3] He
insisted that Christ had built His Church on the Bible and not on Peter.
Hence he could affirm that "a declaration of the canonical Scriptures is of
greater authority than an assertion of the Christian Church".[4] Excerpts
like that enable us to realize why Luther warmed to the teaching of the
Occamists.

Despite the strictures of his more mature judgment, Luther was
indebted to Occam and his school to a greater degree than he was prepared
to admit. If on the one hand it is too much to claim that Luther is nothing
but an "ossified Occamist", it is unrealistic on the other hand to dismiss
this influence entirely.[5] Boehmer is quite right to point out that in all its
essential features Luther's Christianity was the greatest conceivable antithesis to Occamism.[6] Yet it cannot be denied that Occam made it easier
for Luther to overcome the medieval religion. This remains true in spite
of the adverse effect of his idea of God as an arbitrary tyrant. It was
Occam who put Luther on the track of a biblical grasp of justification
with his talk about the non-imputation of sin. For Occam that was a
hollow phrase, but as he brooded over the Word, Luther was able to fill
it with saving content. "I know what Scholastic theology did for me: I
know also how much I owe to it," Luther confessed. But he added
significantly: "and I am glad that I am delivered from it, and give thanks
for my deliverance to Christ the Lord."[7]

[1] WAB. 1. 66.   [2] LCC. 16. 266–73.
[3] Paul Tschackert, *Peter von Ailli* (1877), Appendix, p. 9.
[4] Ibid., p. 10.   [5] Boehmer, op. cit., p. 140.
[6] Ibid., p. 141.   [7] Cole, 1. 8.

Before we discuss what Luther derived from Augustine, as representing the fathers of the Church, mention must be made of another Schoolman who forms a link between the two. Peter Lombard (*c.* 1100–1160) taught in the Cathedral school in Paris and later became Bishop of the diocese. His *magnum opus* was the *Sentences* (1148–1150), which was adopted as the standard textbook of theology throughout the Middle Ages. Only at a later date was it superseded by the *Summa Theologica* of Thomas Aquinas. Luther studied the *Sentences* for his doctorate and lectured on them at Erfurt. He came to Lombard as already a convinced Occamist and thus tended to read him through Nominalist spectacles. He spoke of him as "a great man", and valued him because above all the Scholastics he stressed faith rather than reason.[1] Peter followed Augustine in his conception of sin, predestination, grace, faith and justification. With Anselm, Abelard and Bernard, however, he refused to accept the unqualified impotence of man's will after the fall and held that grace is not irresistible. Rupp notes that Peter Lombard represents the twelfth century conflation of the Scriptures and the fathers before the major infiltration of Aristotle in the next century.[2] No doubt Luther outgrew his unqualified admiration for Peter Lombard as *summus theologis*, but he expressed his approval of him at a later date, with the exception of his views on justification which were "too thin and weak".[3]

It is hardly surprising that as a member of an Augustinian order, Luther should have devoted much of his time to examining the works of the great African father. He must have been introduced to some of these at quite an early stage. His marginal notes in the *Opuscula*, the fifteen books *Concerning the Trinity* (Augustine's principal dogmatic systematization), and *The City of God* prove how thoroughly he mastered them. We know that Luther had his own copy of Augustine's exposition of the Psalms. Before he had started to read him – perhaps before he entered the cloister – Luther admitted that he had very little room for Augustine.[4] How different it was now! He positively "devoured Augustine", and obviously relished the meal.[5] As Jean Cadier puts it, Luther read the works of Augustine "with passion", and Rupp explains that it was "the rapture of a younger theologian for his first theological love".[6] So familiar did Luther eventually become with Augustine's writings that Melanchthon could report that he held most of their contents in his memory.[7]

Luther had chosen his master well, for Augustine was essentially a

[1] LW. 54. 26. No. 192; cf. 260. No. 3698 – "a very diligent man with a superior mind"; WATR. 2. 575. No. 2544a.
[2] Rupp, *Righteousness of God*, p. 92.   [3] End. 25. 258.   [4] LW. 48. 24.
[5] LW. 54. 49. No. 347. Luther added that when he came to understand justification "it was all over with Augustine".
[6] Jean Cadier, "St. Augustin et la réforme", *Recherches Augustiniennes*, Tome IV (1958) p. 358; Rupp, *Luther's Progress*, p. 21.
[7] CR. 6. 159.

biblical thinker. "God's Word is always the rule of truth," he affirmed.[1] It is a serious error, if not a sin, to doubt it. "Everything written in Scripture must be believed absolutely."[2] Hence "we unhesitatingly give credence to the divine Scriptures".[3] They carry "paramount authority to which we yield assent in all matters".[4] They are "the work of God's fingers because they have been completed by the operation of the Holy Spirit, who works in the holy authors".[5] Thus they are altogether reliable, for "God's Scripture neither deceives nor is deceived".[6] There is such unaminity that "they were spoken as if by one mouth".[7] The Bible is "both clear and obscure, simple and profound, lucid yet full of mystery".[8] "If it were nowhere plain, it would not feed you; if it were nowhere hidden, it would not exercise us."[9]

The Scriptures are to be accepted as the sole and supreme standard in "all matters that concern faith and the manner of life".[10] No one should be believed, however wise or saintly, unless he bases his arguments on Holy Writ.[11] Quoting this last injunction with evident approval, Luther added that here we learn how the fathers are to be read, namely, that we ought not merely to ask what they say, but whether they use clear texts of Scripture and sound reasoning from it.[12] In his sermon on the shepherds, Augustine told his hearers that they must disdain everything outside the Scriptures if they were not to be lost in the mists.[13] The peril of abandoning the rule of God's Word was grave: "If the authority of the divine Scripture is undermined, faith itself will become undermined, and once faith is shaken, love will abate."[14]

One of the most helpful distinctions in Augustine was that between the spirit and the letter. In this he was an heir of Origen, although he made more of it than the Alexandrine genius. Augustine also relates the differentiation to that between *signum* and *res* – the sign and the thing signified. In reading the Bible, the believer must pay attention to the spiritual significance lest he should be "put in subjection to the flesh by a blind adherence to the letter".[15] The letter itself is dead until it is quickened by the Spirit. It is only as the Spirit who inspired the Word breathes again in the heart of the Christian that Scripture again becomes alive. This distinction constituted one of the major principles in Luther's hermeneu-

---

[1] *De Sermo in Monte*, 30. 2. On Augustine's attitude to Scripture, *vide* A. D. R. Polman, *The Word of God According to Augustine* (E.T. 1961) from which this and other quotations have been derived. Cf. A. Skevington Wood, *The Principles of Biblical Interpretation* (1967), Chap. III, "Augustine", pp. 53–66.
[2] *De Civitate Dei*, 21. 6. 1; cf. *Contra Faustum*, 11. 5.
[3] *Epistolae*, 147. 39, 40; *De Peccatorum Meritis et Remissione*, 3. 7.
[4] *De Civitate Dei*, 11. 3.   [5] *Enarrationes in Psalmos*, Ps. 8:7.   [6] *De Patientia*, 26. 22.
[7] *Contra Faustum*, 11. 5.   [8] *De Civitate Dei*, 20. 23; *Prooemium in Ps. 118.*
[9] *Enarrationes in Psalmos*, Ps. 140:2; *De Sermo in Monte*, 352. 6.
[10] *De Doctrina Christiana*, 2. 4.   [11] Cf. *Epistolae*, 82. 2. 5; *Contra Faustum*, 11. 5.
[12] LW. 27. 156; cf WA 1. 647.   [13] *De Sermo in Monte*, 46. 24.
[14] *De Doctrina Christiana*, 1. 41.   [15] Ibid., 3. 5.

tics, although he was to insist more strongly on the primacy of the literal
sense than his mentor. It is thought that Luther may have first encountered
this feature of Augustine's exegetical methodology in the writings of
Jacques Lefèvre from Étaples (c. 1455–1536). The French humanist, who
was sometimes known by his latinized name of Faber Stapulensis, inherited
the Augustinian tradition. Luther made use of his commentaries on the
Psalms and Romans in compiling his own lectures on those books.
Lefèvre accepted the Bible as "the sole rule of Christians".[1] When he
issued his exposition of the Epistles in 1512, he told young Guillaume
Farel: "My son, God will renew the world and you will be a witness of
it."[2] That prophecy of the reformation was destined to be fulfilled and
Lefèvre was one of those who paved the way for it.

In the preface to the Wittenberg edition of his German writings, the
initial volume of which appeared in 1539, Luther paid one of many
tributes to Augustine to be found in his remains. Luther asked his readers
not to allow their interest in his books to prevent them from weighing
the Scriptures themselves. In making such a recommendation he was
following "the example of St. Augustine, who was, among other things,
the first and almost the only one who was determined to be subject to
the Holy Scriptures alone, and independent of the books of all the fathers
and the Saints".[3] Then Luther drew this salutary lesson for his own time.
"And if the example of St. Augustine had been followed, the pope would
not have become Antichrist, and that countless mass of books, which is
like a crawling swarm of vermin, would not have found its way into the
Church, and the Bible would have remained in the pulpit." That is but
one example amongst many which could be adduced to show that Luther
virtually equated "our theology and St. Augustine".[4] Although he re-
nounced his monastic vows, he remained doctrinally an Augustinian for
the most part to his dying day.

[1] Pierre Imbart de la Tour, Les origines de la réforme, Tome III, L'Évangelisme (1521–1538)
(1914), p. 127; DTC. 9. 145–6.
[2] A. L. Herminjard, Correspondance des réformateurs (1866), Tome I, p. 15.
[3] LW. 34. 285.
[4] Ibid.

CHAPTER IV

LUTHER'S THEOLOGICAL DEVELOPMENT

T HOSE WHO USED TO PORTRAY MARTIN LUTHER ON
the grand scale as an outsize Gothic hero figure, viewed him as one who
stood like a giant at what Thomas Carlyle in a vivid phrase once described
as "the conflux of eternities".[1] In him, it was said, the pressure of the past
was gathered up. In him the ferment of the present found its outlet. In
him the shape of things to come began to appear. This was only an attempt
to indicate in at times excessively hyperbolic terms the plain and hardly
deniable fact that Luther was one of those men whom God matches to
the hour. It is no longer fashionable to adopt such dramatic, even apocalyptic imagery, but whilst endeavouring to avoid the extremism of Protestant
mythology, we may nevertheless find ourselves compelled to conclude on
the soberest reflection that the influence of Luther over the last four centuries serves to vindicate a prophetic interpretation of the pioneer reformer.
    Our concern at the moment, however, is to amplify the less arresting
and therefore less controversial assertion that in the context of his theological development Luther was also affected by the contingencies of
time. He was profoundly indebted to the past, as we have seen. He was
equally susceptible to the impact of the present. His beliefs were hammered
out on the anvil of experience, which means that we cannot consider his
maturing theology apart from his spiritual quest. There is an impressive
existential quality about Luther's thinking. His doctrinal principles were
formulated as and how the actual demands of living determined. This
goes far to explain the enormous appeal of Luther's teaching. This was
no doctrinaire theory, dreamily conceived in the solitude of a monastic
cell but quite out of touch with life. Monk though he was, Luther was no
recluse. His duties as a member of the teaching faculty at the University
of Wittenberg brought him into contact with the youth of the period
with all their vitality and all their frustrations too. It was in these years,
when he took up his chair of biblical exegesis in 1512 and embarked on his
series of expository lectures until the ferocity of his opponents compelled
him to seek refuge in Wartburg in 1521, that his doctrinal position was
consolidated.

----

[1] Thomas Carlyle, *The French Revolution: A History*, in *The Works of Thomas Carlyle*
(Centenary Edition), Vol. II (1896), p. 134. The reference was to 4th May 1789 – "the baptism
day of democracy" (ibid., p. 133).

The determinative factor in his advance towards an integrated theology was, of course, his increasing conviction that the Bible alone must be his guide. "The Sacred Scriptures in which his mind became so saturated," explains Vivian Green, "formed the central feature of his study".[1] When Luther was promoted to the doctorate in Wittenberg it is significant that, according to the custom, the ceremony included the presentation of a Bible to the candidate, as a token of his office. The institution was conducted by Andreas Bodenstein von Karlstadt, who was later to emerge as leader of what we have now come to call the radical Reformation. After reading a selection of Scripture passages, he handed Luther first a closed and then an open Bible. He placed a woollen beret on his head, and on his finger a silver ring, which can still be seen in the museum at Braunschweig.[2] Thus was Luther installed as a Doctor of Sacred Scripture. That was on the 19th October 1512. On the 25th. he started his professorial duties with the first lecture of a series on Genesis (so it would seem), and for the next seven years the nature of his vocation compelled him to dig deeper and yet deeper into the Word of God. As yet he had not seen the light, as he himself afterwards confessed.[3] But these were to prove the decisive days both for mind and soul.

Before we trace the earlier stages of this development in its theological aspect, up to the time of Luther's spiritual illumination, it is necessary to justify the assumption that he can rightly be called a theologian at all. It is too readily supposed that this was not in fact his forte. He is regarded as a preacher, a prophet, a protester, a reformer, but not as one at all versed in theology. It is conceded that Luther was a genius in religion and that as a historical figure he changed the face of Europe. But it is almost proverbial in some quarters to take it for granted that Luther was no theologian. Even so sympathetic a critic as Sydney Cave could fall into the trap, and announce that to refer to Luther's theology is to use a phrase without a meaning.[4] Hugh Ross Mackintosh similarly spoke about "Luther's system of belief, if system it may be called".[5]

Such a depreciation of Luther as a systematic theologian is wide of the mark, as Philip Watson shows.[6] On the other hand, we can see why the impression has gained currency. Luther made no effort to amass anything remotely resembling Calvin's *Institutes* or the *Summa Theologica* of Aquinas. But if the production of an exhaustive compendium is a *sine qua non*, then many of the recognized theologians of the past would fail to qualify. Luther coordinated theology in a creative fashion by seizing on the biblical fulcrum of justification by faith and using it to move the entire

[1] Green, op. cit., p. 47.   [2] Schwiebert, op. cit., pp. 195–6.   [3] WA. 45. 86.
[4] Sydney Cave, *The Doctrine of the Person of Christ* (1925), p. 148.
[5] Hugh Ross Mackintosh, *The Doctrine of the Person of Jesus Christ* (1912), p. 230.
[6] Philip S. Watson, *Let God be God! An Interpretation of the Theology of Martin Luther* (1947), pp. 4–6.

structure of belief into a new position. Whereas others have systematized the doctrines of the Word by arranging them in logical sequence with impressive cohesion, Luther did so by using a single though crucial article to interpret the whole.

Here is the apposite comment of Joseph Sittler on this matter. "There is, to be sure a sense of the term *systematic thinker* before which Luther would not qualify – which in fact he would not understand. If, that is, the connotation of system which is proper to propositional logic is made absolute, then Luther was not systematic. But we must decidedly reject any such presumption. There is a system proper to the dissection of the dead; and there is a system proper to the experience and description of the living. There is a system proper to the inorganic; and there is a system proper to an organism. A crystal has a system. But so does a living personality in the grip of a central certainty. If, then, by system one means that there is in a man's thought a central authority, a pervasive style, a way of bringing every theme and judgment and problem under the rays of the central illumination, then it must be said that history shows few men of comparable integration."[1] For Luther, of course, the "central authority" and the "central illumination" was the truth of justification, which he declared is "master and prince, lord, ruler, and judge over all kinds of doctrine, which preserves and governs all ecclesiastical doctrines".[2]

It was once presumed that a great gulf was fixed between the earlier and later Luther. Recent scholarship, however, has shown that this is not the case. Luther's theological development took place, as we have already noted, within a comparatively brief space of time. Indeed, the basic principles were established as he worked on Romans shortly after his decisive encounter with God, and can even be detected incipiently at least in his *Dictata Super Psalterium* (1513–1515). To be sure, there were further advances within this framework, especially under the impact of controversy. But, as Regin Prenter makes clear, "the development is within the new evangelical view of life and not away from it. It is a development, therefore, which does not signify any modification of the basic view, but is rather a progressive and final struggle with the traditional views based on the unchanged fundamental conclusion."[3]

Whilst the Bible was the major factor in bringing about Luther's reorientation, we must not overlook the help he received from some of his mentors. In a letter to Jodocus Trutvetter – nicknamed "Doctor Eisenach" after his native town – Luther admitted that it was from him he first learned that Christian faith must be based only on the Bible, and that all other writers must be tested by it.[4] Trutvetter, however, became

[1] Joseph Sittler, *The Doctrine of the Word in the Structure of Lutheran Theology* (1948), pp. 3–4; cf. LW. Companion Volume, pp. 42–43.
[2] WA. 39. i. 205.   [3] Regin Prenter, *Spiritus Creator* (E.T. 1953), p. xvi.
[4] End., 1. 189–90.

so obsessed with Aristotelian logic – Luther dubbed him "the king of dialectic philosophers in our day" – that he failed to heed his own advice.[1] Bartholomeus Arnoldi from Usingen, another of Luther's teachers at Erfurt, insisted that the Scriptures must be accepted as the unerring guide to truth and that the tradition of the Church and the works of the fathers must be evaluated in relation to the Word. Arnoldi, it seems, was infected by the same virus as Trutvetter and succumbed to the fever of dialectic philosophy, for which Luther had to take him to task.[2] But he continued to send a kindly greeting to him in his letters.[3]

Luther's debt to his vicar-general, Johann von Staupitz, was much more substantial. We have seen how he acted as a spiritual counsellor. His theological advice was equally profitable. Luther could allude to him as "my very first father in this teaching" – that is, the doctrine of justification which lay at the heart of the Reformation.[4] In a letter he wrote to Staupitz in May 1518, he recalled his superior's "most delightful and helpful talks, through which the Lord Jesus wonderfully consoled me".[5] Then he went on to remind Staupitz that it was through him that he began to grasp the real meaning of repentance. As a result of the conversation, Luther set out to explore the biblical connotation of *metanoia* and was eventually led into the light. It was Staupitz, too, who dragged Luther out of the seclusion of the cloister, almost against his will, and convinced him that his most effective sphere lay in teaching the Bible. He gave up his own chair so that Luther could take it. Referring to the mystical devotions to which he was then attracted, Luther wrote: "These are mere Satanic illusions, among which I would have been imprisoned as a monk had not Staupitz recalled me to the public profession of theology."[6] In his last letter to Luther in 1524, Staupitz was not ashamed to describe himself as "a precursor of the evangelical doctrine".[7] Giovanni Miegge doubts whether Staupitz can be claimed in the strict sense of the word as a forerunner of the Reformation, but he agrees that Luther's obligation to him was considerable.[8] The debt, however, was reciprocal, as Staupitz acknowledged when in the same letter he told Luther: "You have led us from the husks of swine back to the pastures of life."[9]

The critical period in Luther's theological development fell between his promotion to the doctorate with the Wittenberg chair and his spiritual awakening in the tower experience, in the autumn of 1514 most probably. After his enlightenment, he was working from a turning-point as he continued to prepare his lectures on Romans, and later those on Galatians, Hebrews and the second set on Psalms. Prior to the *Türmerlebnis*, he was

[1] LW. 48. 57.   [2] Ibid., 52; cf. End. 4. 31.   [3] LW. 48. 139, 151.
[4] *Dok.* 512.   [5] LW. 48. 65.   [6] *Dok.* 472.
[7] Boehmer, op. cit., p. 108.
[8] Giovanni Miegge, *Lutero* (1946), p. 110; cf. Rupp, *Righteousness of God*, p. 118.
[9] Boehmer, op. cit., p. 108.

straining towards that watershed. "When I became a doctor, I did not yet know that we cannot expiate our sins."[1] Despite the objections of Uuras Saarnivaara, it would appear that Luther is there referring to the fact that he had not as yet fully gained his evangelical insight into the nature of justification.[2] But he was on the way to doing so.

It is not at all certain which was the first course of lectures delivered by Luther as a professor in Wittenberg. There is reason for thinking that it may have been on the book of Genesis.[3] Luther himself included it in the list when he looked back on this period in 1539, in his treatise *On the Councils and the Churches*. "I, too, read the fathers, even before I opposed the pope so decisively. I also read them with greater diligence than those who now quote them so defiantly and haughtily against me; for I know that none of them attempted to read a book of Holy Scripture in school, or to use the writings of the fathers as an aid, as I did. Let them take a book of Holy Scripture and seek out the glosses of the fathers; then they will share the experience I had when I worked on the letter to the Hebrews with St. Chrysostom's glosses, the letter to Titus and the letter to the Galatians with the help of St. Jerome, Genesis with the help of St. Ambrose and St. Augustine, the Psalter with all the writers available, and so on."[4] In his footnote in the American edition, Eric W. Gritsch assigns these lectures to the period between 1513 and 1517.[5] The rest can be checked, but there is no direct evidence about a series on Genesis. It is argued that if Luther did in fact tackle it, then it can only be fitted in during 1512–1513. This would make it the course which he commenced as soon as he was appointed as a professor. Boehmer believes that he began on the 25th. October, 1512.[6] There are no extant manuscripts, however, and the riddle must remain unsolved. The last commentary Luther published from 1535 to 1545 was on Genesis and may conceivably have incorporated some of the previous material.

We are on more solid ground when we come to deal with Luther's *Dictata Super Psalterium* of 1513 to 1515.[7] These lectures are to be distinguished from a set Luther gave from 1518 to 1521 entitled *Operationes in Psalmos*. They were prepared during the summer of 1513 and begun on the 13th August. The journal of Johann Oldecop, a priest from Hilder-

---

[1] WA. 45. 86.

[2] Uuras Saarnivaara, *Luther Discovers the Gospel: New Light on Luther's Way from Medieval Catholicism to Evangelical Faith* (1951), p. 57. Saarnivaara prefers to relate Luther's statement to "the reviving of faith in the forgiveness of sins and grace in Christ" which he thinks occurred under the influence of Staupitz late in 1512. Luther's illumination, by which he came to grasp the meaning of justification by faith, Saarnivaara places as late as 1518, and equates with the *Türmerlebnis*.

[3] Schwiebert, op. cit., pp. 196, 282; cf. Heinrich Boehmer, *Luthers erste Vorlesung* (1924), p. 4.

[4] LW 41. 19.   [5] Ibid., n. 17.   [6] Boehmer, *Luthers erste Vorlesung*, p. 3.

[7] For an analysis of these lectures, *vide* Rupp, *Righteousness of God*, pp. 138–57, from which material has been drawn.

sheim, confirmed that Luther was lecturing on the Psalms in 1513.[1] He
used an edition of the Psalter which came from the press of Johann
Decker from Grünenberg in 1510. It is still preserved in the library at
Wolfenbüttel. Luther's notes are there for visitors to see. But we are not
at present concerned with Luther's methods of exposition: we are enquir-
ing about his theological development. It was his study of the Psalms that
led Luther to a new comprehension of God's righteousness which was to
prove determinative in his thinking.

The exegetical factors, however, were not altogether unrelated to the
doctrinal. Erich Vogelsang saw in the combination of Christological and
tropological interpretation, reflected in these lectures, the key to Luther's
ultimate discovery of God's righteousness.[2] It came when Luther applied
the concept of divine justice first to the work of Christ and then to the
soul on the ground of faith. Taking a hint from Jacques Lefèvre, he was
enabled to transcend the limitations of medieval exegesis and eventually
to penetrate to the heart of the gospel. Lefèvre distinguished a twofold
literal sense: the literal-historical which relates to the time when the
Psalmist wrote, and represents the letter which kills, and the literal-
prophetic which points to Christ and reflects the intention of the Spirit.
It was this grounding of the prophetic interpretation – which in itself was
familiar enough in the Middle Ages – on Augustine's differentiation
between the letter and the spirit which constituted Lefèvre's contribution.
Through it Luther was able to equate the righteousness of God – which
he had formerly regarded exclusively in terms of punitive justice – with
the person of Jesus Christ, whom he had now come to recognize as full of
grace and integrity. This made it possible for him to take the further step
of relating righteousness to the individual through faith by applying the
tropological rule. In this curious intermingling of the exegetical and the
theological, Luther began to move towards a resolution of his doubts and
fears.

Vogelsang discerned signs of tension early in the *Dictata*. But, he went
on, "the real wrestling begins from Psalm 30/31 onwards".[3] Yet even
here the solution and goal were not reached. The climax was to come
with Psalm 70/71. We have an indication of Luther's preconceptions in
a report from the *Table Talk*. "When under the papacy I read, 'In thy
righteousness deliver me' (Ps. 31:1) and 'in thy truth', I thought at once
that this righteousness was an avenging anger, namely the wrath of God.
I hated Paul with all my heart when I read that the righteousness of God
is revealed in the gospel (Rom. 1:16, 17)."[4] Later, in the tower experience,
to which this extract is related, Luther came to realize that the righteous-

[1] WA 3. 1.
[2] Erich Vogelsang, *Die Anfänge von Luthers Christologie nach des ersten Vorlesung* (1929), p. 50.
[3] Ibid., p. 43.   [4] LW. 54. 309. No. 4007.

ness of God is His mercy through which He makes us righteous by faith. This was to prove the remedy for his affliction. But as yet he was only beginning to glimpse it.

When he came to Psalm 70/71, Luther found the same phrase staring at him again in v. 2 – "In thy righteousness deliver me." He was led to comment at greater length than he had done in Psalm 30/31, where he had merely underlined *"thy* righteousness" by adding: "not in mine, which is nothing."[1] Now he expanded on this theme. "The righteousness of God is wholly this: to humble oneself to the depths. Here he speaks properly of Christ, who is the power and righteousness of God through His utter and profound humility."[2] Then he showed how he had been influenced by Lefèvre's interpretative principles. "The righteousness of God when considered tropologically, for thus it is most often regarded in Scripture, is that by which God condemns us and makes us condemn what we are in ourselves, the old man as a whole with all his works (even our righteousness, Isaiah 64). So humility is actually humiliation. . . . For this is called the judgment of God, as the righteousness, power and wisdom of God are those by which we are made wise, strong, righteous and humble, or by which we are judged."[3] "Thus whoever wants to understand the Scriptures wisely needs to understand all these things tropologically. The truth, wisdom, salvation, righteousness are those by which he makes us strong, saved, righteous, wise. So the works of God and the ways of God are all in the literal sense Christ. In the moral sense, all this is faith in Him. . . . . In fact the old law only prophesied the first coming of Christ, in which He reigns in a benign and salutary judgment, because it is the advent of grace and loving kindness. Therefore the apostle says in Romans 3, 'The righteousness of God . . . through Jesus Christ.'"[4] "No one can . . . 'be delivered by the righteousness of God' unless he hopes in the God who justifies the ungodly. . . . He does not say that he desires to be freed by something other than righteousness. For we are delivered from unrighteousness by righteousness, just as we are delivered from sickness by health, and from ignorance by knowledge."[5]

It is apparent that, when he reached this point in his *Dictata Super Psalterium,* Luther had come very close to an evangelical appreciation of righteousness. He was on the edge of it, but not yet quite there. We do not go all the way with Vogelsang in identifying Luther's notes on Psalm 70/71 as the specific moment of his illumination, preferring to connect this with the tower experience; but we can agree with Rupp and others that Luther in all likelihood came to a fuller insight into the meaning of God's righteousness at some time during his lectures on Psalms.[6] Wendorf's

[1] Saarnivaara, op. cit., p. 64.   [2] WA. 3. 458.
[3] Ibid., 465.   [4] Ibid., 458.   [5] Ibid., 453.
[6] Rupp, *Righteousness of God,* p. 136; cf. Vogelsang, op. cit., p. 50.

attempt to push the transition even further back to the exposition of
Psalm I is hardly convincing.[1]

Attention must also be drawn to Luther's reaction to Psalm 21/22 with
its unmistakable anticipations of the cross. It begins with the words
which Christ took upon his own lips as he hung on the tree: "My God,
my God, why hast thou forsaken me?" Luther was brought to a halt by
that cry of dereliction. Whatever could it mean? Christ had evidently felt
Himself to be deserted, abandoned and estranged from the Father. This
was just what Luther himself had gone through. But why should it
happen to the Lord Jesus? Luther knew very well why he felt forlorn: it
was because his sin separated between him and God. But Christ had no
sin to sever Him from the Holy One. Why then was He forsaken? And
the answer dawned on Luther with the force of a fresh revelation. He who
knew no sin was made to be sin for the sake of sinners. He so identified
Himself with sinful humanity that he took upon Him the iniquity of us all.
This introduced Luther to a totally new conception of Christ, as Bainton
enables us to appreciate. "The judge upon the rainbow has become the
derelict upon the cross. He is still the judge and must be, so long as truth
judges error and right judges wrong. But in the very act of judging the
sinner He has made Himself one with the sinner, assuming His punishment
and sharing in his very guilt."[2]

But a new view of God is involved as well. The All-Great is the All-
Loving too.[3] At the cross righteousness and peace have kissed each other.
Wrath and mercy meet. Redemption is achieved by the only availing
sacrifice, and pardon is made possible for guilty men. "Luther, as no one
before him in more than a thousand years, sensed the import of the
miracle of divine forgiveness," declares Bainton.[4] That was the heart at
once of Luther's theological reorientation and his spiritual renewal.
Henceforward he was to realize that "the cross of Christ runs through the
whole of Scripture".[5]

There is no extended discussion of original sin in the Dictata, as there
was in the lectures on the Sentences. Luther was to take up this theme more
thoroughly in dealing with Romans. "Luther's doctrine of sin was in a
transition stage," Adolf Hamel declared, with reference to the Dictata,
and "remnants of Occamist teaching and Augustinian notions are mingled

[1] Hermann Wendorf, Der Durchbruch der neuen Erkenntnis Luthers im Lichte der handschrift-
lichen Überlieferungen (1932), pp. 124, 285; Rupp, Righteousness of God, pp. 136–7.

[2] Bainton, op. cit., pp. 34–35.

[3] The Poetical Works of Robert Browning, ed. Augustine Birrell (1896), Vol. I, p. 515, "An
Epistle".

> "The very God! think, Abib; dost thou think?
> So, the All-Great, were the All-Loving too –"

[4] Bainton, op. cit., p. 35.

[5] WA. 3. 63.

together".[1] In commenting on the *Sentences*, Luther had denied the continuance of original sin beyond baptism, in spite of what Peter Lombard had written on the matter. But now he could quote the Master of the Sentences with acquiescence. The guilt of sin may indeed have been remitted in the sacrament, but the "misery of infirmity" remains as a "weakness in the memory, a blindness in the intellect, or a disorder in the will", as well as "a dolour of conscience."[2] These are only gradually healed by grace, in the inn where Christ as the Good Samaritan has lodged us.[3]

Thomas McDonough sees in the relationship between law and gospel "not a mere aspect of Luther's theology but the very heart and core of his basic conviction".[4] In the *Dictata* this feature of Luther's developed doctrinal synthesis is already discernible, though not yet so definitive as, for instance, in his great commentary on Galatians of 1535. "For in this the difference between the gospel and the law is indicated," Luther wrote. "The law is the word of Moses to us; the gospel, on the other hand, is the word of God in us."[5] "All that pertains only to the body and the senses and not to the spirit is letter. . . . But the new law conveys spiritual gifts and grace, by which the carnal and literal things are made void."[6] The clear-cut distinction between law and gospel, so vital for the biblical concept of justification, was not yet fully drawn by Luther. He tended to interpret it in terms of the Augustinian and neo-Platonic contrast between the shadow and the reality. The law "stays outside, speaks in figures and in the shadows of what will one day become visible".[7] The gospel, on the other hand, "comes inwardly and speaks of inward, spiritual and true things".[8] "All that the law says and does is but mere words and signs. The works of the gospel, however, are the works and reality thus signified."[9]

For Luther the gospel flows out of the law. "The gospel was hidden in the law and was therefore unseen, like water in a rock, until Christ tore it apart and broke it open."[10] "The new law was hidden, enclosed in the old law, but it was intended to be brought out and disclosed by the advent of Christ."[11] It may be concluded that on the whole Luther's idea of the connexion between law and gospel at this time was basically Augustinian.[12]

Lennart Pinomaa reports that the *Dictata* are "almost drenched" with the theme of divine wrath.[13] It must be borne in mind, however, that there are few books in the Bible in which this aspect of God's nature is more

[1] Adolf Hamel, *Der junge Luther und Augustin*, Bd. I (1934), p. 129; Rupp, *Righteousness of God*, p. 153, n. 3.

[2] WA 3. 453, 231. [3] WA. 4. 211. [4] McDonough, op. cit., p. 146.
[5] WA. 4. 9. [6] WA. 3. 37. [7] WA. 4. 9.
[8] Ibid. [9] WA. 3. 258. [10] Ibid., 271.
[11] WA 4. 285.
[12] Saarnivaara, op. cit., p. 70. But cf. Hamel, op. cit., Bd. I, pp. 169–78 for minor differences.
[13] Lennart B. Pinomaa, *Der Zorn Gottes in der Theologie Luthers* (1938), p. 19; Rupp, *Righteousness of God*, p. 155.

prominent than the Psalms. Augustine's commentary on the Psalms, on which Luther drew, makes repeated reference to the wrath of God and its implications. As Rupp points out, Luther was at pains to safeguard this conception from anthropomorphic association.[1] "For His wrath is not as He is in Himself."[2] "For the punitive effects of God are His wrath – not as He Himself is in Himself."[3] Luther also followed Augustine in distinguishing between the merciful wrath of God and the wrath of His severity. The former is shown to the saints and brings them to repentance and faith. The latter is reserved for the ungodly and impenitent, leading up at last to the eternal punishment of hell itself.[4]

It will be realized that, even in the brief period between his entry upon his duties as a professor at Wittenberg and the tower experience in the autumn of 1514, Luther had come, in the course of his scrutiny of the Scriptures, within sight of his theological goal. Not all was yet sharply defined, but his eyes were unwaveringly focused on the vision of the King in His beauty and the land that once seemed so very far off.

[1] Rupp, *Righteousness of God*, p. 155; Pinomaa, op. cit., p. 80.
[2] WA. 3. 35.
[3] Ibid., 591.
[4] Rupp, *Righteousness of God*, p. 156; Pinomaa, op. cit., p. 73.

CHAPTER V

LUTHER'S ENCOUNTER WITH GOD

REFORMATION, LIKE REVIVAL, HAS TO START SOME-
where. More accurately, it has to start in someone, since it is no impersonal
phenomenon. It has to do with the Church, and the Church is a body
made up of living members. Martin Luther was the chosen instrument
through whom God designed to bring renewal in the sixteenth century.
The Reformation in that sense began in this man.

But can we determine precisely when it did so? It was neither so soon
as the scene on the steps of the Scala Sancta in Rome, where pious legend
has overlaid the tale, nor so late as the nailing of the Ninety Five Theses to
the door of the Castle Church at Wittenberg, which was intended to
inaugurate a discussion rather than to touch off an explosion. The birthplace of the Reformation was in the tower of the Augustinian monastery
at Wittenberg, where Luther sat before an open Bible and met God face
to face. This was the divine-human encounter which preceded the movement for reform, and from which it sprang. A man, a Bible – and God:
that is how it all began. When God aims to act, it is always through his
Word and its impact on personality.

This experience in the tower was at once the climax of Luther's quest
for theological clarification, and the issue of his struggle for faith. These
two cannot be divorced, as Boehmer reminds us.[1] The inner spiritual
experience of Luther and his intellectual enlightenment were intertwined.
The event which proved to be the decisive moment in his life involved
both these factors. Through it he came to embrace the truth of justification
both in the heart and in the head. Luther has left us his own account of the
Türmerlebnis in his letters and in his *Table Talk*. But the most detailed
description is to be found in the preface which he wrote for the collected
edition of his Latin works in 1545. He traced his career down to 1519. He
continued like this (and we must quote the extract in full because of its
significance): "Meanwhile I had already during that year returned to
interpret the Psalter anew. I had confidence in the fact that I was more
skilful, after I had lectured in the university on St. Paul's epistles to the
Romans, to the Galatians, and the one to the Hebrews. I had indeed been
captivated with an extraordinary ardour for understanding Paul in the
Epistle to the Romans. But up till then it was not the cold blood about

---

[1] Boehmer, *Road to Reformation*, p. 91.

the heart, but a single word in Chapter 1 (17), 'In it the righteousness of God is revealed,' that had stood in my way. For I hated that word righteousness of God,' which, according to the use and custom of all the teachers, I had been taught to understand philosophically regarding the formal or active righteousness, as they called it, with which God is righteous and punishes the unrighteous sinner.

"Though I lived as a monk without reproach, I felt that I was a sinner before God with an extremely disturbed conscience. I could not believe that He was placated by my satisfaction. I did not love, yes, I hated the righteous God who punishes sinners, and secretly, if not blasphemously, certainly murmuring greatly, I was angry with God, and said, 'As if, indeed, it is not enough, that miserable sinners, eternally lost through original sin, are crushed by every kind of calamity by the law of the decalogue, without having God add pain to pain by the gospel and also by the gospel threatening us with His righteousness and wrath!' Thus I raged with a fierce and troubled conscience. Nevertheless, I beat importunately on Paul at that place, most ardently desiring to know what St. Paul wanted.

"At last, by the mercy of God, meditating day and night, I gave heed to the context of the words, namely, 'In it the righteousness of God is revealed, as it is written, He who through faith is righteous shall live.' There I began to understand that the righteousness of God is that by which the righteous lives by a gift of God, namely by faith. And this is the meaning: the righteousness of God is revealed by the gospel, namely, the passive righteousness with which merciful God justifies us by faith, as it is written, 'He who through faith is righteous shall live.' Here I felt that I was altogether born again and had entered paradise itself through open gates. There a totally other face of the entire Scripture showed itself to me. Thereupon I ran through the Scriptures from memory. I also found in other terms an analogy, as, the work of God, that is, what God does in us, the power of God, with which He makes us strong, the wisdom of God, with which He makes us wise, the strength of God, the salvation of God, the glory of God.

"And I extolled my sweetest word with a love as great as the hatred with which I had hated the word 'righteousness of God'. Thus that place in Paul was for me truly the gate to paradise. Later I read Augustine's *The Spirit and the Letter*, where contrary to hope I found that he, too, interpreted God's righteousness in a similar way, as the righteousness with which God clothes us when He justifies us. Although this was heretofore said imperfectly and he did not explain all things concerning imputation clearly, it nevertheless was pleasing that God's righteousness with which we are justified was taught. Armed more fully with these thoughts, I began a second time to interpret the Psalter."[1]

[1] LW. 34. 336–7.

To this account of the tower experience in the preface to his Latin works must be added a further description collected by Conrad Cordatus in the *Table Talk*. "The words 'righteous' and 'righteousness of God' struck my conscience like lightning. When I heard them I was exceedingly terrified. If God is righteous (I thought), He must punish. But when by God's grace I pondered in the tower and heated room of this building, over the words, 'He who through faith is righteous shall live' (Rom. 1:17) and 'the righteousness of God' (Rom. 3:21), I soon came to the conclusion that if we, as righteous men, ought to live from faith and if the righteousness of God should contribute to the salvation of all who believe, then salvation will not be our merit but God's mercy. My spirit was thereby cheered. For it is by the righteousness of God that we are justified and saved through Christ. These words (which had before terrified me) now became more pleasing to me. The Holy Spirit unveiled the Scriptures for me in this tower."[1] Other versions of the same conversation are almost identical in content.[2]

Another statement by Luther reported by Anthony Lauterbach would also appear to be relevant. "That expression 'righteousness of God' was like a thunderbolt to my heart. When under the papacy I read, 'In thy righteousness deliver me' (Ps. 31:1) and 'in thy truth,' I thought at once that this righteousness was an avenging anger, namely the wrath of God. I hated Paul with all my heart when I read that the righteousness of God is revealed in the gospel (Rom. 1:16). Only afterward, when I saw the words that follow – namely, that it is written that the righteous shall live through faith (Rom. 1:17) – and in addition consulted Augustine, was I cheered. When I learned that the righteousness of God is His mercy, and that He makes us righteous through it, a remedy was offered to me in my affliction."[3] This excerpt is of particular value and interest in that it harks back to Luther's wrestling with Psalm 30/31, and then shows how "only afterward" in the tower experience did he come to a genuine understanding of God's righteousness. Two more passages in the *Table Talk* corroborate this.[4]

In yet another conversation, recorded this time by Caspar Heydenreich, Luther looked at the same event from a somewhat different angle. "For a long time I went astray (in the monastery) and did not know what I was about. To be sure, I knew something, but I did not know what it was until I came to the text in Romans 1:17, 'He who through faith is righteous shall live.' That text helped me. There I saw what righteousness Paul was talking about. Earlier in the text I read 'righteousness'. I related the abstract ('righteousness') with the concrete ('the righteous One') and

[1] LW. 54. 193–4. No. 3232c.
[2] WATR. 3. 228. Nos. 3232a and 3232b; cf. WATR. 2. 177. No. 1681.
[3] LW. 54. 308–9. No. 4007.   [4] WATR. 5. 26. No. 5247; 234–5. No. 5553.

became sure of my cause. I learned to distinguish between the righteousness of the law and the righteousness of the gospel. I lacked nothing
before this except that I made no distinction between the law and the
gospel. I regarded both as the same thing and held that there was no
difference between Christ and Moses except the times in which they lived
and their degrees of perfection. But when I discovered the proper distinction – namely, that the law is one thing and the gospel is another – I made
myself free."[1]

These extracts will have sufficed to show that what happened to Luther
in the tower was of determinative significance. This was no incidental
occurrence. It was an encounter with God which changed both the man
and the course of his life. But before we consider its meaning more
fully, the minor questions of where and when it took place must be
raised. It is not disputed that the location was somewhere in the
tower of the Augustinian (or Black) cloister at Wittenberg. But which
room was it? The accounts set down by Cordatus and Lauterbach
mentioned not only the tower but also a "heated room" or *hypocaustum*.[2]
This is also referred to by Luther in a letter to Justus Jonas in 1529.[3] Does
it mean that Luther was simply in the monastic calefactory, or communal
warming-room, or is it not more likely that the private study which he
occupied as sub-prior was supplied with a fire? Schlaginhaufen closed his
entry with a mysterious abbreviation which has been the cause of much
speculation.[4] This visitation of the Holy Spirit occurred in a place which
is indicated only in shorthand as "cl." Some have thought that it should
really be "sl." – for *solus*, meaning that the Holy Spirit alone had given
Luther this exegetical insight. Others have taken it as "cap." referring to
Chapter One in Romans. But it appears to be quite clearly "cl.", which
has been taken by a number of scholars to be an abbreviation of *cloaca* –
the toilet. But the context makes this improbable in the extreme. In any
case, the pronoun which precedes it is neuter (*das*) whilst the noun is
feminine (*cloaca*).[5] The same objection could be raised against the theory
that cl. stands for *cella*. The noun *claustrum*, however, is neuter and
Saarnivara thinks this the most likely interpretation.[6] All Luther would
then be telling us in Schlaginhaufen's account would be that his illumination occurred "in this monastery". Within the cloister was to be found the
heated study from which, as he put it, "he had stormed the Pope".[7] This
Stüblein is thought to have been situated on the second floor of the old tower
seen in the south-west corner of the building in contemporary etchings.

More complicated is the problem of when this encounter is to be dated.

[1] LW. 54. 442–3. No. 5518.   [2] Ibid., 193. No. 3232c; 308–309. No. 4007.
[3] End. 6. 117.   [4] WATR. 2. 177. No. 1681.
[5] Saarnivaara, op. cit., p. 48 n. 104. Some texts, however, read "diss" (WATR. 2. 177. No.
1681) or "dieser" (Rörer, Cordatus: WATR. 2. 177 n. 1).
[6] Saarnivaara, op. cit., p. 48 n. 104.   [7] Schwiebert, op. cit., p. 287.

Luther's detailed review in the preface to his Latin works does not really make it clear. At first glance it might be imagined that he is referring throughout to the year 1519 when he was in contact with Karl von Miltitz, a Saxon nobleman who was the emissary of the pope. But a closer examination of the text will show that, after speaking about his second set of lectures on the Psalms, begun in 1518, he goes back in his mind still further to his lectures on Romans (1515–1516). "Up till then" he had not grasped the import of righteousness. But "at last" he began to understand, and as he contemplated Rom. 1:17, he felt that he was indeed born again. Now all this seems to point to some time during his lectures on Romans, or his preparation for them, or it could be even whilst he was delivering his first series on the Psalms in 1513 to 1514. It is enough to state here that, whilst this must be regarded as an open question still, the evidence on the whole would appear to favour a date in the period between late 1513 and early 1515 – perhaps most probably in the autumn of 1514. However, as Kooiman wisely cautions us, the last word has not yet been spoken on this matter.[1]

The 'where' and 'when' of Luther's climacteric experience is much less important than the 'what.' That is to say, it is the nature of the event which matters, not its place or time. It is with what happened that we are chiefly concerned. We are warned by the more recent writers on Luther not to rest more weight on the tower encounter than it will bear. We must be careful, so we are told, not to read into it anything like an evangelical conversion. To speak, as Bainton does, about Luther's Damascus road, is regarded with considerable suspicion.[2] The same sort of reticence now inhibits those who examine the evidence relating to John Wesley's heart-warming in Aldersgate Street, London, in 1738. Of course, it may well be argued that the two instances are not altogether parallel, and that Luther's own testimony is much less explicit. Whilst, then, we must be on our guard, as Rupp admonishes us, against reading into Luther's Türmerlebnis any preconceived pattern, we cannot disregard the profound effect it indubitably had on his whole life and mission.[3] Without it he would not have become reformer. The significance of what happened to Luther in this formative period must be measured by what he eventually became as a result of it.

Nevertheless, it has to be recognized that the actual circumstances in which the light broke in upon him were at the last remove from the spectacular. "The third great religious crisis which resolved his turmoil was as the still small voice compared to the earthquake of the first upheaval in the thunderstorm at Stotternheim and the fire of the second

[1] Kooiman, op. cit., p. 43 n. 2.
[2] Roland H. Bainton, *Here I Stand: A Life of Martin Luther* (1950), p. 60.
[3] Rupp, *Luther's Progress*, p. 38.

tremor which consumed him at the saying of his first mass," writes
Bainton. "No *coup de foudre*, no heavenly apparition, no religious ceremony,
precipitated the third crisis. The place was no lonely road in a blinding
storm, nor even the holy altar, but simply the study in the tower of the
Augustinian monastery. The solution to Luther's problems came in the
midst of the performance of the daily task."[1]

Nor in treating the tower experience as decisive do we at all intend to
suggest that it was unassociated with what had gone before. This was not
something which came out of the blue, as we say. It was a crisis which
emerged from a prolonged process, as Luther grappled with the Word
of God. What rose to the surface in the moment of illumination had been
brewing for a long time. That is why André Jundt can rightly conclude
that "the discovery he made of the true sense of God's Word was the
outcome not of a sudden inspiration but of long and patient strivings".[2]
Imbart de la Tour similarly likens Luther's enlightenment, not to the
lightning flash which strikes without warning, but to the brightness of
sunrise, gradual and almost imperceptible.[3] Whilst not perhaps being
prepared to press those analogies to their limits, we must agree that what
happened to Luther in the Black Cloister lay at the end of a long quest as
well as at the beginning of a life's work.

Some attempts have been made to draw a line between the religious
and theological aspects of Luther's encounters with God. Boehmer warns
us very strongly about the danger of doing this.[4] The spiritual and doctrinal
crises were inter-related, as the struggles which preceded them had been.
For this reason we find it hard to follow Saarnivaara as he separates Luther's
personal attainment of faith from his intellectual apprehension of it by as
much as six years.[5] The first he would place in 1512 under the influence
of Staupitz. The second – the tower event – he postpones to 1518 and
interprets primarily as an enlightening of the mind. Whilst preferring to
regard Luther's religious and theological emancipation as being achieved
in a single experience, we would nevertheless seek to accord due recognition to the intellectual element involved. Luther's own word for what
happened to him is *illuminatio*.[6] Light flooded his mind and heart.

When he met God in this way, Luther had no idea where his new
insight would lead him, claims Boehmer. "He perceived at first only the
liberating and reviving effect it had upon him. The oppression which had
weighed so long upon his soul had suddenly vanished. The brazen wall

[1] Bainton, *Here I Stand*, pp. 60–61.
[2] André Jundt, *Le développement de la pensée religieuse de Luther jusqu'en 1517 d'apres de
Documents inédites* (1905), p. 3.
[3] de la Tour, op. cit., Tome II, *L'Église catholique. La crise et la renaissance* (1909), pp. 24–25.
[4] Boehmer, *Road to Reformation*, pp. 115–17.
[5] Saarnivaara, op. cit., pp. 34, 121–2.
[6] WA 43. 537; cf. WATR. 2. 177. No. 1681; WATR. 3. 228. No. 3232c.

against which his thought had beaten in vain was finally broken down. Now the stream of his ideas could pour forth unhindered and flow onward in a constantly rising flood. But he was still permitted to mature for four full years without suspecting what his real destiny would be. What he then proclaimed to the world was almost entirely the acquisition or at least, the fruit of those four quiet years in which, still pursuing his own needs, he was able to deepen and extend his new 'insight'."[1]

To this period of preparation for his reforming task we must now turn. We shall see how his encounter with God and his theological realignment in terms of justification by faith was to be reflected in the lectures he continued to deliver in the discharge of his professorial obligations. He had obtained the key to the Scriptures. There now shines through his expositions, declares Schwiebert, "the rich soul-experience through which he understood St. Paul better than had been the case for a thousand years. The God of the New Testament, who had been lost in the maze of medieval fusion of pagan and Christian elements, was once more brought to the light of day. The Bible once more became Christocentric, and Luther's lectures breathed the atmosphere of first-century Christianity".[2]

Of course, this did not happen all at once. There is no dramatic and unmistakeable transition. If that were so, then we should be in less doubt as to when exactly the illumination took place. Whilst the discovery of justification by faith crystallized in the tower, the actual change which came over Luther's articulated thinking was not immediate. After all, as Karl Holl explains, he had to undergo a radical reappraisal of his whole conception of God.[3] Assuming, as we have done, though tentatively, that the Türmerlebnis took place sometime in the autumn of 1514, we should expect to see the first signs of Luther's new outlook in his lectures on Romans, on which he embarked in November 1515. That this is in fact the case may be judged from James Mackinnon's description of this notable commentary as "a Reform manifesto".[4] It is indeed a declaration of theological independence.

Henri Strohl regarded it as a work of genius "of very great span, of remarkable clarity and vigour".[5] Holl went even further and judged it to be Luther's greatest achievement along with his Galatians in 1535, and thought it still unsurpassed.[6] In his Romans, Luther shows that what Anders Nygren called his Copernican revolution has been effected.[7] The centre of gravity in his theology has been transferred from subject to

[1] Boehmer, Road to Reformation, p. 117. [2] Schwiebert, op. cit., p. 289.
[3] Karl Holl, Gesammelte Aufsätze zur Kirchengeschichte, Bd. I (1921), p. 188.
[4] James Mackinnon, Luther and the Reformation, Vol. I, Early Life and Religious Development to 1517 (1925), p. 176.
[5] Strohl, op. cit., p. 12. [6] Holl, op. cit., Bd. I., p. 420.
[7] Anders Nygren, Agapé and Eros, Part II, The History of the Christian Idea of Love (E.T. 1939), Vol. II, pp. 463–6. Cf. Heinrich Boehmer, Luther and the Reformation in the Light of Modern Research(E.T. 1930), p. 80; Watson, op. cit., pp. 33–38.

object, from man to God. *Soli Deo gloria* was the motto of Luther no less than of Calvin. "Let God be God!" he cried.[1] This Godward reinterpretation of theology is the theme of his lectures on Romans, sounded out like a trumpet in the introduction, and reiterated throughout.[2] "The sum and substance of this letter is: to pull down, to pluck up, and to destroy all wisdom and righteousness of the flesh..., no matter how heartily and sincerely they may be practised, and to implant, establish, and make large the reality of sin.... For God does not want to save us by our own but by an extraneous righteousness which does not originate in ourselves but comes to us from beyond ourselves, which does not arise on our earth but comes from heaven."[3] The whole relationship between God and man thus rests on a divine basis, not a human one. Luther's revised view of righteousness stems from his God-orientated approach.

Other noticeable features in the lectures on Romans include a more thorough-going treatment of sin, although, as Paul Tschackert points out, Luther has not yet fully worked out his theory of concupiscence.[4] This does not mean sensuality so much as self-love. It is the essence of that egocentricity which thwarts the gracious overtures of God at every turn. Luther parted company with Augustine in recognizing no justifiable self-regard. Original sin is interpreted as implying more than mere deprivation in a purple passage without even a Rembrandtian ray of light to relieve the picture, as Mackinnon put it.[5] "The central motif of these lectures," according to Kooiman, "is that God's Word causes us to see our sin."[6]

In his comments on Romans, Luther plainly interpreted the gospel in terms of grace. The glory of God is seen in His grace.[7] Salvation hangs solely on His merciful will. It is beyond the scope of human effort.[8] The whole root and fount of redemption is in God.[9] Luther agreed with Augustine that grace is not grace unless it is free. Gift and grace are almost interchangeable terms. Grace is creative and regenerative.[10] It is always to be thought of as the personal action of God, and never as the infusion of an abstract quality. In his teaching on justification itself – the crux of his new theology – Luther deviated from Augustine and remained strictly biblical. He preferred to insist rigorously on imputation, which, as Seeberg showed, was for Luther just another name for forgiveness.[11] The imparting of righteousness does not properly belong to justification, but to the resultant process of sanctification. The place of faith is recognized

---

[1] WA. 10. i. 25.

[2] Cf. A. Skevington Wood, "The Theology of Luther's Lectures on Romans", *Scottish Journal of Theology*, Vol. 3 (1950), pp. 1–18, 113–26

[3] WA. 56. 157–8. LCC. 15. 3–4.

[4] Paul Tschackert, *Die Entstehung der lutherischen und der reformierten Kirchenlehre* (1910), p.34.

[5] Mackinnon, op. cit., Vol. I, p. 182.   [6] Kooiman, op. cit., p. 61.

[7] WA. 56. 520.   [8] Ibid., 382.   [9] Ibid., 421.

[10] Ibid., 379.   [11] Seeberg, op. cit., Bd. IV, p. 113.

without jeopardizing the sovereignty of grace. Luther defined faith as confidence in God, or belief in the reality of His promises in the Word.[1]

We have been able to do no more than touch and glance upon the salient features of Luther's theological *bouleversement* as evidenced in the pages of his lectures on Romans. He was still advancing toward his fully developed position, for he was one who, as he himself confessed, made progress whilst he wrote and taught. But, as Wilhelm Pauck observes, "we can clearly recognize in these writings the thinker who was to become the reformer of the Church and, as such, the one who introduced a new biblical theology into Christendom."[2]

We can only mention the other lectures belonging to this period. They do not, however, stand in quite the same outstanding category as those on Romans. They continue all the same to bear the stamp of a growing appreciation on Luther's part of what is meant by the evangelical message. The series on Galatians is rather disappointing, and not to be compared with the classic commentary on this epistle published in 1535.[3] Luther himself tended to discount his earlier work. Yet it is not altogether without value, and the recent English translation in the American edition makes it easier for us "to examine at first hand the engagement with Sacred Scripture out of which Luther's reformatory work and thought emerged".[4] The distinction between law and gospel is more comprehensively suggested – partly, of course, because the text of Galatians demands it. The law tells us what must be done and left undone, or rather, it exposes what has been done or left undone. The gospel, on the other hand, announces that sins have been remitted and that all that is needed has been effected.[5] The law says: "Pay what you owe;" the gospel says, "Your sins be forgiven you."[6] In this tension, the centrality of Christ becomes apparent. It was as the law made its full demand on the Son of God as He endured the cross for us that the way to forgiveness was opened. Hence our sins are no longer ours, but Christ's; and Christ's righteousness is no longer only His, but ours.[7] The extent of Luther's emancipation from medieval distortions may be measured by his stress on the fact that "in the Scriptures the righteousness of God is almost always taken in the sense of faith and grace, very rarely, in the sense of the sternness with which He condemns the wicked and lets the righteous go free, as is the custom everywhere nowadays."[8]

If the lectures on Galatians are not in Luther's best vein, those on Hebrews (1517–1518) contain some of his most noteworthy comments. Here he was almost out of the chrysalis. His theology is about to take flight. James Atkinson claims that it is all in view, even though not yet

<hr/>

[1] WA. 56. 46, 225-6.
[2] LCC. 15. xxxviii.
[3] Holl, op. cit., Bd. III (1923), p. 134.
[4] LW. 27. x.
[5] Ibid., 183-4.
[6] Ibid., 184.
[7] Ibid., 241.
[8] Ibid., 242.

completely worked out and coordinated.¹ The major themes are unmistakably evident: the centrality of Christ, the Word of God, the doctrine of
the cross, faith and works, law and gospel, and, of course, his fundamental
principle of justification by faith alone. The primacy of Scripture is everywhere implied – there are over a thousand biblical references. God works
all things only by the Word, and no-one can cooperate with Him who
does not hold fast to the Word by faith. It is "over and above all things,
beyond all things and within all things, before all things and behind all
things," and therefore inescapable.² Faith is nothing else but adherence to
the Word. It is the Word which breaks down the sinner by the law and
which raises up the believer in the gospel.

Luther's second series of lectures on the Psalms – *Operationes in Psalmos*
– stand at the end of this formative period, just as the first series – *Dictata
super Psalterium* – stand at the beginning. Although Luther himself was
later to deplore its immature theology in some places, what he had said
about faith and the Word in expounding Hebrews is here considerably
amplified, and his theology of the Cross is movingly set forth. "To know
Christ is to know the cross, and to understand God in the midst of the
crucifixion of the flesh: this is the design of God, this is the will of God,
yea, this is God."³ Some of the comments are unmistakably autobio-
graphical. Luther must have been recapitulating his own spiritual journey
when he wrote: "For a man is not truly converted until he has tasted both
of hell and heaven: that is, until he has experienced what an evil and
miserable creature he is in himself, and how sweet and good God is."⁴
It was as one who had gone through the mill in this way, that Luther was
destined to become the prophet of his age. As he confessed in the *Table
Talk*, he did not learn his theology all at once. He had to search deep for
it, where his trials took him.⁵ But he found a firmer faith his own as a
result, and his ministry was the more effective because of what he had
endured. Hence he could declare in a classic dictum: "For a man becomes
a theologian by living or rather by experience, death, and condemnation,
not by mere understanding, reading, and speculation."⁶

¹ LCC. 16. 22.   ² Ibid., 95–96.
³ Cole, 1. 148; cf. 260 – "The theology of the cross is our theology".
⁴ Ibid., 510.   ⁵ LW. 54. 50. No. 352.   ⁶ Cole, 1. 243.

CHAPTER VI

LUTHER'S STAND FOR THE TRUTH

THE EXEGETICAL LECTURES GIVEN BY LUTHER AT Wittenberg, which we examined in the previous chapter, spanned the gap between his encounter with God and the beginnings of his protest against abuses in the Church. The affixing of his Ninety Five Theses to the door of the *Schlosskirche* is usually regarded as the first salvo in the battle, although Luther's intention was scarcely so dramatic. Indeed, he may well be described as in one sense a somewhat reluctant reformer. His temperamental inclinations were not such as to endue him with an appetite for controversy, much as he later appears to have relished it, if we are to judge by the vigour of his expressions. But he would not himself have chosen to make a stand unless he had been compelled to do so by the Word of God.

In the preface to his Latin works, Luther opened a window in his heart which lets us see how diffident he must have been at the start. This presents a very different picture of Luther from that painted by his detractors, and even by some of his more partisan admirers. "At first I was alone and certainly very inept and unskilled in conducting such great affairs," he confessed. "For I got into these turmoils by accident and not by will or intention. I call upon God himself as witness."[1] Here, then, is no self-confident enthusiast, foolishly rushing in where angels fear to tread. It was only in obedience to the Word of God that Luther dared to venture forth. It was through the Scriptures that he had been brought to a personal experience of saving grace. It was through the Scriptures that he had come to recognize justification by faith as the criterion by which all teaching must be tested. It was inevitable therefore that, however much he himself shrank from it, he should be led to speak out against the apostasy of his day, from the viewpoint of his new-found faith. It was thus the Bible that made him a reformer. Others had begun to see the need for a return to a more completely scriptural outlook, but with Luther it became a ruling passion. Henceforward he was a man of one book.

> . . . In his hand
> The Thing became a trumpet; whence he blew
> Soul-animating strains.[2]

[1] LW. 34. 328.
[2] *The Poetical Works of William Wordsworth*, ed. Thomas Hutchinson (revised edn. 1950), p. 207. The reference is to John Milton and the sonnet.

In a perceptive introduction to Luther's reforming career, Harold J. Grimm has indicated the sequence of events which led up to his emergence as a prophet of renewal. He points out that Luther's programme did not begin with his attacks upon the corruption in the Church, "but with questions raised concerning his own salvation in the quiet of his monastery cell. It was there that he found an unequivocal and satisfying answer to the question which had long perturbed him and many of his contemporaries: 'How may I be certain of salvation?'"[1] The search was ended when Luther came to an understanding of what the Bible means by righteousness: this was the essence of his tower experience. Both in his mind and in his heart he embraced the justifying grace of God. "This doctrine of justification by faith and not by works, which became the fundamental principle of Protestantism, he had found in the Bible and not in the textbooks of the medieval Schoolmen. Therefore he turned from the works of men to the Word of God and enunciated the second evangelical principle which formed the basis of Protestantism: the recognition of the Bible as the sole authority in religious matters. When, finally, he came to the conclusion that the ecclesiastical hierarchy as it had developed in the Middle Ages hindered rather than aided the Christian in his personal, direct approach to God, he formulated the third fundamental principle of the Protestant Reformation: the universal priesthood of believers."[2]

Once Luther had arrived at his evangelical standpoint, it was really only a matter of time before some issue would arise which would compel him to speak, and thus bring him into conflict with the leaders of the Church. That occasion presented itself when Johann Tetzel came hawking papal indulgences within twenty miles of Wittenberg. This was more than Luther could stomach. He took his first public stand for truth as he pinned his theses to the sturdy wooden door of the church. Although he may not have been fully aware of what was involved, the die was now cast. Luther was destined to be a reformer. We must take note in this chapter of how at each point of challenge, in the stormy years from 1517, when he published the Theses, to 1521, when he was hauled before the Diet of Worms, Luther rested his defence exclusively on Scripture. We can only mark the major crises.

In 1510 the "warrior pope", Julius II, instituted a jubilee indulgence in order to pay for the new basilica of St. Peter's in Rome.[3] It was revived in 1515 by his successor Leo X, who later permitted Albrecht of Brandenberg, Elector and Archbishop, to recoup his debts to the banking house of Fuggers by pushing it in his dioceses and sharing the profits. He appointed

---

[1] LW. 31. ix.   [2] Ibid., x.
[3] Julius II was dubbed the "warrior pope" because he joined in the League of Cambrai against Venice.

a Dominican friar from Leipzig named Tetzel to be his publicity man. Tetzel had considerable experience in this sort of thing, for he had been doing it for a number of years in various parts of Europe. He had brought the sales technique to near perfection, and backed up his travelling exhibition with "patter worthy of an Autolycus".[1] Johann Tetzel was a curious mixture of the mountebank and the revivalist missioner. It seems that he quite genuinely regarded himself as an evangelist of sorts. According to Friedrich Myconius, who wrote the first history of the Reformation and had actually heard Tetzel preach, he claimed that he had saved more souls through indulgences than St. Peter had through the preaching of the gospel.[2]

Luther opened his attack in a sermon on All Saint's Eve, the 31st October 1516, in the parish church of Wittenberg. On the following day a plenary indulgence was being offered to those who venerated the relics housed there. There were so many of them that they occupied eight aisles as they were displayed. Two years later their number was no less than 17,443, and it has been calculated that those who prayed before them could gain the equivalent of 127,709 years and 116 days of indulgences.[3] Luther objected on the ground that the peddling of indulgences militated against true and inward repentance. On St. Matthew's Day, 24th February 1517, he spoke out even more sternly. Indulgences are well named, he declared, for their effect is to indulge the sinner.[4] Luther's sermon ended with this ejaculatory peroration: "Oh, the dangers of our time! Oh, you snoring priests! Oh, darkness deeper than Egyptian! How secure we are in the midst of the worst of all our evils."[5] There spoke a prophet indeed.

The Elector Frederick of Saxony would not allow Tetzel into the city of Wittenberg, but he came as near as he could. In the autumn of 1517 Luther saw a copy of the instructions issued by Archbishop Albrecht to those who were involved in the indulgence traffic. In it he suggested that it should be used as a means of reconciling men to God. It was this prostitution of the gospel which stung Luther into action. He thereupon decided to arrange a disputation on the subject in the University. He drew up a long list of the items he wanted to debate and, according to the custom, advertised them on the church door. There was nothing intentionally spectacular about what he did. As Erikson explains, it was "not a defiant gesture in itself but rather scholastic routine".[6] Luther made it plain in the preamble that he took this step "out of love and zeal for truth and

[1] *Times Literary Supplement*, 23rd February 1946, p. 86.
[2] Friedrich Myconius, *Historia Reformationis*, ed. E. S. Cyprian (1718), pp. 17-20.
[3] Schwiebert, op. cit., p. 312. Cf. Johannes Hausleiter, *Die Universität Wittenberg vor dem Eintritt Luthers* (1903), p. 26 n. 2.
[4] LW. 51. 31.   [5] Ibid.
[6] Erik H. Erikson, *Young Man Luther* (1958), p. 215.

the desire to bring it to light".[1] Not so much because of what went into
it but much more because of what came out of it, the 31st October 1517
has come to be regarded as a historic date.

Luther's jealousy for the Word of God is evident throughout. He left
no doubt that this was the ground on which he took his stance. "53. They
are the enemies of Christ and the pope who forbid altogether the preaching of the Word of God in some churches in order that indulgences may
be preached in others. 54. Injury is done to the Word of God when, in
the same sermon, an equal or larger amount of time is devoted to indulgences than to the Word. . . . 62. The true treasure of the Church is the
most holy gospel of the glory and grace of God."[2] The first four theses
lay down the scriptural definition of repentance. "1. When our Lord and
Master Jesus Christ said, 'Repent' (Matt. 4:17), He willed the entire life of
believers to be one of repentance. 2. This word cannot be understood as
referring to the sacrament of penance, that is, confession and satisfaction,
as administered by the clergy. 3. Yet it does not mean solely inner repentance; such inner repentance is worthless unless it produces various
outward mortifications of the flesh. 4. The penalty of sin remains as long
as the hatred of self, that is, true inner repentance, until our entrance into
the kingdom of heaven."[3] "These four statements introduce a world-
historical revolution," asserts Bornkamm. "They rend the tie between
the Catholic sacrament of penance and Christ's words on penitence. They
deprive the sacrament of penance of any binding power, for it would be
ridiculous for a Christian to pursue a mode of penance which does not
conform to Christ's demand."[4]

But the punch-lines in the theses are kept until later in the argument.
"35. They who teach that contrition is not necessary on the part of those
who intend to buy souls out of purgatory or to buy confessional privileges,
preach unchristian doctrine. 36. Any truly repentant Christian has a right
to full remission of penalty and guilt, even without indulgence letters.
37. Any true Christian, whether living or dead, participates in all the
blessings of Christ and the Church; and this is granted him by God, even
without indulgence letters."[5] Whereas the Roman sacrament of penance
was designed to make things easy for a man by relaxing the punishment
he deserved, Luther taught that genuine penitence will be ready to suffer
for sin and to make amends. It will be noted that a certain pseudo-
evangelical presentation of the cross offers the same soft option, which
Luther was to repudiate as sharply as the tactics of Tetzel. He would have
nothing to do with what Bonhoeffer has dubbed "cheap grace".[6]

The theses reach a ringing climax. "92. Away then with all those

[1] LW. 31. 25.   [2] Ibid., 30.   [3] Ibid., 25–26.
[4] Heinrich Bornkamm, *Luther's World of Thought* (E.T. 1958), p. 45.
[5] LW. 31. 28–29.
[6] Dietrich Bonhoeffer, *The Cost of Discipleship* (E.T. 1959), p. 35.

prophets who say to the people of Christ, 'Peace, peace,' and there is no peace! (Jer. 6:14). 93. Blessed be all those prophets who say to the people of Christ, 'Cross, cross,'' and there is no cross! 94. Christians should be exhorted to be diligent in following Christ, their head, through penalties, death, and hell; 95. And thus be confident of entering into heaven through many tribulations rather than through the false security of peace (Acts 14:22)."[1] Boehmer rightly concludes that the Ninety Five Theses are not only a religious-historical document but also a world-historical document of the first order. "When Luther attacked indulgences he involuntarily – nay, against his will – touched the pope's crown and forced the hierarchy to engage with him in a struggle which was to be the signal for half the world to revolt against Rome."[2]

It is not often noticed that nobody came to the disputation which Luther tried to convene through the medium of his theses. But when they were printed and circulated – by Luther's friends without his approval – they spread like wildfire. Myconius reported that within a fortnight they had covered the whole of Germany, and added piously: "It was as though the angels themselves were the messengers carrying the news to all peoples."[3] No doubt only the angels could have achieved such an astonishing distribution rate in so short a time, but even allowing for the exaggerations of Luther's well-wishers, it seems clear that the theses soon began to cause a stir throughout the land, and beyond. We might say that never did a meeting which failed even to take place have such an effect on mankind!

Late in 1517 Luther planned his *Explanations of the Ninety Five Theses* in order to correct misinterpretations which had already been voiced. The statement was ready in February, but in the end it did not come out until August. As Carl Folkemer remarks, it is one of the most important documents written during Luther's formative years, and "illustrates how inexorably his doctrine of justification by faith alone was compelling him to break with the past".[4] What is presented here is something much more radical than simply an elucidation of the theses. "They contain, rather, an independent reform programme of basic importance," as Boehmer discerns.[5] The *Explanations* are of the highest scholarly value.

In his opening declaration Luther laid down the biblical basis of his arguments. "First, I testify that I desire to say or maintain absolutely nothing except, first of all, what is in the Holy Scriptures and can be maintained from them; and then what is in and from the writings of the church fathers and is accepted by the Roman Church and preserved both in the canons and the papal decrees."[6] This was not an appeal to Scripture *and* tradition as set over against each other: it was an appeal to Scripture *in*

[1] LW. 31. 33.   [2] Boehmer, *Road to Reformation*, p. 189.
[3] Myconius, op. cit., p. 23.   [4] LW. 31. 79.
[5] Boehmer, *Road to Reformation*, p. 197. [6] LW. 31. 83.

c

tradition, which was always Luther's line. He did not equate tradition
with biblical doctrine, but wherever it was plainly based on Scripture he
was prepared to acknowledge it. Throughout the *Explanations* the Bible
is quoted in a plethora of references. An extract will indicate how Luther
relied on the Word of God to advance his propositions. "It is impossible
for one to be a Christian unless he possesses Christ. If he possesses Christ,
he possesses at the same time all the benefits of Christ. For the holy
apostle says in Rom. 13 (:14), 'Put on the Lord Jesus Christ.' And in
Rom. 8 (:32) he says, 'Will He not also give us all things with Him?' And
in 1 Cor. 3 (:21–22) he says, 'All things are yours, whether Cephas or
Paul, or life or death.' And in 1 Cor. 12 (cf.:27) he says, 'You are not your
own, but individually members of the body.' And in other places, where
he describes the Church as one body, one bread, we are altogether in
Christ, members one of another (cf. 1 Cor. 10:17). And in the Song of
Solomon we read, 'My beloved is mine and I am His" (Song of Sol. 2:16).
By faith in Christ a Christian is made one spirit and one body with Christ.
'For the two shall be one flesh' (Gen. 2:24). 'This is a great mystery, and I
take it to mean Christ and the Church' (Eph. 5:31, 32.)."[1]

Luther did not conceal his concern at the abuses in the Church and his
desire for renewal. "The church needs a reformation which is not the
work of one man, namely, the pope, or of many men, namely, the
cardinals ... but ... the work of God alone. However, only God who
has created time knows the time for this reformation. In the meantime
we cannot deny such manifest wrongs. The power of the keys is abused
and enslaved to greed and ambition. The raging abyss has received added
impetus. We cannot stop it. 'Our iniquities testify against us' (Jer. 14:7),
and each man's own word is a burden to him (cf. Gal. 6:5)."[2]

In the Ninety Five Theses, and in Luther's detailed *Explanation* of them,
we hear the first blasts of reform. Luther leaves us in no doubt as to where
he made his stand for truth. It was unambiguously on the basis of the
Word. Now we must notice how he defended himself against his accusers
in a series of interrogations. As in the writings we have just examined,
Luther was content to rest his case on the Scriptures. We need only mention the Heidelberg Disputation, which had in fact taken place before the
Explanation appeared in print. Luther was not on trial here. He was
simply attending the triennial general chapter of his order, which as a
provincial superior he was obliged to attend. Staupitz invited Luther,
with Leonhard Beier as respondent, to hold an academic disputation,
with a view to familiarizing the brethren with the new theology, as it
was considered to be.[3] The items discussed dealt with original sin, free

[1] Ibid., 189–90.   [2] Ibid., 250.
[3] Schwiebert, op. cit., pp. 327–8. Cf. Theodor Kolde, *Die deutsche Augustiner-kongregation
und Johann Staupitz* (1879), pp. 313–14.

will and grace. There was no reference to the indulgence controversy. As a result, most of the debate was directed against Aristotle and Occam. The Heidelberg professors were not unduly disturbed by this onslaught on Scholastic philosophy. One junior instructor, however, was more agitated, and interrupted: "If the peasants heard that, they would stone you"; but his outburst was only greeted with laughter.[1] Amongst those present was young Martin Bucer, a Dominican from Schlettstadt, who was much impressed by Luther and later became one of his staunchest supporters. He was struck by the way in which Luther had "got so far away from the bonds of the sophists and the trifling of Aristotle, one who is so devoted to the Bible, and is so suspicious of the antiquated theologians of our school."[2] He admired "his answers, so brief, so wise, and drawn from the Holy Scriptures" which quickly won over his hearers.[3]

This is borne out when we consult the forty theses Luther had drawn up in preparation for this dialogue at Heidelberg. Right at the start Luther disclaimed any dependence on his own wisdom, according to the counsel of the Holy Spirit, "Do not rely on your own insight" (Prov. 3:5).[4] His sole concern was that the debate might decide whether or not he had rightly interpreted the Scriptures. In the proofs which followed, Luther appealed to the Word in almost every other sentence. As in the *Explanations*, the argument is littered with texts. He resorted to the biblical evidence to substantiate his teaching about sin and grace, about righteousness and works, about the bondage of the will, and about the theology of the cross.[5] "Heidelberg was a triumph for Luther," observes Todd, "his last in the old world of his early monastic and university life."[6] Soon the heat was to be turned on, but his determination to stick to the truth of revelation did not falter.

The confrontation with Cardinal Cajetan at Augsburg in the summer of 1518 was more testing, although it did not match the tense inquisitions at Leipzig and at Worms. Thomas de Vio, general of the Dominican order, was the apostolic legate in Germany. He was known as Cajetan from his birthplace of Gaeta in Italy.[7] He himself had pressed the cause of reform before the Lateran Council of 1512. He was reputed to be the outstanding theologian of his time. He treated Luther with the utmost patience in the earlier part of the examination at the imperial diet, where Luther had been eventually summoned to answer for himself instead of in Rome.[8] Cajetan attempted to concentrate the enquiry on the two matters of indulgences and the efficacy of faith.[9] Whereas Cajetan repeatedly

---

[1] This was Georg Schwarz von Löwenstein (WAB. 1. 173–4 and 174 n. 8).
[2] LC. 1. 80. [3] Ibid., 82. [4] LW. 31. 39.
[5] Ibid., 53, 55–56, 58–70. [6] Todd, op. cit., p. 134.
[7] His Christian name was Jacopo, but he assumed that of Thomas in deference to Aquinas.
[8] LW. 31. 261. [9] Ibid.

appealed to the canons of the Church and papal pronouncements, Luther resolutely adhered to the testimony of Scripture.[1] He pleaded that nothing he had said or written was consciously contrary to the Word. His conscience refused to allow him to recant unless he could be convinced by Scripture.[2] "The more Cajetan insisted upon the infallibility of the papacy the more Luther relied on the authority of Scripture," according to Grimm.[3]

This attitude was maintained in the written statement which Luther presented on the third day at Augsburg. He again appealed to Scripture in upholding the doctrine of justification by faith.[4] He firmly rejected the bull of Clement VI relating to the treasure of the Church, being unwilling to "discard so many important clear proofs of Scripture on account of a single ambiguous and obscure decretal of a pope who is a mere human being. Much rather I considered it proper that the words of Scripture, in which the saints are described as being deficient in merits, are to be preferred to human words, in which saints are said to have more merits than they need. For the pope is not above, but under the Word of God, according to Gal. 1(:8): 'Even if we, or an angel from heaven, should preach to you a gospel contrary to that which you received, let him be accursed.' Furthermore, it was not unimportant to me that the bull stated that this treasure was committed to Peter, concerning which there is nothing either in the gospel or any part of the Bible."[5] In the outcome, Cajetan wilted under this continuous barrage of Scriptural proof, and brought the interview to an abrupt though inconclusive close.

Luther deplored the fact that there was such an unwillingness on the part of officialdom to settle these issues solely in terms of what had been revealed in the Word. His complaint against Cajetan was that "he never produced a syllable from the Holy Scriptures against me".[6] This failure Luther regarded as symptomatic. "Therefore, since the sacred Scriptures are abandoned and the traditions and words of men are accepted, it happens that the Church of Christ is not nourished by its own measure of wheat, that is, by the Word of Christ, but is usually misled by the indiscretion and rash will of an unlearned flatterer. We have come to this in our great misfortune that these people begin to force us to renounce the Christian faith and deny Holy Scriptures."[7]

In November 1518, Luther appealed from the pope to a general council. Meanwhile Karl von Miltitz was sent as a papal agent to try to settle the affair of Luther. This smooth diplomat – "a kind of ecclesiastical von Ribbentrop", as Rupp delineates him – persuaded Luther to pen a

---

[1] Ibid., 278.   [2] Ibid., 262.
[3] Ibid., 263. When Cajetan declared that the Pope possessed power over everything, Luther broke in with "Salva Scriptura – except the Scripture" (W. 15. 681).
[4] LW. 31. 265–7, 271–4.   [5] Ibid., 266–7.
[6] Ibid., 275.   [7] Ibid., 276.

pacific letter to Leo X in March 1519.[1] At the same time, however, the reformer gave himself to research into the history of the papacy.[2] He had been convinced from the Scriptures that indulgences were wrong. Now he found that it still remained technically the case that the authority of Scripture was in fact above that of the pope, and that, in any event, it was possible to regard a council as superior to a papal decree. Armed with this information, Luther was ready to answer the summons to appear in Leipzig for a public disputation with Johann Eck, in July of the same year.

Johann Meier, from Eck in Swabia, was a distinguished controversialist at the University of Ingoldstadt. He was a man of real mettle. Indeed, "if quickness and repartee could have won the victory," remarks Owen Chadwick, "Eck would have laid Luther low with ease."[3] However, his wit was not matched by a comparable mastery of the true source of theology in the Word of God. The debate "showed forth Luther's unrivalled knowledge of the Bible", as Todd concedes.[4] That all arguments must be based on the Scriptures was made plain by the professor of poetry at Leipzig, Peter Mosellanus, in his rather dreary opening oration. The first debate was between Eck and Karlstadt, in which the former was considered to have scored a triumph, although it was only a superficial one. It was thus with boosted confidence – though he had little need of such encouragement – that Eck faced Luther in the second part of the proceedings. Once again, as at Augsburg, Luther refused to be drawn away from his unequivocal reliance on Scripture. No other arguments would he employ himself and no other arguments would he allow to his opponent than those based on the Word. He knew that his position was unassailable. No one could overthrow him without at the same time jeopardizing the Scriptures.

It was as he maintained his stand that Luther became even more assured that he was right. Schwiebert has shown how important was the contest with Eck in consolidating his own convictions. "In the Leipzig Debate he came face to face with the orthodox Roman position on sin, grace, justification, the Church, and papal power, and he began to realize how far he had really drifted. Eck's blind fanatical acceptance of a position that seemed untenable on the basis of the clearly revealed Word of God made Luther realize that the whole Roman hierarchy rested on a very flimsy foundation. He determined that the principle of *Sola Scriptura* would have to be the basis for testing all decisions of church councils and the official

[1] Rupp, *Luther's Progress*, p. 64.
[2] CR. 1. 96. Cf. Ernst Schäfer, *Luther als Kirchenhistoriker* (1897), pp. 53–55.
[3] Owen Chadwick, *The Reformation, The Pelican History of the Church*, Vol. III (1964), p. 49.
[4] Todd, op. cit., p. 164. Mosellanus reported concerning Luther at Leipzig: "He is so wonderfully learned in the Bible that he has almost all the texts in memory. He has learned enough Greek and Hebrew to form a judgment of the translations. He has no lack of matter in speaking, for an immense stock of ideas and words are at his command" (LC. 1. 261).

decrees of the papacy as recorded in Canon Law."[1] It may well have been this increasing disenchantment which prompted Luther, in the highlight of the whole debate, to take his stand quite openly as one in the line of John Hus. This has been regretted by some as a tactical error, but it was in fact a prophetic *tour de force*. The words "fell like a stone into the hall", reported an eye-witness.[2] Luther had nailed his colours to the mast. He was ready to pay the price of reform.

Luther's parting shaft at the Leipzig Disputation was directed at Eck's refusal to meet Scripture with Scripture. "I regret that the holy doctor penetrates the Scriptures as deeply as a spider does the water: in fact, he runs away from them as the devil from the cross. Therefore, with all my regard for the fathers, I prefer the authority of the Scriptures, which I commend to those who will judge me."[3] "The Leipzig debate cast down the last barrier which restrained his antagonism to Rome," writes Owen Chadwick, with reference to Luther. "He had publicly and irrevocably identified himself, in part, with a man condemned by the authorities of the Universal Church. Henceforth he expected antipathy and incompatibility between the Bible and ecclesiastical authorities as now constituted, between the truth taught in the Word of God and the errors taught in the human tradition of papal churchmen."[4]

All this helps us to see Luther's historic stance at the Diet of Worms in perspective. It was no sudden, unpremeditated inspiration. It represented the crystallization of convictions which had been maturing over several years. He had long been captive to the Word. Now he said so in the presence of the Emperor and to the world. Forty-one propositions set forth by Luther were condemned as heretical in the bull *Exsurge Domine* of the 15th June 1520. He was given sixty days to recant. His books were to be burnt, and in Louvain and Cologne the flames consumed them. Luther retorted by casting a copy of the bull, together with the text of canon law and the papal decretals, into a bonfire in a meadow down by the River Elbe at Wittenberg.[5] On the 3rd January 1521 his excommunication was ratified, and the battle was on. "All Germany is in revolution," wrote the papal nuncio, Girolamo Aleander; "Nine tenths shout 'Luther!' as their war-cry; and the other tenth cares nothing about Luther, and cries: 'Death to the court of Rome!'"[6]

This was the setting for the notorious Diet of Worms. The Emperor gave Luther a safe-conduct, but it was a brave decision when he decided

[1] Schwiebert, op. cit., p. 416.
[2] W. 15. 1430. The eye-witness was Sebastian Fröschel.
[3] WA. 2. 282.   [4] Chadwick, op. cit., p. 51.
[5] This was outside the Elster Gate. Afterwards the students held their own celebration. Green (op. cit., pp. 92–93) describes it as "a theatrical demonstration that was half-way between an academic occasion and a university bump supper".
[6] *Die Depeschen des Nuntius Aleander von Wormser Reichstage 1521*, ed. Paul Kalkoff (1886), SVR. 17. 43.

to accept it. Hus had gone to the council of Constance under similar protection and had been burnt at the stake. But Luther nevertheless assured Georg Spalatin that he would go to Worms "in spite of all the gates of hell and the powers in the air".[1] His interlocutor was another Eck, not to be confused with the Ingoldstadt professor who tilted with him at Leipzig. This was Johann von Eck, secretary to the Archbishop of Trier. He was an experienced jurist, but not so ebullient as his namesake. At first Luther was simply asked whether the books which had been put out in his name (some twenty of them were piled on the table in full view of all) were in fact his, and then whether he wanted to retract anything in them.[2] After Jerome Schurff, professor of law at Wittenberg, who acted as Luther's adviser, had demanded that the titles be read, the reformer asked that, since the issue concerned "the divine Word, which we are all bound to reverence, for there is nothing greater in heaven or on earth", he might have time to consider his answer.[3] The hearing was thereupon adjourned until four p.m. on the following day, the 18th April 1521.

Then it was that Luther made a considered statement, over which we know he spent much prayer as well as time. The notes are still to be seen in the Weimar archives. Not all his books fell into the same group, he explained.[4] Some had to do with faith and morals, and did not raise any query even in the minds of his critics.[5] Some were attacks on the papacy, which if he retracted would open not only windows but doors to tyranny and godlessness.[6] Some were directed against individuals who had upheld the *status quo* and, although he admitted that his tone had been more violent at times than became his calling, since what was at stake was the truth of Christ, he could not withdraw.[7] Luther then declared that he would seek no other protection for his books than that which the Lord Jesus Christ offered for his teaching: "If I have spoken wrongly, bear witness to the wrong" (John 18:23).[8] He was not surprised that he had caused such commotion. "To see excitement and dissension arise because of the Word of God is to me clearly the most joyful aspect of all in these matters. For this is the way, the opportunity, and the result of the Word of God, just as He (i.e. Christ) said, 'I have not come to bring peace, but a sword. For I have to come to set a man against his father, etc.' (Matt. 10:34–35). Therefore we ought to think how marvellous and terrible is our God in His counsels, lest by chance what is attempted for settling strife grows rather into an intolerable deluge of evils, if we begin condemning the Word of God."[9]

---

[1] WAB. 2. 298. Luther had written to Melanchthon from Gotha: "I shall enter Worms under Christ's leadership in spite of the gates of hell" (WAB. 2. 296 n. 3). The *Table Talk* has "even though there should be as many devils in Worms as tiles on the roof I would still enter" (WATR. 5. 65. No. 5342a).
[2] LW. 32. 106.   [3] Ibid., 107.   [4] Ibid., 109.   [5] Ibid., 109–10.
[6] Ibid., 110.   [7] Ibid., 110–11.   [8] Ibid.   [9] Ibid.

When Luther had finished, Eck reproached him for having evaded the question, and demanded not a horned response (i.e. a sophistical, ambiguous reply), but a simple one. Did he or did he not wish to retract?[1] Then it was that Luther uttered his most famous words, as he stood for the truth on the ground of the Scriptures. "Since then your serene majesty and your lordships seek a simple answer, I will give it in this manner, neither horned nor toothed: Unless I am convinced by the testimony of the Scriptures or by clear reason (for I do not trust either the pope or in councils alone, since it is well known that they have often erred and contradicted themselves), I am bound by the Scriptures I have quoted and my conscience is captive to the Word of God. I cannot and will not retract anything, since it is neither safe nor right to go against conscience."[2] Then he added: "May God help me. Amen." It was in the earliest printed version of the story that the now familiar words were inserted: "Here I stand; I cannot do otherwise."[3] Bainton thinks that the saying may indeed be authentic, though not recorded on the spot, because the hearers were too moved to write.[4] But whether or not the words were actually uttered, they sum up all that Luther intended to convey by his heroic defence.

There was an uproar as Luther left. Outside, he raised his arms, like a knight who had unhorsed his opponent, and shouted: "I've come through!"[5] And so he had, with the sword of the Spirit, which is the Word of God, as his weapon. Kierkegaard called him "the knight of faith," and such he proved to be.[6]

---

[1] Ibid., 112.   [2] Ibid.   [3] Ibid., 113.
[4] Bainton, *Here I Stand*, p. 185. The words may have been drowned in the ensuing commotion, for Conrad Peutinger reported that "there was a great noise·" (Johannes Kühn, *Luther und der Wormser Reichstag 1521*, Voigtländer Quellenbücher (1914), Bd. LXXIII, p. 75 n. 4).
[5] *Deutsche Reichstagakten unter Kaiser Karl V*, ed. Adolf Wrede, Bd. II (1896), p. 853.
[6] Søren Kierkegaard, *Concluding Unscientific Postscript* (E.T. 1941), p. 452.

PART II

Luther and the Bible
(a)

LUTHER'S USE OF SCRIPTURE

CHAPTER VII

LUTHER AS A COMMENTATOR

IT IS ALL TOO EASILY IMAGINED THAT MARTIN
Luther was mainly, if not exclusively, cast in the mould of an agitator
and controversialist. He is commonly regarded as a prophet of fire, but
little more. In consequence, his considerable scholarship is altogether overlooked, and it is assumed that his serious exegetical achievement was
virtually negligible. His name is not associated, in the uninformed mind,
with the production of biblical commentaries. Calvin is more often seen
in this context, but hardly Luther. This failure to realize the scope of
Luther's varied gifts – not least those of the intellect – is not always confined to popular misconceptions of his capabilities. It sometimes even
vitiates what claims to be an expert assessment. Hence a contributor to a
standard encyclopedia could announce that "of the reformers Luther did
little strictly exegetical work apart from his preaching".[1]

It is incredible that such a verdict could be passed on one who held the
chair of biblical exegesis at a highly reputable German university for
over thirty years, and whose published commentaries cover so many
books of the Bible. It was in the fulfilment of his professorial duties that
Luther was brought to understand that the key to Scripture lies in a
proper interpretation of God's righteousness. It was in this same capacity
that he pinned his Ninety Five Theses to the door of the Castle Church at
Wittenberg. It was as holding this office that he sounded the trumpet of
reform. When he died in 1546, he was still Professor Luther, Doctor of
Sacred Scripture.

Indeed, we have to be yet more explicit and point out, as Bornkamm
has done, that if Luther belonged to a modern faculty, he would not
occupy the chair of New Testament exegesis, still less that of systematic
theology or dogmatics.[2] If we are to judge from his actual courses in the
classroom, he would be a teacher of the Old Testament. Jaroslav Pelikan
reminds us that "the most ironic feature of the reinterpretation of Luther's
thought on the basis of his exegetical work is that this rediscovery of
Luther as a biblical theologian will bring Luther scholarship back into
line with Luther! For it was as a biblical theologian that Luther understood himself and wanted others to understand him."[3] He goes on to say

[1] H. S. Nash, 'Hermeneutics', NSH. 4. 244.
[2] Heinrich Bornkamm, *Luther und das Alte Testament* (1948), p. 6.
[3] LW Companion Volume, 46.

75

that *Doctor in Biblia* more than any other title summarizes Luther's own sense of vocation and mission.[1]

In his exposition of the Sermon on the Mount, Luther met the challenge of an imaginary critic who asked: "Why do you publicly attack the pope and others, instead of keeping the peace?"[2] Here is Luther's answer: "A person must advise and support peace while he can and keep quiet as long as possible. But when the sin is evident and becomes too widespread or does public damage, as the pope's teaching has, then there is no longer time to be quiet but only to defend and attack, especially for me and others in public office whose task it is to teach and warn everyone. I have a commission and charge, as a preacher and a doctor, to see to it that no one is misled, so that I may give account of it at the Last Judgment (Heb. 13:17). So St. Paul (Acts 20:28) commands the preachers to watch and guard their whole flock against the wolves that were to appear among them. Thus it is my duty to chastise public sinners so that they may improve, just as a judge must publicly condemn and punish evildoers in the performance of his office."[3] It will be noted that Luther had as high a conception of his teaching function as he did of his calling as a preacher. In those days the two belonged together. Each professor had to preach, and each preacher had to teach his congregation. Pulpit and desk were related. Luther taught from the pulpit and exhorted from the desk, as well as *vice versa*.

His call to be an instructor in the Word came to him through the instrumentality of Staupitz.[4] One day in September 1511, a group of monks at Wittenberg were sitting in the shade of a pear tree. As a member of the university senate the vicar-general had just been recognizing four candidates for the doctorate. He caught sight of Luther and, knowing something of his uncertainties, said to him: "Herr Magister, you must become a doctor and preacher; then you will have something to do." A few days later Luther came to Staupitz with a string of fifteen objections. "Why, my dear fellow," replied Staupitz, "you don't want to set yourself up as wiser than the whole community and all the fathers too!" Luther retorted: "Herr Staupitz, you will bring me to my death. I will never endure it for three months." But his kindly counsellor refused to let the earnest young monk take himself too seriously. "Don't you know," he added playfully, "that our Lord God has many great matters to attend to? For these He needs clever people to advise Him. If you should die, you will be welcomed into His council in heaven, for He too has a vacancy for one or two doctors."[5]

It was through the good offices of Staupitz that Luther first presented

[1] Ibid.   [2] LW. 21. 44.   [3] Ibid.
[4] LW. 54. 320. No. 4091 – "Staupitz drove me to it"; cf. WATR. 2. 245. No. 1878.
[5] WATR. 2. 379. No. 22552; 3. 188. No. 3143b; cf. 5. 98. No. 5371, C.R. 6. 160.

himself for the doctorate, which he gained at the exceptionally early age of twenty-eight, and then took up the *lectura in Biblia*, which Staupitz relinquished in his favour. Thus in 1512 Luther committed himself to the task of biblical exposition as a life-work. The terms of his contract required him to stick to the post for the rest of his career. Luther was not slack concerning the promise implicit in his vocation. From then on he delivered at least two or three lectures each week, unless prevented by sickness or his multifarious activities in the cause of the Reformation. In one sense, Luther's onslaught on the evils in the Church and his stand for Scriptural truth are almost incidental. They both emerged in the line of duty. In his commentary on Psalm 82 which appeared in 1521, Luther tried to explain his position to those who enquired why, since he was a professor and preacher at Wittenberg, he wished to reach the whole world through his books. "I answer: I have never wanted to do it and do not want to do it now. I was forced and driven into this position in the first place, when I had become Doctor of Holy Scripture against my will. Then, as a doctor in a general free university, I began, at the command of pope and emperor, to do what such a doctor is sworn to do, expounding the Scriptures for all the world and teaching everybody. Once in this position I have had to stay in it, and I cannot give it up or leave it yet with a good conscience, even though both pope and emperor were to put me under the ban for doing so. For what I began as a doctor, made and called at their command, I must truly confess to the end of my life. I cannot keep silence or cease to teach, though I would like to do so and am weary and unhappy because of the great and unendurable ingratitude of the people."[1] There spoke a man who was clearly under authority to God and to the Word.

In dealing with Luther as a commentator, we can base our estimate, of course, only on those lectures of his which were eventually published or have been preserved in students' notes. But we know of others which have not survived. The complete catalogue, so far as it can be ascertained, is as follows.[2] Those that are in print are marked with an asterisk.

1512–1513 Genesis (?)
1513–1515 *Psalms
1515–1516 *Romans
1515–1516 Galatians
1517–1518 *Hebrews
1518–1521 Psalms; *Galatians (revised), Titus, Judges (?)
1523–1525 Deuteronomy

[1] LW 13. 66. Luther's inaugural oration as a doctor was probably an encomium on the Scriptures (Fife, op. cit., p. 18 n. 2).
[2] Cf. A. Skevington Wood, *Luther's Principles of Biblical Interpretation* (1960), pp. 9–10.

Despite this considerable productivity, springing from more than competent technical equipment, Luther modestly disclaimed any title to distinction. After thanking Johann Brenz, a learned pastor in Schwäbisch-Halle, for a sight of his commentary on Amos, he added: "Far be it from me to suggest any alterations, for I cannot set up as a master in the divine writings. I only wish to be a learner in that school."[1]

The noticeable omission from the curriculum, of course, is that of the four Gospels. But, as Gerhard Ebeling explains, there was no exclusion on principle.[2] Luther had once announced a series on the pericopes, or Gospel passages in the liturgy, in 1521, but he was prevented from delivering it because of his summons to the Diet of Worms. Moreover, the task of instruction was shared by his colleagues in the faculty, and we know that Melanchthon gave a course on Matthew and John, whilst Dolsch lectured on Luke and a little later so did Lambert and Agricola. Luther himself handled the Gospels not in the classroom but in the pulpit. This is not to suggest, however, that his treatment is therefore unworthy of serious consideration. Our accepted modern distinction between preaching and biblical exegesis was unrecognized by Luther. As we have seen, the functions of pulpit and desk coalesced. Luther's preaching was always expository in character, and his exegetical lectures invariably contained a homiletical element not nowadays associated, for good or ill, with scholarly comment. As J. W. Heikinnen makes clear, Luther's exegesis was essentially kerygmatic.[3]

In our estimate of Luther as a commentator we shall concentrate on his methodology. His principles of interpretation will be discussed in a later chapter.[4] By reference to Luther's earlier lectures in particular, we will try to discover how he freed himself from the shackles of medieval exegesis, and arrived at a new way of approaching Scripture and elucidating its meaning. In doing so, however, we must avoid the pitfalls of an undue denigration of scholastic attitudes. We cannot dismiss the Middle

[1] LML. 196.
[2] Gerhardt Ebeling, *Evangelische Evangelien-Auslegung* (1942), p. 13.
[3] Jacob W. Heikinnen, "Luther's Lectures on the Romans", *Interpretation*, Vol. VII (1953), p. 180.
[4] See below, pp. 159–168.

Ages as altogether barren in this field. Important work in biblical exposition was pressed forward in this period, as Miss Beryl Smalley has shown in her definitive book on *The Study of the Bible in the Middle Ages*, which should be consulted by all who seek an honest and impartial assessment. Nevertheless, it remains true that, as E. C. Blackman points out, "there had developed a regrettable shift of emphasis from the Bible to the fathers, and from seeking the direct guidance of the Spirit to reliance on established usage, so that the main task of the reformers in the sixteenth century was to redress the balance and put the Bible back in its place".[1]

The real weakness of medieval exegesis lay in its rigid insistence that Scripture must always be interpreted in a fourfold sense. According to Guibert of Nogent, these are the rules on which the sacred page revolves as if on wheels.[2] The *quadriga* can be traced back to John Cassian.[3] In each part of Scripture four different meanings could be found. The first was literal and explained the historical contents. The allegorical clarified matters of faith, by revealing the hidden spiritual significances. The moral sense indicated rules of human conduct, whilst the anagogical dealt with the future to be hoped for. This method still persisted in the sixteenth century and, indeed, tended to dominate the lecture rooms. It is mentioned in the famous Complutensian polyglot Bible, produced by Cardinal Ximenes and published in 1520 at Alcala. In the first volume this couplet is quoted:

> *Littera gesta docet: quid credas allegoria.*
> *Moralis quid agis: quo tendas anagogia.*
> ("The letter teaches what has been done, the allegory what you are to believe, the moral what you must do, and the anagogy where you are heading for.")

It is not difficult to realize what inhibitions such a method of exegesis could impose. It puts the Scripture in a straightjacket. Luther sought to release the Bible from its bondage and restore the primacy of the plain, literal sense. This had never been entirely obscured during the Middle Ages, and in Thomas Aquinas the balance was considerably redressed in its favour. He believed that "all interpretations are based on one, that is the literal, from which alone we can argue".[4] He was not the pioneer in this matter, however, as Miss Smalley has demonstrated, although it was his own great authority which gave weight to the tendency. Miss Smalley ascribes the credit to Albert the Great, whose pupil Thomas was, and who insisted that his custom was not to concern himself

[1] Edwin C. Blackman, *Biblical Interpretation: The Old Difficulties and the New Opportunity* (1957), p. 109.
[2] Guibert de Nogent, *Quo Ordine Sermo Fieri Debet*, PL. 156. 25.
[3] John Cassian, *Conlationes*, 14. 8.
[4] Thomas Aquinas, *Summa Theologica*, 1. 3. 10.

"with divisions which cannot be deduced from the letter."[1] Richard
of St. Victor must share the honour, and Nicolas of Lyra – the Jerome
of the fourteenth century – continued the trend.[2] Luther, then,
was not altogether an innovator as he championed a return to the
straightforward meaning of Scripture. He picked out of the past what he
felt was in line with the way in which the Bible itself demanded interpretation.

The first assumption of medieval exegesis which Luther challenged
was the acceptance of the Vulgate as the basis of comment. There was as
yet no suggestion in the Church that the Hebrew and Greek texts might
take the place of the official Latin version for the purpose of research. The
Vulgate was venerated as if it were inspired. The humanist movement
was still in its infancy. Reuchlin's *De Rudimentis* appeared only in 1506,
Lefèvre's *Quintuplex Psalterium* in 1509, and Erasmus' New Testament not
until 1516. It was only after this date that Luther began to pay greater
deference to the original texts. By the time that he was ready to embark
on his translation of the Bible in 1521, he had unreservedly recognized the
need to work from the Hebrew and Greek. This factor becomes increasingly apparent in his commentaries. In the *Dictata Super Psalterium* he
still showed a preference for the Vulgate, and expressed his opinion
that it did justice to the spiritual sense better than any other version. But
when he treated the Psalms a second time in the *Operationes in Psalmos*,
he did not hesitate to use the Hebrew text. In his lectures on Romans
there is quite a dramatic turning-point. In the first eight chapters his
acquaintance with the Greek text was limited to what he could glean
from Lefèvre's translation and comment. But by the time he reached
the ninth chapter, Luther was using the New Testament in Greek
published by Erasmus, and from then on his notes fairly bristle with
references.[3]

Luther's debt as a commentator to the biblical humanists did not end
there. Not only did he learn from them to accord the primacy to the
original texts. He was able to avail himself of the lexical aids they provided.
Reuchlin's *De Rudimentis* was a combined Hebrew grammar and lexicon,
of which it has been said that "it placed the hitherto almost neglected
scientific study of the Hebrew language on an entirely new basis and
became a powerful incentive to the study of the Old Testament in the
original".[4] This was exactly its effect on Luther. There were also extended

[1] Beryl Smalley, *The Study of the Bible in the Middle Ages* (1940), p. 299. Cf. I. M. Vosté,
S. Albertus Magnus, ii. *In Vetus Testamentum* (1932–1937), p. 6.
[2] LCC. 10. 321. A. Skevington Wood, "Nicolas of Lyra", *Evangelical Quarterly*, Vol.
XXXIII (1961), pp. 196–206.
[3] Quanbeck, op. cit., p. 77.
[4] ODCC 1159. Luther obtained Reuchlin's *De Rudimentis* in the early days of his studies at
Erfurt (WAB. 2. 547).

philological annotations in Reuchlin's edition of the *Seven Penitential Psalms*, which Luther obtained in 1512.[1] Later he produced a treatise on Hebrew accents and orthography. Lefèvre and Erasmus rendered Luther a similar service so far as Greek was concerned, and afterwards he had Melanchthon to give him expert help. He used the lexicon of Girolamo Aleander, the papal envoy, who introduced humanist studies into France as rector of the University in Paris. Ironically, it was Aleander who officially denounced Luther at the Diet of Worms. Luther was also indebted to John Chrysostom, the golden-mouthed orator of the fourth century, who was no mean scholar and supplied valuable lexical notes in his commentaries.

Thus by providing a better text of the Bible and a number of tools for the job, the biblical humanists enabled Luther to pioneer a new exegetical methodology. It is here that his significance as a commentator lies. Warren Quanbeck summarises the process we have just been describing: "By making available the Hebrew and Greek texts of the Scriptures, Reuchlin and Erasmus opened the way to freedom from the limitations and restrictions of medieval methods. The combination of new theological insights, improved textual and lexicographical tools, and doctrinal controversy with Rome, enabled Luther to outgrow the exegetical methods in which he had been trained. Beginning with the *Operationes in Psalmos* of 1519, Luther began his search for new forms to accord more aptly with his new and almost mature exegetical principles."[2]

Luther not only broke free from the stranglehold of the fourfold sense, and reinstated the original text of Scripture. He also shed the traditional technique of exposition by means of glosses and *scholia*. When he started lecturing, he adopted the conventional approach, as his notebooks show. But he was soon to achieve a much more flexible and effective manner of presentation. In the customary routine, students were given a printed copy of the Latin text of Scripture in a special edition. Luther got Johann Decker from Grünenberg, a fellow monk, to prepare such a book with wide margins and ample space between the lines.[3] The lecturer would then begin by dictating the glosses, to be inserted into the text in the interlinear gaps. By this means, almost every word was paraphrased. Longer notes would be added in the margins. These *glossula* would deal with especially difficult expressions. Much of this material would have been borrowed in the first place from the *Glossa Ordinaria*, ascribed to Walafrid Strabo, a ninth-century abbot of Reichenau, but now thought

---

[1] This was the first Hebrew text printed in Germany. It was published on the 1st August 1512 by Thomas Anshelm of Tübingen.

[2] Quanbeck, op. cit., pp. 71-72.

[3] Karl A. Meissinger, *Luthers Exegese in der Frühzeit* (1916), pp. 1-2.

to have been a composite work.[1] It was a collection of comments from the outstanding exegetes of the Church, and proved a valuable mine of information for the teacher who either had no opportunity or no inclination to do his own research. This was supplemented by the *Glossa Interlinearis*, linked with the name of Anselm from Laon.[2]

After the lecturer had exhausted the glosses on the text under examination, he turned to more extended and detailed comments on passages of special interest or difficulty. These were known as *scholia*. They gave the teacher much more scope. He could choose whatever portions he wished to dilate upon, and could really spread himself. Yet once again, the tendency was not to indulge in speculation nor even in creative comment, but simply to rehearse what the established expositors had said.[3] Bound up with the *Glossa Ordinaria* and the *Glossa Interlinearis* were to be found in most cases what were known as the *Postilla* and the *Annotationes* or *Additiones*.[4] Six folio volumes altogether comprised this popular set. The *Postilla* were the work of Nicolas of Lyra, and perhaps so named since the comments came "after those, i.e. words of Scripture" (*post illa*).[5] Later, a postil meant a homily on the Gospel or Epistle for the day, or a book of such homilies. The *Annotationes* were the additions to Lyra by Archbishop Paul of Burgos, mentioned by Luther along with Lyra as preferring the Hebrew text to that of the Vulgate.[6]

Although Luther does not explicitly refer to the *Glossae*, it is likely that, in common with his contemporaries, he resorted to them at first. Certainly his early lectures were divided in the traditional way into glosses and *scholia*. This can be seen in the published lectures on Romans and Hebrews. In the translation of the latter in the *Library of Christian Classics*, the editor has used the *scholia* as the meat of the comment, with the glosses incorporated *ad loc*.[7] In his introduction to Luther's commentary on Romans, Wilhelm Pauck sees him liberating himself from the restrictions of this medieval methodology. "In his first exegetical course, the *Dictata super Psalterium*, he was still very closely bound to this established manner of interpretation. Later on, he gradually freed himself from it. Indeed, from 1519 on, he abandoned it altogether. In the lectures on Romans, he exhibits a use of it that we may regard as characteristic of his way of doing

---

[1] Cf. Smalley, op. cit., p. 56: "a bibliographical legend". J. de Ghellinck accepted the traditional ascription (*Le mouvement théologique du XII siècle* (2nd edn. 1948), pp. 104–12, but J. de Blic administered the *coup de grâce* ("L'oevre exégétique de Walafrid Strabon et la *Glossa Ordinaria*", *Recherches de théologie ancienne et médiéval*, Tome XVI (1949), pp. 5–28); cf. ODCC. 1434. In view of this it is surprising to find that the fiction is still perpetuated in some recent works on Luther – e.g. Quanbeck, op. cit., p. 68; LCC. 15. xxvi (Pauck); but cf. LW. 8. 209 n. 9.
[2] ODCC. 59. Cf. Smalley, op. cit., pp. 60–62; Lcc. 15. xxvi.
[3] Quanbeck, op. cit., p. 61.   [4] Ibid., p. 69.
[5] ODCC. 1094.   [6] WA. 3. 518.
[7] LCC. 16. 29–250.

intellectual work: under his hands the interlinear gloss often becomes a very succinct restatement of the words and ideas of the apostle. For he explains the individual passages of the letter by illuminating them through reference to its other parts. Moreover, he formulates his explanatory comments and paraphrases so as to exclude meanings that the apostle could have had in mind when he wrote the letter.

As far as Luther's marginal glosses are concerned they are no longer mere collectanea from the writings of the fathers, but brief incisive comments on selected short passages or individual terms or phrases. He combines them with quotations from Scripture or with critical or commendatory remarks on the writings of certain ones of the fathers (chiefly Jerome, whom he makes the butt of many criticisms, and especially Augustine, on whom he generally bestows high praise) or with references to the interpretations of recent scholars (mainly Faber Stapulensis and Erasmus)."[1] In the *scholia*, too, Pauck tells us, Luther's style is often highly impassioned and personal, quite unlike the conventional academic manner of his day.[2]

By the time Luther came to handle Galatians in the autumn of 1516, he rid himself more completely of the legacy he had inherited. The *glossae* and *scholia* have disappeared altogether. The *quadriga* has been largely replaced by a major stress on the literal sense, in conjunction with a spiritual interpretation arising from it. But Luther criticized the accepted notion of a spiritual sense, since it ignored Augustine's distinction between the spirit and the letter. It was not until after his confrontation with the papal theologians, however, that Luther finally discarded the multiple pattern of exegesis, and relied on what he came to call the historical sense. In this Luther may rightly be hailed, not only as the father of Protestant exegesis, but of modern exegesis too.

The gains he made in these formative years were developed in the lectures he gave so regularly until his death in 1546. His presentation grew more free and flexible. His method of preparation changed, for, as experience increased, he no longer required the extensive notes on which he formerly relied. His mind was so stored with scriptural content that, as Kooiman puts it, "he could lecture from the overflow".[3] His mastery of the material had left far behind the cramping impediment. of medieval exposition, with its microscopic scrutiny of the text. Luther now ranged freely over the whole of Scripture, and stressed the need for a synoptic view of each book in itself and of each book in its setting. "I am the first to place primary emphasis on the importance of laying hold upon the meaning of the book, that which it wants to say, the essential viewpoint of the author," he wrote, when he was working on Ecclesiastes. "If we

---

[1] LCC. 15. xxvi-xxvii.   [2] Ibid., xxvii.
[3] Kooiman, op. cit., p. 193.

do not know this central fact, it is impossible to understand a book."[1] Whilst realizing the significance of the minutiae in Scripture – since he believed each single word to be inspired – Luther sought in his later years to see the whole as well as the part.

When in 1535 he started on his study of Genesis he had a premonition that it would be his swan song as a commentator. "This will be my last work," he wrote, "with which, if God wills, I will end my life."[2] Already in a lecture on Psalm 90, he had announced his intention of devoting the remaining years which the Lord might still grant him to an exposition of the books of Moses.[3] When he had completed this course, he promised: "Later we shall if the Lord lengthens my life, interpret Genesis; thus, when our end comes, we shall be able to die joyfully, being engaged in the Word and work of God."[4] And when the first part of Genesis was published, he reiterated the conviction that this would be his final commentary.[5] Luther's last lecture on Genesis was on the 17th November 1545. "So Joseph died. . . and was put in a coffin." (Gen. 50: 26): that was the verse with which he closed. It seemed to be prophetic. "This is now the dear Genesis," he concluded. "God grant that after me others will do better. I can do no more. I am weak. Pray God for me that he may grant me a good and blessed last hour."[6] Luther finished as he began – as a Doctor of Sacred Scripture. But his best commentary was not written with pen and ink, nor printed in a book. It was his life, lived in obedience to God and to his Word. In his faithful, though not faultless, witness to the truth he had embraced, Luther was a living commentary, known and read by all.

[1] Ibid., p. 194.   [2] Ibid., p. 197.   [3] LW. 13. 75.
[4] Ibid., 141.   [5] Kooiman, op. cit., p. 197.   [6] LW. 8. 333.

CHAPTER VIII

LUTHER AS A PREACHER

In the year 1947 an excellent study of Calvin as a preacher was prepared by T. H. L. Parker. The title was *The Oracles of God*. It introduced a neglected aspect of the man who led the work of reform in Geneva. John Calvin was not exclusively a theologian whose motto was "Theology for theology's sake." Nor was he merely an administrator. He was primarily a preacher. He only became a reformer as he wrestled with the Word. Throughout his career he conceived his first duty to be that of preaching.

A similar book is needed on Luther's preaching. It would point in precisely the same direction. But no such survey exists. No exhaustive monograph on this subject has yet been presented, not even in Germany.[1] The usual accounts in homiletical textbooks and histories of preaching are woefully inadequate, and sometimes inaccurate too. There is a certain amount of material in the standard biographies of Luther and now and again in the accounts of his theology which have multiplied in recent years. There is a useful introduction in the volume in the American Edition of Luther's works which starts off the series containing his sermons, and a similar preface in the Weimar Edition.[2] It is to the latter that we have to turn also for the opportunity to examine Luther's homiletical output. The bulk is considerable, for Ebeling has classified 1,978 complete sermons delivered by Luther, and with the addition of some that are unfinished, over two thousand are included in the Weimar collection.[3] Not even this contains all the sermons of which transcripts are available Sixteen volumes are filled with nothing but sermons, six more record the postils, and there are others elsewhere in the series. One of the reasons why no detailed research into Luther's preaching has yet been done is that the task of examining all the sources available is a formidable one indeed. "Every Luther scholar knows that this requires years of labour," said Emanuel Hirsch.[4]

Luther did not become a preacher when he became a priest.[5] A priest

[1] The lacuna mentioned by Mackinnon (op. cit., Vol. IV, *Vindication of the Movement (1530–1546)* (1930), p. 318 n. 66) still remains; cf. LW. 51. xi. Some material contained in this chapter has been presented in A. Skevington Wood, "Luther as a Preacher", *Evangelical Quarterly*, Vol. XXI (1949), pp. 109–21.

[2] LW 51. xi–xxi; WA. 10. iii. III–VII, IX–XV.

[3] Ebeling, op. cit., Anlage I, Tabelle I. LW. 51. xii.

[4] LW. 51. xi.   [5] Scheel, op. cit., Bd. II, pp. 551–553.

was not automatically required to preach. Luther was ordained in 1507. As far as we know, he did not begin to preach until 1510. When he embarked on his course for the doctorate at the University of Wittenberg it was part of the statutory requirements that he should be able to preach. Luther received a summons to deliver sermons first in the refectory of his convent at Erfurt, and then in the *Stadtkirche* at Wittenberg.[1] It is not at all certain whether these have been preserved, but two manuscripts were discovered in Zwickau by Georg Buchwald which may belong to this initial period. They came from the remains of Andreas Poach, the Erfurt preacher, who supplied this note: "From an autograph of Luther discovered in the monastery of the Augustinians, Erfurt."[2] The text of one is John 3:16 and of the other Matthew 7:12. John W. Doberstein thinks that the latter may perhaps represent Luther's first sermon.[3] At least we may agree with Vogelsang that it is the earliest of his that we possess.[4] It was with much trepidation that Luther essayed his maiden speech. "O how frightened I was at the sight of the pulpit!" he confessed later in the *Table Talk*.[5] Yet this diffidence was a contributory factor to his subsequent effectiveness. Great preachers are often nervous, though not all nervous preachers are great!

Luther was first and foremost a preacher, for as we have seen, he did not differentiate, as is now the custom, between his lectures in the classroom and his messages in the church. "For the reformers," according to von Schubert, "the pulpit was a kind of popular professorial chair, and the professorial chair a kind of students' pulpit".[6] Preaching was the spearhead of the Reformation. What was later printed and circulated throughout the length and breadth of Germany was much of it first preached at Wittenberg. Moreover, Luther was not only a preacher: he was a pastoral preacher. He was not an itinerant. In addition to being a university professor, he acted as assistant to Johann Bugenhagen at the parish church of Wittenberg. To this one congregation he was attached for the rest of his days. It is true now and again he preached elsewhere, but from 1510 until his death in 1546 he was associated with his local church. This was *his* congregation – "*ecclesia mea*" he called it – and for it he knew he would be responsible at Judgement Day.[7] He only permitted himself to be drawn away from Wittenberg on exceptional occasions – to attend the Leipzig Disputation and the Diet of Worms, or to seek refuge in the Wartburg when the seas of opposition were running high.

Usually he preached two or three times a week. Sometimes it was even

[1] Ebeling, op. cit., p. 15; Fife, op. cit., pp. 184-5.   [2] LW. 51. 5.
[3] Ibid. Cf. H. S. Bluhm, "The Significance of Luther's Earliest Sermon", *Harvard Theological Review*, Vol. XXXVII (1944), pp. 175-84.
[4] CL. 7. 19-20.   [5] WATR. 3. 188. No. 3143b.
[6] Hans von Schubert and Karl A. Meissinger, *Zu Luthers Vorlesungstätigkeit* (1920), p. 3.
[7] WA. 49. 318.

more. "Often I preached four sermons on one day," he told Bucer. "During the whole of one Lent I preached two sermons and gave one lecture every day. This was when I first preached on the Ten Commandments to a large congregation, for to preach on the catechism was then a new and uncommon thing."[1] The reference was to the years 1516 and 1517. In 1529 Luther preached eighteen times in eleven days from Palm Sunday to the Wednesday after Easter.[2] When Bugenhagen was absent – as in this instance – the whole burden of the pastorate devolved on Luther, and his preaching rate was stepped up accordingly. The festival seasons also increased his commitments. "I am not only Luther," he declared, "but Pomeranus, Registrar, Moses, Jethro and what not – all things in all."[3] These incessant pulpit labours lasted on to the very end, for his swan song was delivered only four days before his death. He modestly claimed to have equalled the preaching activity both of Augustine and of Ambrose.[4]

It must be remembered that the church at Wittenberg, as the Reformation progressed, was regarded more and more as a sort of test case. The eyes of all the world were on it. Protestantism might rise or fall according to the success or failure of this one congregation. Yet the members of this trial church were not hand-picked. They did not represent a specially selected circle of super-Christians.[5] They were very ordinary folk who needed the ministry of men who took their preaching and pastoral responsibilities seriously. Luther showed himself to be a true shepherd of souls who fed and tended his flock. But this was a mission church, too. Luther preached not only to the converted, but to the common people. The fervent exhortations with which his sermons closed made it quite evident that he was out for a response from the hitherto unawakened.[6]

There are no finer specimens of Luther's congregational preaching than the eight sermons he gave in Wittenberg after his return from the Wartburg in 1522.[7] In his absence, Karlstadt, Zwilling and the Zwickau prophets had been sowing seeds of discord. The city was in an uproar when Luther came back. On the 9th March, the first Sunday in Lent, he mounted the pulpit and preached the first of a series of sermons covering such controversial subjects as the mass, images, fasting, and confession. But if the subjects were debatable, the tone was conciliatory. These remarkable discourses were delivered in a *vox suavis et sonora*.[8] Their message was one of peace and love. "Let us, therefore, feed others also with the milk which we received, until they, too, become strong in faith."

[1] LW. 54. 282. No. 3843.   [2] WA. 29. 132–3.
[3] End. 8. 326. Pomeranus was Bugenhagen, who hailed from Pomerania.
[4] WATR. 5. 659. No. 6434; cf. 3. 437. No. 3590a.
[5] Ebeling, op. cit., p. 16.   [6] Ibid., pp. 473–5.
[7] Cf. Philip Schaff, *History of the Christian Church. Modern Christianity: The German Reformation 1517–1530* (1888), Vol. II, pp. 388–91; Félix Kuhn, *Luther: sa vie et son oeuvre*, Tome II (1884), pp. 70–75.
[8] LC. 2. 115.

For there are many who are otherwise in accord with us and who would also gladly accept this thing, but they do not yet fully understand – these we drive away. Therefore, let us show love to our neighbours: if we do not do this, our work will not endure. We must have patience with them for a time, and not cast out him who is weak in faith; and do and omit many other things, so long as love requires it and it does no harm to our faith. If we do not earnestly pray to God and act rightly in this matter, it looks to me as if all the misery which we have begun to heap upon the papists will fall upon us. Therefore I could no longer remain away, but was compelled to come and say these things to you."[1]

These eight sermons produced immediate results. Jerome Schurff wrote to the Elector on the 15th March (after sermon number six): "Oh, what joy has Dr. Martin's return spread among us! His words, through divine mercy, are bringing back every day misguided people into the way of truth. It is as clear as the sun, that the Spirit of God is in him, and that he returned to Wittenberg by His special providence."[2] Zwilling openly confessed that he was wrong, and declared that Luther "preached like an angel".[3] Karlstadt was silenced, and the city council acknowledged Luther's intervention by substantial gifts. The eloquence of one man had restored law and order to the frenzied populace. Those who think that Luther preached faith without works other than in the matter of justification, should ponder what he had to say in the first of these memorable sermons: "A faith without love is not enough – rather it is not faith at all, but a counterfeit of faith, just as a face seen in a mirror is not a real face, but merely the reflection of a face."[4] It is noticeable that Luther consistently appealed to Scripture.

Involved as he was in this orgy of sermonizing, Luther had no time to superintend the publication of his discourses. He did not even write out his manuscript in full before entering the pulpit. He prepared a careful outline, but left the language to look after itself. Occasionally he even forgot his line of thought and preached a better sermon than he had intended. "Our Lord God himself wishes to be the preacher, for preachers often go astray in their notes so that they cannot go on with what they have begun. It has often happened that my best outline came undone. On the other hand, when I was least prepared my words flowed during the sermon."[5]

Luther's sermons would never have been preserved for posterity if the matter had been left in his own hands. We are indebted to a little band of scribes who devoted themselves to the tedious task of noting Luther's discourses, and then preparing them for publication. This labour of love dates from 1522 onwards, and it is significant that, whereas prior to this year the sermons handed down were comparatively few in number and

[1] LW. 51. 74–75.   [2] End. 3. 307; cf. LC. 2. 102.   [3] End. 3. 307.
[4] LW. 51. 71.   [5] LW. 54. 213. No. 3494.

badly authenticated, those preserved after this year represent no less than
ninety-two per cent of the total in this period and are much more carefully recorded.[1] A fascinating story surrounds the names of Georg Rörer
and Kaspar Cruciger, Luther's principal shorthand writers, and Johannes
Aurifaber and Veit Dietrich, who supervised the printing of the sermons.

The salient feature of Luther's preaching was its biblical content and
reference. It was subject to Scripture throughout. Luther submitted to a
rigorous discipline. He was bound by the Word. His preaching was never
merely topical. He could never turn a text into a pretext. "I take pains to
treat a verse, to stick to it," he explained, "and so to instruct the people that
they can say, 'That is what the sermon was about.'"[2] His preaching was
never a movement from men to the text: it was always a movement from
the text to men. The matter never determined the text: the text always
determined the matter. He was not in the habit of treating subjects or issues,
but doctrines. But when he did so, he invariably followed a prescribed
Scripture passage step by step. He considered one of the major qualifica-
tions of the preacher to be familiarity with the Word. He must be *bonus
textualis* – a good man with the text.[3] Luther never dispensed with a text
from Scripture, and never approved of the practice in others. "It is
disgraceful for the lawyer to desert his brief; it is even more disgraceful for
the preacher to desert his text."[4]

Luther's subjection to Scripture in his preaching was illustrated in his
choice of texts. He adhered most strictly to the official list of pericopes,
invariably selecting his text from the passage for the day.[5] Whilst he freely
criticised the contents of the lectionary and amended it in the *Formula of
the Mass* (1523) and the *German Mass* (1526), he never sought to replace it.
The result of this method was that Luther's sermons were nearly all based
on the appointed Gospels and Epistles. Within this framework, Luther
gave by far the greater prominence to the Gospel portions, on which a
high percentage of his sermons were based. Even the continuous expositions on Sunday afternoon tended to be from one of the four Gospels. We
have noted that in his university lectures Luther devoted more time to
the Old Testament than to the New, and did not deal at all with the
Gospels. These were covered exclusively (and exhaustively) in his preaching. He believed that a Christian congregation should be thoroughly
grounded in the story of Christ.

In describing Luther as essentially a biblical preacher, we must not
overlook his broader conception of the Word. He did not equate the
Word of God with the Bible, although he accepted the Bible as the Word
of God. For Luther the Word of God was not static, but active. It could

---

[1] Ebeling, op. cit., p. 16.   [2] LW. 54. 160. No. 1650.
[3] WATR. 4. 356. No. 4512.   [4] End. 1. 149.
[5] Ebeling, op. cit., p. 21.

never be imprisoned in a book – not even in God's book. The Word is God speaking. It is God confronting man in personal encounter. It is the establishment of what Martin Buber called an "I-Thou" relationship between God and man.[1] For only as man sees God in relation to himself can he see himself in relation to God.[2] Now this meeting between man and God can take place – indeed must take place – through the medium of Scripture. But it is in no passive sense that the Bible is the Word of God, according to Luther. It is as the Spirit who inspired it breathes upon it afresh, and applies it to the reader, that God speaks again through the Scriptures, as He spoke when they were first set down. But for Luther, it is supremely in preaching that the Word of God in the Scriptures is made alive in the present. The living Word of God, once spoken through the prophets and apostles, now recorded in the Scriptures, speaks again through His servants who are called to preach. Luther would have agreed with Kierkegaard's description of the Bible as a letter from God with our address on it, but he would have wanted to add that it comes to us like that most forcibly when it is read to us in the living voice of the preacher.[3]

That is made very clear in his *Operationes in Psalmos*. "Christ did not write anything, but He spoke it all. The apostles wrote only a little, but they spoke a lot. . . . Notice: it says let their voices be heard, not let their books be read. The ministry of the New Testament is not engraved on dead tablets of stone; rather it sounds in a living voice. . . . Through a living Word God accomplishes and fulfils the gospel."[4] In the *Church Postil* of 1522 Luther put the same point in a more popular way. "The church is not a pen house, but a mouth house. For since the advent of Christ the gospel, which used to be hidden in the Scriptures, has become an oral preaching. And thus it is the manner of the New Testament and of the gospel that it must be preached and performed by word of mouth and a living voice. Christ himself has not written anything, nor has he ordered anything to be written, but rather to be preached by word of mouth."[5]

There is thus a distinctly existential quality about Luther's preaching. One feels that through it God is speaking directly to His people, and to those who still reject Him – and this immediacy is conveyed even in the printed record. It was this factor which ensured that Luther's preaching should always be decisive. There was nothing vague or cloudy about it. It was clear-cut and definite. A sense of reality prevailed. Luther was no mystic. Christ and Antichrist, God and the devil – these were objective personalities to him, and this awareness gave a peculiar urgency to his

---

[1] Martin Buber, *I and Thou* (E.T. 1937), p. 3.
[2] Paul S. Minear, *Eyes of Faith: A Study in the Biblical Point of View* (1948), p. 11.
[3] Søren Kierkegaard, *For Self Examination and Judge for Yourselves!* (E.T. 1941), p. 51.
[4] WA. 5. 537.
[5] WA. 10. i. 48; cf. Regin Prenter, "Luther on Word and Sacrament", *More About Luther*, ed. Gerhard L. Belgum (1958), p. 73.

preaching. He believed, as Doberstein expresses it, that "preaching continues the battle begun by the saving event and is itself the saving event."[1] This is made clear in one of Luther's own comments. "When I preach a sermon I take an antithesis."[2] That is to say, he never proclaimed God's great Yes, His acceptance of man in the gospel, without at the same time proclaiming His No, his rejection of all man's presumption and pretence.[3] Every sermon for him was a struggle for souls. Eternal issues were being settled in the moment of preaching – the issues of life and death, light and darkness, sin and grace, the kingdom of Christ and the kingdom of Satan. There was an *Einmaligkeit*, a once-for-allness, about Luther's preaching which stimulated his hearers to respond. They were made to feel that the offer of the gospel was here and now, and now or never. Dr. John Ker said of this element in Luther's sermons: "He was taking aim at the heart, with arrows which reached their mark."[4]

It was not enough, Luther asserted, simply to preach the facts of the gospel. The historical evidence, though valuable, has no power to save. Christ must be preached as the One who lived and died to redeem men from sin. What He did was not for His own benefit, but for ours. "Christ ought to be preached to the end that faith in Him may be established that He may not only be Christ, but be Christ for you and me, and that what is said of Him and is denoted in His name may be effectual in us. Such faith is produced and preserved in us by preaching why Christ came, what He brought and bestowed, what benefit it is to us to accept Him."[5] There were preachers of repentance and grace even in his day, Luther went on, but they did not explain how a man might repent and how he might know the grace of God.[6] Repentance proceeds from the law of God, but grace from the promise of God. "Faith comes from what is heard, and what is heard comes by the preaching of Christ" (Rom. 10:17). "Accordingly man is consoled and exalted by faith in the divine promise after he has been humbled and led to a knowledge of himself by the threats and the fear of the divine law."[7]

This stress on faith, which is so typical of Luther, found expression in a celebrated sentence in *The Freedom of a Christian*, from which the above quotations have also been taken. It may be translated: "If you believe it, you have it. If you do not believe it, you do not have it" (*Glaubstu so hastu. – Glaubstu nit so hastu nit*).[8] This dictum assumes that the Word of God is always effective, claims Regin Prenter. "If it does not work salvation through faith, it works condemnation through unbelief. That does not imply that man decides, through his belief or unbelief, whether God succeeds or not in His saving work. God cannot be defeated by man. But

[1] LW. 51. xx. [2] WA. 36. 181. [3] LW. 51. xx.
[4] John Ker, *Lectures on the History of Preaching* (1888), p. 102.
[5] LW. 31. 357. [6] Ibid., 364. [7] Ibid.
[8] Ibid., 348–9.

it does imply that God saves through a personal Word. For that reason He can save men only through their personal faith in that Word. He cannot save them through their personal disregard of His Word."[1]

Mackinnon claimed that Gospel preaching in the evangelical sense began with Luther.[2] It might be more accurate to say that it began again. It had been forgotten for a very long time. Luther himself deplored the lack of such preaching, and denounced the blind leaders of the blind who abounded in the Church of his day. He liberated the sermon from its medieval grave-clothes, and made it once again a means of grace to sinners. He was "importunately evangelical", wrote Peter Bayne.[3] He declared God's great salvation. Like all true gospel preaching, Luther's message moved within the twin orbits of sin and grace. That man has sinned and Christ has died – that was the sum of his evangel. For him to preach the gospel was nothing else than to bring Christ to men and men to Christ.

In order to achieve this end, Luther's sermons were deliberately simple. There was nothing grandiose about his style or matter. He cut out anything that might not be clear to the common man. His preaching was popular in the truest sense of the word. It was for the people. To borrow a phrase from Halford Luccock, he preached to life situations.[4] He used the ordinary speech of every day. He eschewed academic verbiage. His homilies were homespun. He often preached in the house – house postils form a considerable part of his sermons – and all his messages had a homely touch. He always tried to make himself intelligible to the humblest of his hearers. Before he preached, he quaintly said, he would look into the jaws of the man in the street.[5] We are reminded of François de Malherbe's confession: "When I am at a loss for a word or a detail of style, I go and consult the dock-hands at the Port-au-fin."[6] Luther's preaching was like the gospel itself – so simple that a child can grasp some of it, yet so profound that the wise man cannot plumb all of it. It was from the Scriptures that Luther had learned this approach. "To preach simply is a great art," he said. "Christ understood it and practised it. He speaks only of the ploughed field, of the mustard seed, and uses only common comparisons from the countryside."[7]

We have seen that Luther's preaching was essentially congregational and pastoral. It was set in the context of the local church. It was also related to worship. He restored the sermon to prominence in the liturgy of the Church. He virtually raised it to the level of a sacrament. "It was

[1] Prenter, "Luther on Word and Sacrament", pp. 74–75.
[2] Mackinnon, op. cit., Vol. III, *Progress of the Movement (1521–1529)* (1929), p. 62.
[3] Peter Bayne, *Martin Luther, His Life and Work* (1887), Vol. I, p. 260.
[4] Halford E. Luccock, *In the Minister's Workshop* (1944), p. 50.
[5] WATR. 3. 427. No. 3579.
[6] Edmund W. Gosse, *Malherbe and the Classical Reaction in the Seventeenth Century* (1920), p. 21.
[7] WATR. 4. 447. No. 4719.

Luther," claimed Alfred E. Garvie, "who put the sermon in Protestantism in the place held by the mass in Roman Catholicism and made preaching the most potent influence in the churches of the Reformation."[1] We may go further than that. Luther's influence extended beyond Protestantism. As Mackinnon has shown, he revolutionized the preaching of the Roman Church.[2]

The sermon occupied a central position in reformed worship, not as the word of man, but as the Word of God. The preacher was not a free-lance thinker who gave expression only to his personal views. He was the mouthpiece of God. "God, the creator of heaven and earth, speaks with you through His preachers," Luther declared, "baptizes, catechizes, absolves you through the ministry of His own sacraments. These are the words of God, not of Plato or Aristotle. It is God Himself who speaks."[3] Preaching is not what man says about God: it is what God says to man. Only as such can it hold a high place in the worship of the Church.

But Luther did not isolate the sermon from its context in the liturgy There was no sense of tension between the two. Indeed, Luther regarded the sermon as itself an essential expression of worship. The two were not set over against one another. "The conscientious preaching of the divine Word," he could insist ,"is the real worship of the new covenant."[4] In the preface to the *German Mass*, he referred to "the preaching and teaching of God's Word" as "the most important part of divine service".[5] This is not to be taken as meaning that worship is mainly a matter of instruction, and that Luther wanted to turn the Christian liturgy into what has been called the "dry mass" of a synagogue service.[6] Rather he regarded the reading of the Scriptures and the sermon as themselves aspects of worship. He criticized the traditional liturgies of the Church on the ground that they had pushed the Bible into the background – although, of course, much of the language was itself scriptural. Luther sought to restore a balance between the integral parts of worship.

He also stressed the need to relate Word and sacrament. In Rome, the sacrament had gained the ascendancy over the Word. In radical Protestantism there was a danger lest the Word should displace the sacrament. Luther endeavoured to maintain the two in fruitful tension. But he did not regard them as opposites, for the Lord's Supper is after all commanded in Scripture and in itself a proclamation of the Word. Conversely, "the sermon ought to be nothing else than the proclamation of this testament", Luther argued.[7] It is the only ceremony or practice which Christ himself

---

[1] Alfred E. Garvie, *The Christian Preacher* (1920), pp. 115–16.
[2] Mackinnon, op. cit., Vol. III, p. 308.   [3] WATR. 4. 531. No. 4812.
[4] OL. 19. 161.
[5] LW. 53. 68.
[6] Jaroslav J. Pelikan, "Luther and the Liturgy", *More About Luther*, p. 29.
[7] LW. 44. 56.

instituted for his followers to observe when they assemble. Its meaning
must be made plain from the pulpit. "Where this is rightly preached, it
must be diligently heard, grasped, retained, pondered often, and faith must
be strengthened against every temptation of sin. . . . . This preaching
should induce sinners to grieve over their sins and should kindle within
them a longing for the treasure (i.e. of the gospel, which is displayed in
the Supper). Therefore, it must be a grievous sin not to listen to the gospel,
and to despise such a treasure and so rich a feast to which we are bidden.
But it is a much greater sin not to preach the gospel, and to allow so many
people who would gladly hear it to perish, for Christ has so strictly
commanded that the gospel and this testament be preached that He does
not even wish the mass to be celebrated unless the gospel be preached.
As He says, 'As often as you do this, remember me.' And, as St. Paul says,
"You shall preach his death" (I Cor. 11:26). For this reason it is dreadful
and horrible to be a bishop, pastor, and preacher in our times, for no one
knows this testament any longer, not to mention that they ought to
preach it; although this is their highest and only duty and obligation. They
will certainly have to account for the many souls who perish because of
such feeble preaching!"[1]

In an age of liturgical reappraisal such as we live in today, Luther's
welding of Word and sacrament still has a contribution to make. The
sermon gains rather than loses by being incorporated into the wholeness
of worship. Both in the preaching of the gospel and in the breaking of
bread, we proclaim the Lord's death until He comes. In this, as in all else,
Luther was not just ventilating a theory. He was trying to reflect the
pattern of Scripture.

[1] Ibid., 57-58.

CHAPTER IX

LUTHER AS A TRANSLATOR

"THE TRANSLATION OF THE BIBLE INTO GERMAN IS Martin Luther's greatest single work. It is both a literary and a religious achievement of the first order."[1] So writes Heinz Bluhm, and it is no more than the truth. Nothing that Luther ever did had more significant repercussions than when he put the Scriptures into the tongue of the common people in his land. The German Bible is his most enduring monument, and it is fitting that what he should be remembered by best of all has to do with the Word. Here in this singular achievement we see the apotheosis of the man.

Only of late, however, have we begun to measure the magnitude of what Luther accomplished in this respect. In Germany itself, his work has been so familiar to all as to be taken for granted. Outside Germany and German-speaking communities, it has not been fully realized what it means to give a nation the Word of God in the language of man. Luther and his Bible are part of Germany's soul. We are accustomed to being told that the English Bible helped enormously to make England what she is, first in the translations of Tyndale and others and supremely in the Authorized Version. For Germany, Luther was Tyndale and the King James' translators rolled into one. The sheer incredibility of his prodigious feat ought to astonish us, but all too often it passes unacknowledged. However, scholars like Otto Reichert, Wilhelm Walther, Emanuel Hirsch, and Michael Reu have done something in our century to renew our appreciation.[2]

They have enabled us to see the place of Luther's Bible translation, not only in the unfolding of German literature and history, but also in the context of the Reformation itself. The rendering of the Scriptures into the speech of the ordinary man in the street was the greatest single factor in spreading the message of reform. For at heart it was none other than the message of the Word, and to distribute the Scriptures was to further the Reformation. As Luther again and again insisted, it was not what *he* did which effected the transformation of European Christianity: the Word did it all. It was only necessary for it to be let loose, and it would do its

[1] Heinz Bluhm, *Martin Luther: Creative Translator* (1965), p. vii.

[2] Otto Reichert, *D. Martin Luthers Deutsche Bibel* (1910); Wilhelm Walther, *Luthers Deutsche Bibel* (1917); Emanuel Hirsch, *Luthers Deutsche Bibel* (1928); and Reu, *Luther's German Bible*, already cited.

own work. Hence K. R. Hagenbach, in his massive history, could describe Luther's German Bible as "the keystone of the Reformation."[1] More recently, G. R. Elton has expatiated on the same theme. "If there is a single thread running through the whole story of the Reformation, it is the explosive and renovating and often disintegrating effect of the Bible, put into the hands of the commonalty and interpreted no longer by the well-conditioned learned, but by the faith and delusion, the common sense and uncommon nonsense, of all sorts of men. One country after another was to receive its vernacular Bible in this century, and with it a new standard of its language; in 1521–2 Luther, who had for so many people already done so much to bring the gospel to life after its long sleep in the scholastic night-cap, began the work for his Germans."[2]

In order to grasp the timeliness of Luther's work as a translator, we need to appreciate that in the Middle Ages the reading and study of the Scriptures was regarded as the prerogative of the clergy. They alone were qualified to interpret the Word. The layman had to be satisfied to receive it at second hand and on trust. Apart from the few who were versed in Latin, there was no chance of them looking at it for themselves. The likelihood of the Bible ever being made available in the tongue of the people was remote indeed. Even some of the most enlightened men of the age, who saw the need for reform in other directions, suffered from a blind spot here. Johann Geiler from Kaisersburg, who has been nicknamed the German Savonarola, was one of those who advocated the renovation of the Church, yet he believed that to put the Scriptures into the vernacular would be a risky move. "It is a bad thing to print the Bible in German. It must be understood far differently from the way in which the text sounds. It is dangerous to put a knife into the hands of children and let them slice their own bread. They can only wound themselves with it. So also the Holy Scriptures, which comprise the bread of God, must be read and interpreted by people who have requisite knowledge and experience and who are able to determine the true sense."[3]

It was not the case that the Church had explicitly proscribed a translation of the Bible, but it had certainly discouraged the notion. A statement by Pope Innocent III around the turn of the thirteenth century strongly underlined the drawbacks involved in the lay reading of the Bible, if this were allowed without supervision.[4] In January 1486 Archbishop Berthold of Mainz had issued an edict forbidding any unapproved German version in his diocese. He defended his action on the ground that in his office he

[1] Karl R. Hagenbach, *History of the Reformation in Germany and Switzerland Chiefly*, Vol. I (E.T. 1878), p. 143.
[2] Geoffrey R. Elton, *Reformation Europe 1517–1559* (1963). *The Fontana History of Europe*, p. 52.
[3] Georg Buchwald, *400 Jahre deutsche Lutherbibel* (1934), p. 4; Kooiman, op. cit., p. 86 for this reference and that in n. 1 on p. 97.
[4] DTC. 7. 1961–81. PL. 214. 695–9, cf. 793–5.

was required to guard the purity of the divine Word. Those who were trying their hand at turning the Bible into German were for the most part incapable of doing justice to their task, he thought. In any case, he added, it is most dangerous to place the Holy Scriptures in the homes of ordinary people, where even women might read, if they could, or at least hear, since they are unable to come to a right judgment about them.[1] Berthold was giving expression to the general mind of the Church, as Kooiman remarks, even though he put it more bluntly than others might have done.[2]

The result of these inhibitions was that scholars and churchmen rarely concerned themselves with the matter of Bible translation. They took it for granted that there was no market for this kind of enterprise. What little work was done was left to one or two innovators of indifferent calibre, whose acquaintance with Latin was insufficient to enable them to penetrate the considerable depths of the Vulgate. All they attempted was a rather feeble word-for-word rendering into hobbling German. It was the contribution of the humanists which paved the way for something better. Both Reuchlin and Erasmus reached back to the original languages, and thus laid bare the text for an authentic translation. In the preface to his Greek New Testament, Erasmus had looked forward to the day when the Scriptures would be opened up to the people. "I totally disagree with those who are unwilling that the Sacred Scriptures, translated into the vulgar tongue, should be read by private individuals. . . . I wish that they were translated into all languages of all people, that they might be read and known not merely by the Scots and Irish, but even by the Turks and Saracens. . . . I wish that the ploughman might sing parts of them at his plough and the weaver at his shuttle, and that the traveller might beguile with their narration the weariness of the way."[3]

The humanists, however, were not equipped for the task. They were too remote from life as it was and the people as they were. Their idea of the Bible, moreover, was inclined to be legalistic. They lacked the passion of an overmastering sense of mission. This Luther possessed. He knew he was raised up by God for this very purpose. He was driven on by an irresistible compulsion to bring the Word of life to his own people in their native tongue. He could not rest content until the project was complete. Coming as he did from the peasant stock, Luther was essentially a man of the plebs. He knew his own German speech down to the grass roots. He had a unique gift of expression. In him the hour and the task met as he went into enforced retreat in the castle at the Wartburg, after

[1] Karl Mirbt, *Quellen zur Geschichte des Papsttums und des römischen Katholizismus* (4th edn. 1924), No. 332; For Luther's own complaint that the laity had not been allowed to read the Scriptures, *vide* LW. 30. 105.

[2] Kooiman, op. cit., p. 87.

[3] Erasmus, *Novum Testamentum* (2nd edn. 1519), p. 8; cf. Sir Frederic Kenyon, *Our Bible and the Ancient Manuscripts* (1941), p. 212 n. 1.

D

the Diet of Worms. He retired as a fugitive from persecution for the sake of the truth. He emerged with a weapon which would continue to fight the battles of the Lord long after he had been laid to rest. The Word would still do it all.

Heinrich Bornkamm shows how Luther had been prepared for this crowning achievement. "All his previous work impelled him with inner logic to the translation of the Bible. Through the Bible alone he had become what he was. Through it he had learned to rout scholastic theology, and in it he had rediscovered the core of the gospel. The Bible was his only friend in his lonely hours, the sole weapon in his conflict against a thousand-year old system. If he had a right to believe that up to this time he had won all his oral and literary skirmishes, he had to tell himself that he was indebted to the Bible for these victories. Though the plea of his Wittenberg friends gave the final impulse, yet he carried out his very own work, his *opus proprium*. With this work he not only revealed to his people the source of his life, but in it he also found the fullest justification for his previous actions. Henceforth everybody could and should judge for himself and thereby exercise the first duty and the foremost privilege of the universal priesthood; for this was precisely what Luther had discovered in the Scriptures was the basic essence of the Church."[1]

Luther did not suddenly emerge full-grown as a translator when he started on his great work in the Wartburg. Already he had been practising the art. Bluhm has examined his sermons on Matthew's Gospel from 1517 onwards, and the way in which Luther made his own translation of the Greek text.[2] Quite obviously he was still deeply attached to the Vulgate, and there is no need to depreciate the merits of Jerome's version in order to buttress the case for a vernacular rendering. The two issues are quite separate. As he compared the Latin with the Greek, Luther must have learned a lot about how to convert the idiom of one language into that of another. However, Jerome was limited by the self-imposed restrictions of a literal word-by-word method of translation. Luther was able to emancipate himself from this, largely under the influence of Augustine who pioneered what Schwarz calls the inspirational principle of translation.[3]

Bluhm finds no discernible influence on Luther at this period of the already existing German versions.[4] As many as fourteen in High German and four in Low are cited by Oskar Thulin.[5] These range from that printed in Strasburg in 1466 by Johann Mentelin (which ran into fourteen editions in fifty years), through that of Günther Zainer at Augsburg in

---

[1] Bornkamm, *Luther's World of Thought*, p. 274.   [2] Bluhm, op. cit., pp. 4–36.
[3] Werner Schwarz, *Principles and Problems of Biblical Translation: Some Reformation Controversies and their Background* (1955), p. 167.
[4] Bluhm, op. cit., p. 5.
[5] Oskar Thulin, "Die Gestalt der Lutherbibel in Druch und Bild", *Luther, Vierteljahrsschrift der Luthergesellschaft*, Bd. XVI (1934), pp. 60–61: Schwiebert, op. cit., p. 643.

1475 (the best-known of all) to Silvanus Otmar's production, also at
Augsburg, in 1518. Luther was more in debt to the *Plenarium*, the collection of selected Bible passages which he had bought as a schoolboy. This,
as we have seen, was obtainable in German as well as in Latin. Bluhm's
conclusion about Luther's renderings of Scripture in the sermons on
Matthew's Gospel is as follows: "They reveal an expert and an artist in
the handling of highly idiomatic German. Their variety and more than
occasional excellence provide an important clue to what was to be
offered to the world in the *Septembertestament*. When Luther was persuaded
to undertake this formidable task, he was in a position to draw, uncon-
sciously of course, on a large and ready storehouse of previously, and
sometimes frequently, rendered passages. Boundless as this vast supply of
variants would seem to be, in some verses Luther appears to have exhausted the very possibilities of expressing the idea in the vernacular. The
scholar patient enough to peruse these early quotations is impressed by
the apparent ease with which one of the greatest masters of the German
language can render in various superb ways a veritable deluge of biblical
verses."[1]

In the summer of 1519 Luther ventured on the first translation of a
complete pericope. During the Leipzig Disputation he was invited by
Duke Barnim of Pomerania to deliver a sermon for the feast of Peter and
Paul on the 29th June. He selected as his text the Gospel for the day –
Matthew 16:13-19. The vernacular version of this passage prefixed to the
actual sermon represents Luther's earliest attempt to render a pericope in
full. A careful examination of the evidence by Bluhm suggests that
Luther was still using the Vulgate as a basis, although, of course, by now
he was thoroughly familiar with the Greek text of Erasmus.[2] Luther
continued this practice from now on. In a letter to Nicholas Gerbel of
Pforzheim, who helped Erasmus to correct the proofs of his Greek
Testament, Luther spoke about his exposition of the Gospel passage dealing with the ten lepers (Luke 17:11-19). "All this is in German," he
added. "I am born for my Germans, whom I want to serve."[3]

The next stage was the translation of an entire sequence into German.
This was the series of lessons in the Advent Postil. The publication not
only contained a German rendering of the pericopes for the Advent
Sundays, but also a translation of the homilies attached to them. A similar
Christmas Postil was treated in the same fashion. Eventually Luther
intended to link up all the pericopes in a complete Church Postil in four
major parts covering each quarter of the Christian year. His treatment of
the Gospel reading about the ten lepers, already mentioned, fell into
place in the section which included the season of Trinity. In all this work
– done during Luther's confinement in the Wartburg – we can see how

[1] Bluhm, op. cit., p. 36.　　　[2] Ibid., p. 47.　　　[3] LW. 48. 320.

he was being prepared for his overall objective in the translation of the whole Bible into German. In his preface to the Wartburg Postil, entitled *A Brief Instruction on what to look for and expect in the Gospels*, Luther concluded with an impassioned paragraph which lets us see why he was so keen to release the Bible to the people in their own tongue. "Since we abandoned the Scriptures, it is not surprising that He (i.e. God) has abandoned us to the teaching of the pope and to the lies of men. Instead of Holy Scripture we have had to learn the *Decretales* of a deceitful fool and an evil rogue. O would to God that among Christians the pure gospel were known and that most speedily there would be neither use nor need for this work of mine. Then there would surely be hope that the Holy Scriptures too would come forth again in their worthiness."[1]

Similarly, in the Postil itself Luther wound up his coverage of the Christmas lections with this outburst: "O that God would let my interpretation and that of all other teachers vanish altogether, so that every Christian might consider nothing but the simple Scripture itself and the pure Word of God. . . . . Therefore, go to the Scriptures, dear Christians! Go there alone, and let my exposition and that of all other teachers mean no more to you than the scaffolding on a building, so that we might understand the simple, pure Word of God, accept it as our own, and hold it fast."[2]

It is not easy to discover just when it was that Luther conceived the plan of translating the Scriptures in their entirety. It probably began to evolve in the autumn of 1520. The intensified work on the Postil no doubt reflected Luther's growing conviction that soon he would have to tackle the complete project. At the end of 1521 he paid a secret visit to Wittenberg, in all likelihood to discuss with his advisers the possibility of such an undertaking. It seems that Luther's friends encouraged him to pursue the task. He thought of starting with the Old Testament, but he needed more help and toyed with the idea of escaping from his voluntary imprisonment to live under cover in Wittenberg, where he could consult his colleagues. He wrote to Nicholas von Amsdorf on the 13th January 1522 to make a suggestion on these lines, but it was thought to be too hazardous.[3] In the same letter he indicated what he had in mind with regard to the Bible project. He wanted it to be "a worthy translation for all Christians to read".[4] He expressed the hope that it would be an improvement on the past, and that it would do even more for the Germans than the Vulgate had done for those who knew Latin.[5] He recognized, however, that he had shouldered a burden beyond his powers. "Now I

[1] LW. 35. 123-4.
[2] WA. 10. i. 728. On the Advent and Christmas Postils, *vide* LW. 48. 237-43.
[3] LW. 48. 363.   [4] Ibid.   [5] Ibid.

realize what it means to translate, and why no one has previously under-taken it who would disclose his name."[1]

So in what Bornkamm calls "the great breathing spell" afforded by his stay in the Wartburg, Luther set about his task of translation, starting willy-nilly on the New Testament.[2] He told Johann Lang: "I shall be hiding here until Easter. In the meantime I shall finish the *Postil*, and translate the New Testament into German, an undertaking our friends request. I hear that you are also working on this. Continue as you have begun. I wish every town would have its interpreter, and that this book alone, in all languages, would live in the hands, eyes, ears, and hearts of all people."[3] Luther used the Greek text of Erasmus which had been given to him by Gerbel when he was at Worms. He whimsically referred to it as "the bride" to whom he was now married.[4] "She has borne to me the children I mentioned above," he reported in a letter. "You will judge whether the offspring are similar to the mother. She is still fertile and highly pregnant. Christ willing, she will give birth to a son who will destroy the papists, sophists, monks, and Herodians with a rod of iron."[5] Those words proved to be prophetic.

Luther finished off the assignment in the astonishingly short space of eleven weeks. When we consider that this was a time of the year when the days were dark, that the lighting in the castle was minimal, that Luther's health was none too good, and that all the while he was in hiding from his enemies, we can only concur with Kooiman that this was "an almost unbelievable feat".[6] "Rarely, if ever," he added, "has a book that exerted such an influence been written so rapidly."[7] Luther did not only consult the original Greek. He used the Vulgate, and also Erasmus' Latin version contained in the second edition of his New Testament published in 1519.[8] A dictionary was also at his side. There is no evidence that he took account of any of the existing German translation to any marked degree. Bornkamm dismisses the collected lists of alleged loans or adaptation from Zainer's Bible, for example, as displaying "nothing but insignificant trifles".[9] As we have seen, Luther may have drawn to a certain extent on the *Plenarium*, with which he was so familiar, and perhaps also on an oral tradition which is hard to pin down. But this is to be understood only as a work of genius, in which the primary factor was an inspiration which Luther acknowledged had been given from above. Nothing else could account for such an end-product in so brief a period of time. Luther's New Testament was shaped in the white heat of a remarkable spiritual experience.

[1] Ibid.
[2] Heinrich Bornkamm, "Probleme der Lutherbiographie", *Lutherforschung Heute*, Ed. Vilmos Vajta (1958), p. 19; LW. 48. xvii n. 3.
[3] LW. 48. 356.   [4] Ibid., 321.   [5] Ibid.
[6] Kooiman, op. cit., p. 92.   [7] Ibid.
[8] LW. 48. 352. For Luther's use of the Greek text, *vide* WADB. 7. 545.
[9] Bornkamm, *Luther's World of Thought*, p. 278.

In two months, no less than five thousand copies were sold. In twelve years, nearly a quarter of a million New Testaments were distributed amongst the German people. But before the first issue was off the press in September 1522, Luther had got down to his job on the Old Testament. He had now left the Wartburg and resumed his duties at Wittenberg. Here he had the assistance he required for the more exacting demands of Old Testament translation. He could turn to the newly-appointed Professor of Hebrew, Matthäus Aurogallus, for guidance on knotty points. Although he remained modest about his mastery of Hebrew, Melanchthon was also a reliable counsellor. But Luther realized that this was a very different proposition from the New Testament. It was to take twelve years – with considerable interruptions – before he was through. "This tough-minded persistence in an over-busy career," Kooiman thinks is "even more deserving of respect than the speed with which he worked during his period of concealment."[1] And if we ascribe the phenomenal swiftness with which the New Testament was poured out to the enablement of the Spirit, can it not be said that an equal enduement is needed for a hard slog of a dozen years?

In his preface to the first part of the Old Testament – the Pentateuch – which appeared in 1523, Luther frankly confessed the problems involved. "For I freely admit that I have undertaken too much, especially in trying to put the Old Testament into German. The Hebrew language, sad to say, has gone down so far that even the Jews know little enough about it, and their glosses and interpretations (which I have tested) are not to be relied upon. I think that if the Bible is to come up again, we Christians are the ones who must do the work, for we have the understanding of Christ without which even the knowledge of the language is nothing. . . . Though I cannot boast of having achieved perfection, nevertheless, I venture to say that this German Bible is clearer and more accurate at many points than the Latin."[2] Luther's copy of the Hebrew Scriptures, over which he sat for so many long hours, was published at Brescia in 1494, and has been treasured amongst the relics of the reformer to this day. It is thought that the Septuagint he possessed was printed by Aldus in Venice in 1518.[3] He did not, however, rely greatly on the Greek version of the Old Testament, any more than on the Vulgate.

Luther's Old Testament came out piecemeal over the years from 1522 to 1534. It cost him sweat and toil, if not blood and tears. But when the completed Bible was published, in a magnificent edition from the typographical angle, Luther's "crowning accomplishment", as Thulin calls it, was sealed.[4] We cannot begin to estimate its influence, not only in the

[1] Kooiman, op. cit., p. 131.
[2] LW. 35. 249; cf. WA. 10. ii. 60. WAB. 2. 423.
[3] Kooiman, op. cit., p. 131.   [4] Thulin, op. cit., p. 60.

spread of the Reformation message, but in the whole life of the emergent German nation. If ever a people and a book were bound together, since the days when Israel dwelt in their land of old, it was Germany and Luther's Bible. Tributes to his achievement are legion. We can only quote one or two. "Luther's Bible was a literary event of the first magnitude," declares Bernhard Dammerman in the *Cambridge History of the Bible*, "for it is the first work of art in German prose. Luther showed himself to be a poet of genius, and with a true feeling for the properties of other languages."[1] Kenneth S. Latourette refers to it as "one of Luther's major achievements. . . . None other either before or later equalled it in dignity and felicity of expression."[2] He adds that it had an even more profound effect on the German language than the King James Version on English. A front-page article in the *Times Literary Supplement*, commemorating the four hundredth anniversary of Luther's death, passed this judgement: "No other single influence on the German language is comparable to that of his Bible, perhaps the most astonishing, impressive, and highly personal translation ever compassed."[3] In hailing it as "the most important and useful work of his whole life," Philip Schaff went on to explain that "it was a republication of the gospel. He made the Bible the people's book in church, school, and house. If he had done nothing else, he would have been one of the greatest benefactors of the German-speaking race."[4]

Schwarz has described Luther's method of translation as inspirational, following Augustine, rather than traditional (on the lines of the Vulgate), or philological (like Reuchlin and Erasmus).[5] In a letter of the 29th November 1520, Luther chided Spalatin for his rigid imitation of the text in his rendering. "Figures of speech and the liveliness of sentences and arguments can only be conveyed in a free translation," he insisted.[6] But then he went on, significantly, "not to mention the problems involved in reproducing the spirit of the author".[7] According to Schwarz, these two complementary passages contain the basis of Luther's method in transla-tion: content and form must be preserved in a free rendering, yet the underlying spirit of the author must somehow be recreated. At its best, such a treatment can reach the heights.[8] Bluhm considers the translation of the Twenty-Third Psalm, for example, to be a consummate work of art.[9] It surpasses the bounds even of creative translation and touches the border-land of original composition. The text was so to speak reborn in the process of vernacularization. That was Luther's ideal. Men and women

[1] CHB. 103.
[2] Kenneth S. Latourette, *A History of Christianity* (1954), p. 719.
[3] *Times Literary Supplement*, 23rd February 1946, p. 85.
[4] Schaff, op. cit., Vol. I, p. 341.
[5] Schwarz, op. cit., p. 137; cf. pp. 45. 61, 92.
[6] WAB. 2. 220.   [7] Ibid.
[8] Schwarz, op. cit., p. 205.
[9] Bluhm, op. cit., p. 112.

must be able to read God's Word," he declared, "as though it had been written yesterday."[1]

In order to succeed in this, the translator must himself experience what the biblical writer is dealing with. Luther complained that Erasmus had indeed translated the New Testament (into Latin), but he had not felt it.[2] "No one can see an iota in the Scriptures," he asserted, "if he does not have the Spirit of God."[3] In his open letter *On Translating*, with a foreword by Wenceslaus Link, who succeeded Staupitz as vicar-general of the Augustinians, Luther discussed his methodology. He met the objections of his critics who claimed that his free rendering failed to do justice to the Scriptures. Luther believed that just the opposite was the case.[4] He consoled himself with the remembrance that Jerome had to endure much ill-informed comment when he produced the Vulgate.[5]

In the same open letter, Luther defended his version of Romans 3:28 which had come under-fire, and still does today.[6] He had translated it as "by faith *alone*". It was supposed by some that here he had introduced the Reformation principle of *sola fide* unjustifiably in a text where it is not really to be found. But this was no King Charles' head with him, and he was quite ready to give a reason for what he had done. He was perfectly well aware that there is no equivalent for "alone" in the Greek. Those who criticized his rendering stared at it like cows at a new gate, he said.[7] But if the German was to be clear and vigorous, he had no alternative. Incidentally, so distinguished a contemporary New Testament scholar as Joachim Jeremias of Göttingen has recently affirmed that in adding "alone" Luther was linguistically as well as theologically correct.[8]

In providing the German people with the Bible in their own tongue, Luther not only bestowed on them a unique spiritual and literary treasure, which was to become part of the national inheritance. He also ensured, maybe to a greater degree than he realized himself, that the witness of the Reformation would be maintained. Protestantism is the religion of the Word, and by letting loose the Bible in Germany, Luther laid the most stable foundation possible for the future. Nor was this confined to Germany. A chain reaction was set up, which resulted in similar translations into the vernacular all over Europe and beyond. Luther may have been hemmed in by the stout walls of the Wartburg castellan, when he started on his truly monumental enterprise: but the Word of God was not bound, nor could it be.

---

[1] WA. 12. 444. [2] WA. 20. 728. [3] WA. 18. 609.
[4] LW. 35. 189–90. [5] Ibid., 184. [6] Ibid., 185–9.
[7] Ibid., 188.
[8] Joachim Jeremias, *The Central Message of the New Testament* (E.T. 1965), p. 55.

CHAPTER X

LUTHER AS A REFORMER

THERE WAS A STRIKING DIFFERENCE BETWEEN Luther's attitude to the primitive Church and that of the more extreme camp-followers of Protestantism. The latter tended to regard the first century as a kind of Christian Utopia, and as things had gone from bad to worse since then, the only way out in the present seemed to be to reconstitute the idealized structure of those unadulterated beginnings. They saw a great gulf fixed between their own time and that of the early Christians. Their conception of renewal apparently involved a gigantic air-lift over the intervening years, in order to transplant the model community from the first to the sixteenth century. The initial fallacy of this theory lay in the assumption that, even in New Testament times, the Church was ever altogether pure and free from defect. The second was to be found in the impossibility in any case of so shifting the stage scenery of history that the past could be exactly reproduced in the present. No doubt the radicals of the Reformation would have repudiated such a presentation of their views as a caricature, but there were at least some of them who gave the impression that this was how they saw things.

Luther, on the other hand, rejected any such static conception of the Church. He considered it rather as an organism which had maintained its life, now more strongly, now more feebly, throughout the entire period between the first century and his own. It was in the continuing existence of such an organism that his ministry was set and the work of the Reformation proceeded. It is in this sense that Luther showed himself to be a true reformer. His aim was not to scrub everything out and start again from scratch, even if that could have been done. He never hankered after a clean slate, for he knew that Christian history is a serial. He had to deal with the situation as it was, not as it might have been or ought to have been. Of course, he sought under the Spirit's tutelage to wrest the present into shape again. But he recognized that it is the divine prerogative to create *ex nihilo*. As a mere man – even a man in the hand of God – he had to deal with things as they were. It was no use expecting some apocalyptic miracle to make them different overnight. They could only become different as they were made different – the hard way, step by painful step. That, basically, was what Martin Luther understood by reformation. That was the kind of reformer he was. He was no rabid revolutionary. As he took the Word of God as his standard, his intention was not to destroy but to fulfil.

There came a time, certainly, when he abandoned any hopes he may have cherished that Rome itself might respond to a call to self-criticism and initiate a reform from within. Reluctantly he came to the conclusion that she had forfeited her right to be regarded as the true Church at all. But he nevertheless strove to maintain within the emergent Protestant congregations this vital sense of continuity with the past. It was with the Scriptures as his guide that he took up this attitude. Luther's stress on this link with what had gone before goes far to explain why, in his reforming endeavour, he found himself fighting a battle on two fronts. On the one hand, he was up against the traditionalism of Rome, and was constantly seeking on biblical grounds to combat the errors and abuses of that apostate institution, as he believed it to be. On the other hand, as the years went by he was increasingly harassed by and compelled to contend with the advocates of a much more drastic solution than his – the *Schwärmerei*, or fanatical enthusiasts like Karlstadt and Münzer, and the leaders of the proliferating Protestant splinter groups. In some ways, this was Luther's toughest struggle. But, as Herman Preus reminds us, "Luther refused to be the father of left-wing Protestant sectarianism, which disregards the voice of the Church, the fathers, and of the teaching tradition of the Church."[1] It is important for us to be aware that Luther was very far from being what his Roman opponents tried to make out – a schismatic, an individualist, a sectarian, an ecclesiastical anarchist. As we proceed to watch Luther as he carries forward the plan of reform, what will doubtless surprise us is not his impatience but his conservatism.

We can best gain an impression of Luther the reformer as we examine some of the treatises he penned, especially in the earlier days of the movement he almost unwittingly initiated. Before we set out on such an inquiry, we should remember that all this was never unrelated to his Christian experience of a gracious God, and his vocation as a biblical instructor. Gordon Rupp brings out the connection: "The doctrines which Luther had worked out in lecture room, cell, pulpit, which with a Cellini-like intensity he had forged in the fire of his own *Anfechtungen*, are not something apart from what we might call the practical writings of improvization but form the ground base of them all."[2] We shall be concentrating on what Luther wrote from 1520 onwards in a series of what are virtually manifestos of reform. Luther's output was prolific – in his literary *annus mirabilis* of 1520 he produced no less than twenty-four publications.[3] "I have a swift hand and a quicker memory," he revealed.

[1] Herman A. Preus, "The Christian and the Church", *More About Luther*, p. 167.
[2] NCMH. 2. 81.
[3] A. G. Dickens, *Martin Luther and the Reformation* (1967), p. 45.

"When I write, it just flows out; I do not have to press and squeeze."[1] Some half dozen of these constituted the platform of reform. We can only refer to them, and indicate how in each the appeal to Scripture is basic.

In May 1520 his *Treatise on Good Works* appeared.[2] It is an analysis of the Decalogue, and a little compendium of practical theology. Although originally pastoral in intention, it is cast in typical thesis form, the arguments being advanced in a strictly logical way.[3] Luther's new evangelical outlook and spirit is most pronounced. "To his Catholic contemporaries it must have seemed like a book from another world," according to Schwiebert. "Even though there are still some traces of his earlier training, the sermon presented a wholly new interpretation of Christian ethics, which normally flowed from his doctrine of justification by faith."[4] He saw faith as the only foundation of all good works, and allowed no differentiation between the religious and the secular. With this single treatise, it has been said, Luther obliterated the distinction between the two which had dominated the Middle Ages and altered the whole system of Christian ethics.[5] Throughout the exposition of the Ten Commandments which forms the substance of this work, Luther repeatedly compared Scripture with Scripture to prove his point.[6]

In June of the same year, Luther wrote *The Papacy at Rome*, which Köstlin regarded as "one of the most important of his general doctrinal treatises of this period".[7] It is his first major attempt to state his teaching on the Church. Some Roman Catholic historians have sought to argue that Luther's new definition of the Church was the result of his break with the papacy. Just the reverse was in fact the case. It was his new understanding of the Church from Scripture which led to his break with Rome.[8] Previously, "when he thought he touched the hem of the skirt of Mother Church, he found he was touching only the orphrey of a pope or a bishop or a priest – always a man," explains Preus. "By the enlightenment of the Word the day finally came when Luther reached out again for the comfort of the Church – and this time he touched nothing human, but the Body of Christ, the Holy Catholic Church, the Communion of Saints. He touched Christ. He had searched the Scriptures, he had examined the Church fathers, he had seen the unity and the continuity of 'the faith once delivered to the saints'. Through it all he had learned that in spite of his ecclesiastical isolation he was still in the Church."[9]

In what Theodore Schmauk has called "Luther's declaration of

[1] Boehmer, *Road to Reformation*, p. 299.　　[2] LW. 44. 21–114.
[3] Ibid., 17.　　[4] Schwiebert, op. cit., p. 453.
[5] LW. 44. 20 (James Atkinson).　　[6] Ibid., 23, 25–26, 33, et al.
[7] Julius Köstlin and Georg Kawerau, *Martin Luther* (1903), Bd. I, p. 299. For *On the Papacy at Rome* PE. I. 337–94.
[8] Holl. op. cit., Bd. I, p. 288–90.
[9] Preus, "The Christian and the Church", *More About Luther*, p. 132.

emancipation from the spiritual pre-eminence of the Church of Rome", he
had in 1519 replied to the thirteen theses brought against him by Johann
Eck of Ingoldstadt.[1] The Leipzig Disputation was the outcome. Following
it, Luther was the target of so much criticism that he felt he must defend his
position. He was by no means eager to rush into the fray. "You cannot
make a pen out of a sword," he wrote: "the Word of God is a sword. I
was unwilling to be forced to come forward in public; and the more
unwilling I am, the more I am drawn into the contest."[2] *The Papacy of
Rome* is subtitled: *An Answer to the Celebrated Romanist at Leipzig*. This was
Augustine von Alveld, a Franciscan friar whom Adolf, Bishop of Merseberg, had commissioned to counter Luther's arguments.[3] Alveld set such a
pace in scurrility that Luther's response seems mild by comparison.[4] The
reformer was content, as usual, to rest his case on Scripture. He complained that Alveld treated "God's holy words no better than if they were
the fabled pratings of some fool or jester at the carnival."[5] If he did refer to
them at all, it was often with little respect for the context. The word
church, Luther declared, is commonly used in three senses: of a building,
of the Roman organization, and of the spiritual fellowship of believers.[6] He
will only recognize the latter as scriptural. The Church is "a spiritual
assembly of souls in one faith" and "no one is reckoned a Christian for the
body's sake", since "the true, real, right, essential Church is a spiritual
thing, and not anything external or outward, by whatever name it may be
called".[7] This unity of the Spirit "is of itself sufficient to make a Church,
and without it no unity, be it of place, of time, of person, of work, or of
whatever else, makes a Church".[8] Hence it is obvious that "external
fellowship with the Roman communion does not make men Christians,
and so the lack of that fellowship certainly does not make a man a heretic
or an apostate".[9] Of this scriptural Church, Christ is the only head.[10] "All
that the pope decrees I will receive on this condition, that first I test it by
the Holy Scriptures. He must remain under Christ, and submit to be
judged by the Holy Scriptures."[11]

In July 1520 Luther published one of many attacks on the Roman mass.
Already he had written a sermon on the subject in 1519, but in *A Treatise
on the New Testament* (1520) he was clearly moving to a more comprehensively biblical view.[12] The chief external reason for observing this

---

[1] PE. I. 329.   [2] Ibid.
[3] It was the Bishop who had tried to prevent the Leipzig debate on the ground that the
papal decree on indulgences of the 9th November 1518 had settled the matter once and for all
(LW. 31. 319; cf. LW. 48. 164 n. 9).
[4] PE. I. 337 n. 1.   [5] Ibid., 339.   [6] Ibid., 349, 354, 356.
[7] Ibid., 353-4; cf. 349. Luther avoided the normal word *Kirche* and substituted *Christenheit*
to distinguish it from the Roman organization.
[8] Ibid., 349.   [9] Ibid., 351.   [10] Ibid., 352.   [11] Ibid., 391.
[12] *The Blessed Sacrament of the Holy and True Body of Christ* (1513), LW. 35. 49-73; *A Treatise
on the New Testament, that is, the Holy Mass* (1520), LW. 35. 79-111.

sacrament, he stated, is the Word of God, which no one can do without.[1]
Whereas in 1519 Luther had laid emphasis on the service as a communion
with Christ and the saints, now he preferred to regard the words of institution as fundamental. But more importantly still, the treatise "penetrates to the heart of Christian worship and boldly replaces the traditional
notions of the mass as a sacrifice with the scriptural teaching of the Lord's
supper as a testament", as Theodore Bachmann tells us.[2] "The mass is
nothing else than a testament," Luther affirmed, "and a sacrament in which
God makes a pledge to us and gives us grace and mercy." It is not to be
made into a good work from which merit may be obtained. A testament is
not a benefit earned but a benefit conferred. For the first time Luther
unequivocally rejected the Roman interpretation of the mass as a bloodless
repetition of the sacrifice made on Calvary.[3] But it is nevertheless per-
missible to call the mass a sacrifice, "not on its own account, but because
we offer ourselves as a sacrifice along with Christ".[4]

In the same treatise Luther laid the foundation for the distinctively
Protestant doctrine of the believer's priesthood. Since "faith alone is the
true priestly office" it follows that "all Christian men are priests, all women
priestesses, be they young or old, master or servant, mistress or maid,
learned or unlearned. Here there is no difference, unless faith be unequal."[5]
As Green observes, "the priest was . . . the cornerstone of the fabric of
medieval life," and this biblical insistence on the part of Luther demolished
at one blow the entire sacerdotal system of the past.[6] It must not be
supposed, however, that Luther therefore meant to obliterate the distinction between ministers and laymen in the Church, for this was clearly not
accomplished in mainstream Protestantism.[7] His concern was to show that
the difference is merely one of function, and not at all of standing before
God.[8] And in the crucial matter of priesthood – which has to do solely with
the offering of sacrifice – all Christians are one in the need to offer themselves to God through Christ, which is the only sacrifice now required
since the Saviour died once for all on the cross.

Luther's address *To the Christian Nobility of the German Nation Concerning the Reform of the Christian Estate*, which came out in August 1520, dealt
with the details involved in the break with Rome at the regional level.[9]
A. G. Dickens describes it as "one of the great reform programmes of
western literature".[10] The implications of the transfer from allegiance to the
pope are spelled out in practical terms. But first Luther attacked the three

[1] LW. 35. 105. [2] Ibid., 77. [3] Ibid., 93.
[4] Ibid. [5] Ibid., 101. [6] Green, op. cit., p. 17.
[7] "The priesthood of all believers never means for Luther what it has sometimes meant in
degenerate Protestantism, the secularization of the clergy, the doctrine that we are all laymen."
Rupp, *Righteousness of God*, p. 315).
[8] Luther acknowledged a distinction of *Amt* but not of *Stand*.
[9] LW. 44. 123–217. [10] Dickens, op. cit., p. 47.

walls of straw and paper, as he depicted them, which protected the Roman Jericho.[1] He threw them down with the trumpet-blast of the Word. The first was the false division between the spiritual estate and the temporal.[2] Arguing from 1 Corinthians 12 and other passages, Luther claimed that "because we all have one baptism, one gospel, one faith, and are all Christians alike", then "all Christians are truly of the spiritual estate, and there is no difference among them except that of office".[3]

The second wall was yet more loosely built and less substantial. "The Romanists want to be the only masters of Holy Scripture, although they never learn a thing from the Bible all their life long."[4] They assume the sole authority for themselves, and claim that only the pope possesses the key to interpret the Word. They imagine that the Holy Spirit never leaves them, no matter how ignorant and wicked they are. Luther dismissed this pretension as "an outrageous fancied fable", and went on to prove how unscriptural it was.[5] The third wall falls of its own accord when the other two are down. "When the pope acts contrary to the Scriptures, it is our duty to stand by the Scriptures, to reprove him and to constrain him, according to the word of Christ (Matt. 18:15-17)."[6] This can only be effectively done as the whole Church is represented in a general council. But there is no basis in the Bible for the Roman contention that only the pope can convene such a gathering. In Acts 15 it was not Peter, but the apostles and elders who called the council of Jerusalem.[7]

Luther's onslaught on Rome reached its climax in October 1520 with *The Babylonian Captivity of the Church*.[8] This was written in Latin with the clergy in view. The immediate occasion was the renewed claim of Alveld about the power of the pope.[9] Luther used to confess jokingly that men like Prierias, Emser and Eck, as well as Alveld, had been his theological professors since 1517.[10] They forced him to go back to the Word in order to refute their contentions. It was as he faced these vital issues in the light of Scripture that he achieved his full stature as a reformer. *The Babylonian Captivity of the Church* was in essence, as Dickens says, "a plea for the abolition of non-biblical theology and of any man-made ecclesiastical laws."[11] It struck like a dagger at the heart of sacerdotalism and signalized Luther's final and irrevocable breach with Rome.[12]

The title is self-explanatory. The reference is obviously to the Jewish exile, and the thrust of Luther's thesis is that in the same way Christians had been carried away from the Scriptures and subjugated to papal tyranny. This oppression was largely due to a misinterpretation of the

[1] LW. 44. 126.   [2] Ibid.   [3] Ibid., 127.
[4] Ibid., 133.   [5] Ibid., 134.   [6] Ibid., 136.
[7] Ibid.   [8] LW. 36. 11-126.   [9] LC. 1. 206, 283; WAB. 2. 148 n. 6.
[10] LW. 36. 11-12.   [11] Dickens, op. cit., p. 48.
[12] LW. 36. 8. Introduction by Frederick C. Ahrens and Abdel Ross Wentz.

sacraments – especially that of the Lord's Supper. Luther therefore devoted himself to an examination, in the light of Scripture, of the sacramental set-up in Rome. He came to the conclusion that only three of the seven recognized sacraments could at all be substantiated from the Word of God – baptism, penance, and the bread.[1] Indeed, he went so far as to say that if he were to be very strictly scriptural he would speak only of one sacrament – Christ himself – and three sacramental signs.[2] In dealing with the Holy Communion, Luther produced scriptural arguments for administration in both kinds and for the testamental nature of the ordinance.[3] Baptism he immediately related to the promise in Mark 16:16.[4] He utterly rejected the medieval conception of penance as "the second plank after shipwreck".[5] Yet from Matt. 16:19; 18:18 and John 20:23, he sought to reinstate the biblical meaning of forgiveness with a characteristic emphasis on the need for faith.[6] Whilst his exegesis was unexceptionable, he did not really show why this should be recognized as a sacrament, along with baptism and the breaking of bread. In the rest of the work Luther tested the other four sacraments of the Roman Church and found them wanting when judged by Scripture. This comprehensive treatment "represents the culmination of Luther's reformatory thinking on the theological side", according to A. T. W. Steinhäuser.[7]

In considering Luther's resistance to Rome, we have had to limit ourselves to an examination of these seminal writings of the year 1520, when the conflict was at its height.[8] When the Rubicon was crossed, Luther continued to combat the unscriptural deviations of Rome in a spate of publications which we cannot pause to weigh. There were four treatises on the mass which represent "selections from the symphony to which *The Babylonian Captivity* was the prelude".[9] In the third of these Luther announced in memorable terms that the right way to honour God's Word is to hide it within, as the Psalmist did. "The heart is its real gilded ciborium."[10] In the *Formula of the Mass* (1523) and the *German Mass* (1526) Luther translated his theological convictions into liturgical practice – retaining much more than some of his fellow-evangelicals could approve, and yet still seeking to take the Word of God as his guide. He took the view, however, that in the context of worship it is not essential that every item shall be directly derived from Scripture, but only that it must not conflict with Scripture.[11] By the time he wrote *On the Councils and the*

[1] LW. 36. 18.   [2] Ibid.   [3] Ibid., 20–24, 37–46.   [4] Ibid., 58, 59.
[5] Ibid., 61. Jerome, *Epistolae*, 130.   [6] LW. 36. 81–91.   [7] PE. 2. 168.
[8] We have not dealt with the last of these – *The Freedom of a Christian* (LW. 31. 333–377) since it is concerned with the application of theology to life rather than with theology as such. But it represents the quintessence of Luther's biblical thinking at this period in its practical repercussions.
[9] LW. 36. ix. Introduction by Abdel Ross Wentz.
[10] Ibid., 278. *The Adoration of the Sacrament* (1523).   [11] LW. 53. 20.

Church (1539), Luther had become even more disillusioned with Rome, and complained that the pope "makes Holy Scripture subject to himself and tears it asunder".[1] He would try to throw the Protestants not only out of the Church but out of the Bible too, if he could do such a thing.[2] Nevertheless, "God's Word cannot be without God's people and conversely God's people cannot be without God's Word."[3]

We must now turn more briefly to indicate the nature of Luther's confrontation with his opponents on his second front, namely the enthusiasts and the sectarians. These were the wild men of the extreme left, who would have forfeited the gains of the Reformation by going too far and too fast. There has been a reassessment of these radicals in recent years – notably in a definitive study by George Hunston Williams – and it must be made clear that not all can be dismissed as eccentric and incorrigible.[4] But Luther saw for himself what had begun to happen at Wittenberg, whilst he was in the Wartburg and Karlstadt held sway. He visited Zwickau where Thomas Münzer and his self-styled "prophets" ran amok. He did not think that *Schwärmerei* was too strong a term to apply to such men. Gordon Rupp, with his usual penchant for amusing comment, has defined the phenomenon as "too many bees chasing too few bonnets".[5] As he tried to save the Reformation from itself, Luther "found himself locked in a new struggle which made the one at Worms look simple", so Dickens thinks.[6]

It was with the Bible before him that Luther sought to repel this threat to the progress of Protestantism. His *Letter to the Princes of Saxony* (1524) urged the authorities to suppress the unbridled activities of Münzer and his crew.[7] But Karlstadt was a much more subtle antagonist, who had once been a colleague of Luther in the University faculty at Wittenberg. He had been expelled from Saxony, and in the autumn of 1524 visited Strasburg to spread his influence there. The Protestant leaders, under Bucer and Capito, scenting the danger, wrote to Luther asking him to give them some guidance. So he wrote a *Letter to the Christians at Strasburg in Opposition to the Fanatic Spirit*, in which he promised eventually to refute the opinions of Karlstadt, as expressed in eight volumes of his, which Luther had read.[8] "For the moment he only wanted the Strasburgers to realize the errors of Karlstadt, and to counsel them to hold to the Word," explains Conrad Bergendorff. "Dissensions would of course arise, but they were meant to drive Christians closer to the Word. Luther was confident that

[1] LW. 41. 122.   [2] Ibid., 162.
[3] Ibid., 150.
[4] George Hunston Williams, *The Radical Reformation* (1962); cf. also Leonard Verduin, *The Reformers and their Stepchildren* (1964), for a somewhat different viewpoint.
[5] E. Gordon Rupp, "Luther and the Puritans", *Luther Today*, p. 111.
[6] Dickens, op. cit., p. 67.   [7] LW. 40. 45–59.
[8] Ibid., 65–71.

his teachings were based on the Word, while Karlstadt was pursuing notions born of his own fancy."[1]

Luther began with an allusion to God's "salutary Word", through which the Christians in Strasburg had been brought to Christ.[2] They must not be surprised at what has been happening in their midst. "For if our gospel is the true gospel, as I am convinced and have no doubt it is, then it must naturally follow that it will be attacked, persecuted and tested from both sides. On the left the opponents will show open contempt and hate, on the right our own will be guilty of dissension and party spirit."[3] Luther was content that the questions at issue should be settled only by resort to the Scriptures. "I am a captive and cannot free myself," he admitted, in words reminiscent of his brave stand at Worms [4]

The fuller refutation of Karlstadt which Luther had undertaken to supply was presented in 1525, with the title: *Against the Heavenly Prophets in the Matter of Images and Sacraments.*[5] It was from the biblical standpoint that he was able to show how subjective and ill-founded were the mystical dreams of the so-called "spiritualists". Luther began by urging his readers "to pray God for a right understanding and for his holy, pure Word".[6] For him these two belonged together. What he had to say about the sacraments covered by now familiar ground, with his firmness about a plain interpretation of our Lord's pronouncement concerning the bread and wine in the Holy Communion (Matt. 26:26–28). There is also a long discussion of John 6:63.[7] But the first part dealt with another issue that was highly relevant to the current situation – that of the attitude of evangelicals to images. Whilst he was at Wittenberg, Karlstadt had waged an icono-clastic campaign with such misguided zeal that Luther had to take the risk of leaving his retreat in order to set things straight. The most important thing, he affirmed, was that images should first of all be torn out of men's hearts by the Word.[8] Once that had been done, those that were found in the churches would no longer have any meaning for the Christian. Luther went on to show that the only images forbidden in Scripture are those made in the likeness of God Himself.[9] The erection of pillars and stones is expressly prohibited in Leviticus 26:1 if they are treated as idols. But Joshua set up a cairn at Shechem as a testimony (Josh. 24:26), and Samuel raised a stone of help (1 Sam. 7:12). Such things are permitted as memorials. In Scripture, idols were destroyed not by the masses, but by the leaders chosen by God (Gen. 35:4; Judges 6:27; 2 Kings 10:26; 18:4; 23:15).[10] Luther accused Karlstadt of introducing a new legalism into Christianity.[11] He contrasted this with the liberty of the gospel, as expressed in many New

[1] Ibid., 63.   [2] Ibid., 65.   [3] Ibid., 66.
[4] Ibid., 68.   [5] Ibid., 79–223.   [6] Ibid., 80.
[7] Ibid., 173–8, 202–10.   [8] Ibid., 84.   [9] Ibid., 85.
[10] Ibid., 87–90.   [11] Ibid., 91.

Testament passages which he cited. He appealed particularly to Romans
14:2–6 and 1 Corinthians 8:8–10 for the true principle of liberty for the
believer.[1] We are not under obligation to do anything at all for God
except trust and love.[2] This is the authentic freedom of the Spirit, of which
the enthusiasts tended to claim the monopoly.

Luther dealt with another wing of the radical Reformation – the Anabaptists – in 1528.[3] Two pastors had asked him to take up the subject, since
they were faced with the problem of tackling the heresy, as they deemed it
to be, in their own area. Luther did not appear to be too familiar with the
teachings of the Anabaptists, although he had been receiving information
from a number of quarters. The Anabaptist martyr, Balthasar Hubmaier,
had written a book in defence of his beliefs in 1525, but Luther revealed no
acquaintance with it. He challenged the Anabaptists to prepare a more
detailed account of their tenets. He began his reply to the two pastors by
deploring the death of Hubmaier.[4] This was no way to defeat falsehood.
Everyone should be allowed to hold his own convictions, however mistaken we may consider them to be. If a man's faith is erroneous then he will
be sufficiently punished by the fires of hell. It is by the Scriptures and the
Word that we ought to withstand the devil and protect the truth, not by
persecution.[5]

Luther speedily disposed of those who favoured rebaptism simply "to
spite the pope and be free of any taint of the Antichrist".[6] If that were to be
the only motive in reform, then it would be necessary to have a new Bible,
because it has been preserved by the Roman Church.[7] His exposition of the
Protestant doctrine of baptism rested on the fact that it is a promise and
sign contained within God's Word and given to us on that authority.[8] The
real point at issue was not really as to whether those who had been
baptized by Rome ought to be baptized again in the Protestant Church. It
was whether infants should be baptized at all, and whether, if they had
been, even in a Protestant Church, they should not be baptized again on
profession of faith. This led Luther into a defence of paedobaptism, which
he admitted could not be certainly proved from Scripture, but which he
personally contended could not be altogether disproved from Scripture
either.[9] His chief charge against the Anabaptists was that "they teach doubt
not faith, calling this Scripture and the Word of God. . . . Having made up
their minds concerning their peculiar notions, they attempt to make the
Scriptures agree with them by dragging passages in by the hair."[10] Perhaps
Luther did less than justice to those who differed from him, but we must
not question his integrity even if we consider him to have been mistaken.

Concerning Rebaptism was only the beginning of Luther's attempt to

[1] Ibid., 95, 127–8.   [2] Ibid., 127.
[3] Ibid., 229–62. *Concerning Rebaptism* (1528).   [4] Ibid., 229.
[5] Ibid., 230.   [6] Ibid., 231.   [7] Ibid.
[8] Ibid., 252.   [9] Ibid., 255–6.   [10] Ibid., 262.

elucidate this topic from the Word of God. He preached many sermons on the doctrine, and in 1529 he incorporated his teaching into the Small and Large Catechisms. "The keynote of his emphasis affirms that baptism is not the work of man but the work of God," observes Theodore Bachmann. "Therefore the actions of men can neither make nor nullify this sacrament. Baptism is a command of God given us in the Scriptures, notably but not only in such passages as Mark 16:16 or Matt. 28:18, 19. Above all, baptism is exalted for us by Jesus Christ; God honours our baptism in that of His Son."[1]

Whatever verdict we may pass on Luther's logic and the degree of conviction carried by his arguments – especially in refuting the Anabaptists – it cannot be disputed that whether he was contending with the excesses either of Rome or of Protestantism, he strove at all times to be a man of the Word. He was a reformer indeed – one who tried to mould the Church anew according to the pattern of Scripture.

[1] LW 35. 26.

Luther and the Bible
(b)

LUTHER'S VIEW OF SCRIPTURE

CHAPTER XI

LUTHER AND THE AUTHORITY OF SCRIPTURE

"LUTHER WAS NOT BREAKING NEW GROUND WHEN he turned to the Bible," according to Ernst Zeeden, "but only when he cut the Bible off from pope and Church, or subordinated them."[1] The authority of the Word was not seriously questioned. The issue at stake was whether that authority stood on its own feet, or was derived from or needed to be supplemented by that of the Roman Church. This more than anything else was what the Reformation was about. All the other items on its agenda stemmed from the underlying controversy about the magisterial role of Scripture. As we speak of a new reformation in our time, once again biblical authority is the key to the debate.

As we have seen, the exponents of the *via moderna*, under whose influence Luther came at Erfurt, belonged to the Occamist school which laid greater stress on the supremacy of Scripture than most medieval theologians had done. Friedrich Kropatscheck has shown that not only did they accept a thorough-going doctrine of inspiration but also held that the Word of God posits certain propositions of faith which the Christian is obliged to believe on pain of being ejected as a heretic.[2] Occam himself had declared that whoever suggested that any part of the Old or New Testament was false, or need not be recognized by believers, was heretical and must be firmly resisted.[3] Whereas the advocates of the *via antiqua* urged the use of the Scriptures for the edification of the masses, the Occamists were more concerned with underlining the sole authority of the Word. They taught that the only sure foundation for the superstructure of Christian belief was the revealed truth of God.

"Yet this viewpoint could not produce evangelical and reformatory results," added Reu, "since despite all its emphasis and the decided assertion that only accordance with the Scriptures renders truths of faith obligatory, the conviction nevertheless obtained that the teaching of the Church and the teaching of Scripture are identical, and Occam insistently recognized not the pope but the Church as the final judge of the question as to whether

---

[1] Ernst W. Zeeden, *The Legacy of Luther* (E.T. 1954), p. 1.
[2] Friedrich Kropatscheck, *Das Schriftprinzip der lutherische Kirche*, Bd. I, *Die Vorgeschichte. Das Erbe des Mittelalters* (1904), pp. 438–40. Cf. Reu, *Luther and the Scriptures*, p. 134, to which I am indebted for this and certain other references.
[3] Occam, *Dialogue* I.4.vi, in Goldast, op. cit., Vol II, p. 449.

his understanding of the Scripture is correct."[1] In his *Compendium Errorum Johannis Papae* XXII (*c.* 1334–8) Occam had included this disclaimer in the preface: "If I should have written something in this work which is contrary to Holy Writ or the teachings of the saints, or the assertions of the most holy Church, I submit myself and my words to correction by the Catholic Church – not the Church of malignants, or heretics, or schismatics and their protectors."[2] The Erfurt Occamists, however, modified Occam's position by acknowledging the pope and not a general council as the mouthpiece of the Church.[3] Luther's conception of biblical authority therefore, was revolutionary in that it denied that the teaching of Scripture and the teaching of the Roman Church were necessarily identical, and that the pope or a council as representing the Church must ultimately determine the meaning of the Word.

This was not a conviction which Luther reached all at once, even after his illumination. In his *Dictata super Psalterium* (1513–1515), despite the repeated statements about the efficacy of Scripture, he could nevertheless assert that understanding of Scripture does not guarantee truth.[4] He also claimed that the Holy Spirit was given to the leaders of the Church, not only to enable them to interpret the existing Word but also to receive new truths.[5] This continued to be Luther's attitude as he started his lectures on Romans. From this point onwards, however, as a consequence of his tower experience, he began to shake off the shackles of ecclesiasticism and to recognize the sole authority of Scripture. Even as early as 1516 he could declare that "faith surrenders itself captive to the Word of Christ" – a striking anticipation of his testimony at Worms.[6]

We must now seek to analyze Luther's developed teaching about the authority of Scripture. It is this that lies at the heart of the Reformation witness. *Sola Scriptura* was its watchword. Luther would admit no other criterion, even as a corollary. He was content to abide by what he called "the sure rule of God's Word".[7] For him it was *norma normans* not *norma normata*. It was an unregulated regulator. By it everything was to be judged but nothing might judge it. When man attempts to set himself up as one who is capable of critical appraisal he merely displays his ignorance and folly. "Among Christians the rule is not to argue or investigate," wrote Luther, "not to be a smart aleck or a rationalistic know-it-all; but to hear, believe, and persevere in the Word of God, through which alone we obtain whatever knowledge we have of God and divine things. We are not to determine out of ourselves what we must believe about him, but to hear and learn it from him."[8]

[1] Ibid., p. 14.
[2] Occam, *Compendium Errorum Johannis Papae XXII*, in Goldast, op. cit., Vol. II, p. 958.
[3] Boehmer, *Road to Reformation*, p. 27.   [4] WA. 4. 436.
[5] Ibid., 345.   [6] WA. 1. 87.   [7] LW. 7. 21.
[8] LW. 13. 237.

In the empire of the Church the rule is God's Word, Luther insisted.[1]
"We must judge according to the Word of God."[2] Conversely, we must
not try to be its judge. It is the Anabaptists (as well as the Romans) who
think that they can "measure the Word of God . . . with their own yardstick and judge it on the basis of their own education and their own notion
as to its meaning. This settles it for them, and God ends up playing the role
of pupil to all men".[3] The deviationists would pass judgement on Scripture
and say, "That is true, and that is false." "You must cling to His Word. . . .
In brief, you must become God's pupil. If God does not grant you the
Word and faith, you will not believe it. Without this all will fail."[4] Luther
lodged the same complaint against the Jewish exegetes, when they
tampered with the text of the Old Testament. With reference to their
interference with Genesis 19:24, for example, Luther asks: "But who
ordered them to have the audacity to do this in the case of God's Book?
For if one were at liberty to trifle in this way with Holy Scripture, no
article of faith would remain intact. Hence it is a characteristic of the unbelieving Jews and of the godless papists to be teachers of the Holy Spirit
and to teach him what or how to write. But let us be and remain pupils,
and let us not change the Word of God; we ourselves should be changed
through the Word."[5]

It is by the standard of Scripture that the believer is enabled to measure
all other teaching. It is in this way that he will put everything to the proof
and retain only that which is good.[6] "A Christian soon smells from afar
which is God's and which is human teaching. He sees from afar that the
schismatic spirits are speaking their own human mind and opinion. They
cannot escape me, Dr. Luther. I can soon judge and say whether their
doctrine is of God or of man; for I am doing the will of God, who sent
Christ. I have given ear to none but God's Word, and I say: 'Dear Lord
Christ, I want to be thy pupil, and I believe thy Word. I will close my
eyes and surrender to thy Word.' Thus He makes me a free nobleman, yes,
a fine doctor and teacher, who is captive to the Word of God, and is able
to judge the errors and the faith of pope, Turks, Jews and Sacramentarians.
They must fall, and I tread them all underfoot. I have become a doctor and
a judge who judges correctly."[7] In the end, for all their raving, the heretics
have to give way. A Christian who has the Scripture as his guide can
differentiate between true and false doctrine.[8] That is why Paul can claim
that the spiritual man, equipped with God's Word, "judges all things, but
is himself judged by no one" (1 Cor. 2:15). "And though they fall to,
judge and condemn, roar and bellow, murmur and speak defiantly against

[1] LW. 41. 134.
[2] LW. 26. 383; cf. LW. 24. 75 – "We must judge and consider all wonders and miracles in
the light of God's Word, to ascertain whether they are in accordance and agreement with it."
[3] LW. 23. 79.   [4] Ibid., 103.   [5] LW. 3. 297.
[6] I Thess. 5:21.   [7] LW. 23. 230.   [8] Ibid.

others, their judgement is none the less wrong and does not endure as a Christian's judgement endures before God."[1]

We must not rely on man, Luther warned. We must learn to adhere solely to the Word of God. It is not who speaks that matters in the Church, but what is spoken. "The person is of no consequence; nor is the person's name important, whether it be Peter or Paul. The person is acceptable so long as he teaches faithfully. Therefore let the Word of God be your guide, and assure yourself that this is presented correctly. If the preacher does that, he is above suspicion. But if he does not follow that guideline, then may he be accursed, even if it were I myself or an angel from heaven. St. Paul says to the Galatians (1:8): 'But even if we, or an angel from heaven, should preach to you a gospel contrary to that which we preached to you, let him be accursed.'"[2]

Elsewhere Luther referred to the Scriptures as "the proper touchstone"[3] by which all teaching is to be tested. It is "to be the rule or touchstone or Lydian stone by which I can tell black from white and evil from good".[4] Luther did not want to contradict the fathers, "but I will take their books and go with them to Christ and his Word as the touchstone and compare the two."[5] "If anyone says, the Church or the bishops decided this, then answer: Come, let us go to the touchstone and let us measure with the right yardstick and examine whether it agrees with the *Pater Noster* and with the articles of faith and whether he also preaches the forgiveness of sins. If it agrees with what Christ taught us, then let us accept it and do according to it."[6] We can detect here what is to be found again in Luther – namely, a standard even within the standard. The Word is the Word of Christ, and its authority is really his.

Luther sometimes used the analogy of light in relation to Scripture. "It illumines everything just as the sun does. Wherever this light does not shine, you must say: 'I gladly concede that it may appear beautiful before the world, that it may glisten and seem like something precious. But I will never agree that it helps me to God or delivers me from death, no matter how much it may glitter, if it is not in agreement with the Word of God. If such zeal affects my soul's welfare and salvation, I will spit on it and tread it underfoot. I will refuse to tolerate, hear, or see it; for it is not God's Word.'"[7] Again, Luther alluded to the Scripture "alone as the fountain of all wisdom".[8] Hence he could speak about "the commanding Word of God", and declare that God "does all things with the Word alone".[9] Commenting on Galatians 1:9 – "a clear text and a thunderbolt" – Luther showed how Paul subordinated himself, along with an angel from heaven, teachers on earth and any other masters at all to sacred Scrip-

[1] Ibid., 231.   [2] Ibid., 191.   [3] LW. 24. 177.
[4] LW. 23. 174.   [5] WA. 46. 771.   [6] Ibid., 780.
[7] LW. 23. 174–5.   [8] EA. 4. 328.   [9] LW. 9. 7; LW. 8. 275.

ture.[1] "This queen must rule, and everyone must obey, and be subject to her."[2]

In the same section of his lectures on Galatians, Luther nailed "the accursed lie that the pope is the arbiter of Scripture or that the Church has authority over Scripture".[3] And in preaching on John 7:17 he took up the same cudgels: "The pope boasts that the Christian Church is above the Word of God. No, this is not true! We must be pupils and not aspire to be masters, for the pupil must not be above his master."[4] And again: "Years ago all the pope's pronouncements were called Christian truth and articles of faith, yet this was simply based on man. And then it happened that people sank into the abyss and lost everything that pertains to the Word of God and Christ. Therefore we must now declare: 'Pope, council, and doctors, we will not believe you; but we will believe in the Divine Word.'"[5]

Luther took Erasmus to task because he was prepared to submit his mind to the authority of the Church as well as to that of the Scriptures. "What say you, Erasmus? Is it not enough that you submit your opinions to the Scriptures? Do you submit it to the decrees of the Church also? What can the Church decree, that is not decreed in the Scriptures?"[6] When the Church is indeed the Church, its doctrine will coincide with that of the Bible. Luther reversed the assumption of the Occamists. They equated the teaching of Scripture with that of the institutional Church as it then was in its unreformed condition. Luther declared that the true Church is reformed according to the Word of God and that what it teaches is in line with Scripture, not because the Bible has been accommodated to the Church, but because the Church has been aligned to the Bible.

The priority of Scripture over the Church is everywhere stressed in Luther. The Church is the creation of the Word, not vice versa. "The Scripture is the womb from which are born theological truth and the Church."[7] "The Church is built on the word of the Gospel which is the word of God's wisdom and virtue."[8] "The Word of God preserves the Church of God."[9] The Church owes its existence to the Word and is maintained by the same means. The Holy Spirit governs the Church only through the Word.[10] These emphases, which are to be found even in Luther's early lectures, were expanded and clarified in his later writings.[11] In *The Babylonian Captivity of the Church* he gave full expression to them. "The Church was born by the word of promise through faith, and by this same word is nourished and preserved. That is to say, it is the promises of

---

[1] LW. 26. 57.   [2] Ibid., 58.   [3] Ibid., 57.
[4] LW. 23. 231.   [5] Ibid., 297.   [6] BW. 22.
[7] WA. 3. 454.   [8] WA. 4. 189.   [9] WA. 3. 259.
[10] LW. 24. 362.
[11] The references in notes 35–37 are from the *Dictata super Psalterium* (1513–1515). Holl has shown how soon Luther's doctrine of the Church was formulated (op. cit., Bd. I, pp. 288–99).

God that make the Church, and not the Church that makes the promise of
God. For the Word of God is incomparably superior to the Church, and in
this Word the Church, being a creature, has nothing to decree, ordain, or
make, but only to be decreed, ordained, and made. For who begets his
own parent? Who first brings forth his own maker?"[1]

Luther quickly disposed of the argument – still prevalent – that the
Church is superior to Scripture because it was responsible for selecting the
books included in the canon. The thesis of the ecclesiastical sophists ran like
this, according to Luther: "The Church has approved only four Gospels,
and therefore there are only four. For if it had approved more, there
would have been more. Since the Church has the right to accept and
approve as many Gospels as it wishes, it follows that the Church is superior
to the Gospels."[2] "What a splendid argument!" exclaimed Luther
ironically. "I approve Scripture. Therefore I am superior to Scripture.
John the Baptist acknowledges and confesses Christ. He points to Him with
his finger. Therefore he is superior to Christ. The Church approves
Christian faith and doctrine. Therefore the Church is superior to them."[3]
It is noteworthy that four centuries later Hans Lietzmann recognized the
self-authenticating character of the inspired writings in much the same
way as Luther did.[4]

Although the apostolic provenance of the New Testament books
carried weight in the acceptance of the canon, Luther refused to defer to
apostolic authority as such. He only admitted it in so far and because it was
scriptural. Paul in Galatians 2:6 refutes the argument which the false
teachers based on the apostolic tradition. "He says that it is out of order,
beside the point, and therefore irrelevant to the issue," claimed Luther.
"For the issue here is not the distinction amongst social positions; it is
something far more important. It is a divine matter involving God and His
Word, the question whether this Word is to have priority over the office
of an apostle or vice versa. To this question Paul answers: 'To preserve the
truth of the gospel and to keep the Word of God and the righteousness of
faith pure and undefiled, let apostleship go! An angel from heaven or Peter
and Paul – let them all perish!'"[5]

Luther's attitude to the historical creeds was determined by their biblical
content. He accepted them not because they had been adopted by the
councils of the Church but because he found that they conformed to
Scripture.[6] Quite often he linked Scripture and the creeds as his authorities.[7]
This is only another indication that Luther did not regard himself as a rebel

[1] LW. 36. 107.
[2] LW. 26. 57; cf. CC. 27. i. 74 for an example in Politus.
[3] LW. 26. 57.
[4] Hans Lietzmann, *A History of the Early Church*, Vol. II, *The Founding of the Church Universal* (E.T. 1950), pp. 97–98.
[5] LW. 26. 98.   [6] LW. 37. 361–2.   [7] Ibid., 185–6.

against the universal Church, but only against the errors and tyranny of the papal organization. In controversy both with the Romanists and the radicals, he repeatedly referred to the creeds as being grounded in the Scriptures and accepted by the whole Church. In 1538 he published *The Three Symbols or Creeds of the Christian Faith*, in which he elaborated on the brief theses in the first part of his Schmalkald Articles of 1537.[1] In it he declared that the Apostles' Creed is "truly the finest of all" since "briefly, correctly, and in a splendid way it summarizes the articles of faith, and it can easily be learned by children and simple people."[2] But the Nicene and Athanasian symbols were also valued by Luther, and much of his treatise was occupied with showing how the latter sought to safeguard the biblical revelation concerning the person of Christ.[3] There is no question in Luther's mind of setting the creeds above or against Scripture. He simply recognized that they were statements based on Scripture.

The fathers of the Church were subjected to the same test of fidelity to the Word. Although it is true that Luther appealed again and again to the primitive Church as well as to Scripture itself, and quoted the fathers with a profusion and facility which belies the charge that he had little knowledge of their writings, he nevertheless refused to bow to their authority wherever it conflicted with the disclosures of the Word. "I will not listen to the Church or the fathers or the apostles unless they bring and teach the pure Word of God."[4] "Their authority is worth most when it has clear scriptural support," he stated with reference to the fathers.[5] There were those who accused Luther of rejecting all the past teachers of the Church. That was a libel. "I do not reject them. But everyone, indeed, knows that at times they have erred, as men will; therefore, I am ready to trust them only when they give me evidence for their opinions from Scripture, which has never erred."[6] Then he added an apt quotation from Augustine to justify his attitude. Writing to Jerome, the great African father said: "I have learned to do only those books that are called the Holy Scriptures the honour of believing firmly that none of their writers has ever erred. All others I so read as not to hold what they say to be the truth unless they prove it to me by Holy Scripture or clear reason."[7]

"Luther was suspicious of all the fathers," explained Hugh Thompson

[1] This doctrinal statement was drawn up by Luther at the request of Johann Friedrich, Elector of Saxony, to be presented to the proposed General Council convened by Pope Paul III at Mantua in May 1537. The Schmalkald Articles set out the points on which the Protestants felt that no compromise was possible. The Council never met.

[2] LW. 34. 201.

[3] LW. 36. 218–22. The three symbols with which Luther dealt in his treatise were the Apostles' and Athanasian Creeds and the *Te Deum laudamus*. The Nicene Creed was added almost as a postscript. The *Te Deum* was regarded from early times as a declaration of the Christian faith and classed with the liturgical confessions (cf. LW. 36. 199. Introduction by Robert R. Heitner).

[4] LW. 26. 67.   [5] LW. 32. 189.   [6] Ibid., 11.

[7] Ibid. Augustine, *Epistolae*, 82, PL. 33. 286–7.

Kerr, "simply because the Roman Church found it expedient on many occasions to confirm certain practices which he detested by appealing to tradition and the writings of the fathers."[1] An examination of his disputes with Cajetan and the two Ecks will bear that out. In the preface to the Wittenberg edition of his German works (1539) Luther confessed that he hesitated to increase the number of human writings for he felt that they tended to draw men away from the Divine Word. He went so far as to say that he considered it a blessing in disguise that some of the patristic manuscripts had not been preserved, for "if they had all remained in existence, no room would be left for anything but books, and yet all of them together would not have improved on what one finds in the Holy Scriptures".[2] "Neither councils, fathers, nor we, in spite of the greatest and best success possible," he went on, "will do as well as the Holy Scriptures, *i.e.*, as well as God Himself has done."[3] In this he claimed to follow the example of Augustine, who was the first and almost the only one who determined to be subject to the Scriptures alone and independent of fathers and saints.[4] Luther, then, did not repudiate the fathers except where they departed from the biblical norm. He was more thoroughly versed in their works than some of his detractors have cared to concede. But he only cherished those insights which had been gained from the Word. "He was not without a historical sense and a reverence for antiquity," observed Henry E. Jacobs, "provided that it was subjected to the tests of Holy Scripture. Scripture was not to be interpreted by the fathers, but the fathers were to be judged by their agreement or disagreement with Scripture."[5]

Although at the outset of his reforming career Luther entertained hopes that an appeal to a general council might result in the resolution of his dilemma, he nevertheless remained critical of previous conciliar decisions. Once again the Bible was his criterion. He could only approve what the councils had decreed when those pronouncements could be reconciled with the Word of God. Otherwise he was compelled to reject them as merely human declarations. "When anything contrary to Scripture is decreed in a council, we ought to believe Scripture rather than the council. Scripture is our court of appeal and bulwark; with it we can resist even an angel from heaven – as St. Paul commands in Galatians 1(:8) – let alone a pope and a council."[6] "God is more ancient than all the councils and the fathers," Luther argued, against those who rested their case on the precedents of antiquity. "He is also greater and higher than all the councils and fathers. Scripture, too, is higher and more ancient than all the councils and fathers."[7] He conceded that councils could clarify

[1] *A Compend of Luther's Theology*, ed. Hugh Thompson Kerr (1943), p. viii.
[2] LW. 34. 283.   [3] Ibid., 284.   [4] Ibid., 285.
[5] ERE. 8. 201.   [6] LW. 32. 81.   [7] LW. 45. 145.

controverted matters of interpretation, but where the Word is plain we do
not need to wait for conciliar confirmation.[1] It was in his *On the Councils
and the Church* (1539) that Luther spread himself on this theme. "A council
has no power to establish new articles of faith, even though the Holy
Spirit is present. Even the apostolic council in Jerusalem introduced
nothing new in matters of faith, but rather held that which St. Peter
concludes in Acts 16, and which all their predecessors believed, namely, the
article that one is to be saved without the laws, solely through the grace of
Christ. . . . A council has the power – and is also duty-bound to exercise
it – to suppress and to condemn new articles of faith in accordance
with Scripture and the ancient faith, just as the council of Nicaea condemned the new doctrine of Arius, that of Constantinople the new
doctrine of Macedonius, that of Ephesus the new doctrine of Nestorius,
and that of Chalcedon the new doctrine of Eutyches."[2] We must
have "something else and something more reliable for our faith than
the councils. That 'something else' and 'something more' is Holy
Scripture."[3]

For this reason Luther repudiated some of the previous councils as
being unscriptural and therefore unacceptable. Being "outside Scripture",
they were "councils of Caiaphas, Pilate and Herod; as the apostles say in
Acts 4 (:26), They were gathered against the Lord".[4] "Such are the
majority of the pope's councils, in which he sets himself up in Christ's
stead as head of the Church, makes Holy Scripture subject to himself, and
tears it asunder."[5] "Nothing should be asserted in (questions of) faith
without scriptural precedent," Luther demanded.[6] The only hope he had
of a successful appeal to a general council lay in the rather remote likelihood of this principle being recognized by Rome. It is small wonder that
he soon grew sceptical about such a possibility.

Faced with this discrepancy between what was revealed in Scripture and
what had been promulgated by the institutional Church, Luther fell back
on the distinction between the external organization and the genuine
fellowship of the Spirit within it and indeed sometimes beyond it. In dealing with the extent of temporal authority, he made it plain that the rule of
emperor or elector was only to be obeyed in so far as it conformed to the
Word of God. "Hence it is the height of folly when they command that
one shall believe the Church, the fathers, and the councils, though there
be no Word of God for it. It is not the Church but the devil's apostles who
command such things, for the Church commands nothing unless it knows
for certain that it is God's Word. As St. Peter puts it, 'Whoever speaks, let
him speak as the word of God' (1 Peter 4:11). It will be a long time,

[1] Ibid., 148.   [2] LW. 41. 123. Acts 15:11.
[3] LW. 41. 120.   [4] Ibid., 122.
[5] Ibid.   [6] LW. 32. 230.

however, before they can ever prove that the decrees of the councils are God's Word."[1]

Luther's assertion of *sola Scriptura* as over against the counter-claims of the pope, the fathers and the councils must be seen in the perspective provided by his own writings from which we have quoted. We must beware of maintaining a distinction which Luther himself did not recognize. It is not that he set the Bible on one hand, and all that was ever said by the Church on the other, and drew a sharp line of separation between them as if they had no connexion with each other. That would be to exaggerate his emphasis on biblical authority. Rather he used the Word of God as a touchstone by which to test the tradition of the Church. He did not reject tradition outright. He did not invariably disconnect tradition from Scripture. He was ready to allow that where tradition was itself in line with Scripture it had a contribution to make. "Those parts of the tradition of the Church . . . which prove to be based on Scripture also have authority," concludes Althaus in summarizing Luther's view, "even though it is only a derived authority."[2]

To discard the sovereignty of Scripture was for Luther the worst of all apostasies. It could only lead to spiritual anarchy. "For once the pure and certain Word is taken away, there remains no consolation, no salvation, no hope."[3] To overthrow this is to overthrow all. Christianity stands or falls by the Word. Once the foundation is threatened, the structure will soon collapse. "He who does away with the Word and does not accept it as spoken by God does away with everything."[4] Luther realized that in his day. We need to be aware of it in ours.

---

[1] LW. 45. 106. Luther employed the term *Kirche* in two differentiated senses in this passage. Its first appearance in capitalized form (translated "Church") indicates the institutional organization. In the next sentence it is decapitalized (translated "church") and refers to the company of true believers.

[2] Paul Althaus, *The Theology of Martin Luther* (E. T. 1966), p. 7.

[3] LW. 26. 77.   [4] L.W. 3. 272.

CHAPTER XII

LUTHER AND THE REVELATION OF SCRIPTURE

A CCORDING TO JAMES I. PACKER, "THE QUESTION of revelation is at the very heart of the modern theological debate."[1] And in the stimulating contribution he makes to the symposium *Revelation and the Bible*, he explains that, since Christianity claims to be a revealed religion the real subject under discussion is the essential nature of the faith. Its content and character are derived from the revelation on which it rests: hence the outcome of the contemporary debate could well determine the prevalent overall conception of Christianity for many years to come.

In his time, Luther wrestled with this problem too. His conclusions may still provide guidelines for the Church today. We must take care, however, to discover what in fact Luther had to say on this subject. There have been some strange though unconfirmed reports which need to be corrected by reference to the reformer himself. In his Paddock Lectures, Alfred L. Lilley was apparently content to rest on the assumption that "no Christian doctor of the front rank ever disparaged the revelational role of the Scripture more constantly than the great reformer".[2] It would be difficult to miss the mark more comprehensively than that. It is an interesting and significant feature of current trends that, whereas some of the more extreme biblical critics and radical theologians are attempting to depict Luther as the precursor of modern liberalism (by a translation as remarkable as that of Bottom, though we would prefer to regard it as being in reverse), the Church historians, by and large, are increasingly recognizing his decisive influence in establishing the *Schriftprinzip* of the Reformation.[3]

Luther's starting-point in his account of revelation was the premise that all knowledge of God is necessarily dependent on His own self-disclosure. Revelation is thus active, not merely passive. It represents a positive and continuous self-communication. God is essentially the God who speaks and who makes Himself known. Did He not, we should remain in utter ignorance. Behind all revelation we must discern God's gracious will to reveal.

---

[1] James I. Packer, "Contemporary Views of Revelation", *Revelation and the Bible: Contemporary Evangelical Thought*, ed. Carl F. H. Henry (1959), p. 89.
[2] Alfred L. Lilley, *Religion and Revelation* (1931), p. 79.
[3] Cf. A. Skevington Wood, "Luther's Concept of Revelation", *Evangelical Quarterly*, Vol. XXXV (1963), p. 150. The article runs from pp. 149–59, and much of it is reproduced in this Chapter by kind permission of the Editor, Professor F. F. Bruce.

This involves a parallel recognition of the divine reticence. Not all is made known. Revelation is limited and prescribed according to the inscrutable purpose of God. In his debate with Erasmus, Luther was compelled to define revelation as determined by the divine sovereignty.[1] The very fact that God chooses to lift some portion of the covering which hides His presence reminds us that there is much that He refrains from disclosing. This proviso Luther regarded as a safeguard against the implication that the Church could achieve a kind of mastery over God as it manipulated the means of revelation – an implication underlying the Romanist distortion which Luther was raised up to resist.

This led Luther to his distinctively firm and discerning emphasis on the left hand of God, where He works all unknown to men. He is not only *Deus Revelatus* but also *Deus Absconditus*. Luther discussed this hidden God – the expression is scriptural and comes from Isaiah 45:15 – early in his reforming career, as, for instance, when he developed his theology of the cross in the Heidelberg Disputation of 1518.[2] But it must be understood, as Althaus reminds us, that there the concept had quite a different meaning from that which appears in *The Bondage of the Will*.[3] God is hidden in His revelation and is revealed to us not directly but paradoxically in the cross and in suffering. "For this reason true theology and recognition of God are in the crucified Christ, as it is also stated in John 10 (:9)."[4] Luther had in mind the story in Exodus 33, where Moses asked: "Show me thy glory" and God answered: "You cannot see my face; for man shall not see me and live." (Ex. 33:18, 20). Instead, God placed Moses in the cleft of the rock and held His hand before him whilst His glory passed by. When the divine hand was removed, Moses saw God's back but not His face. It is only as He is so concealed that God can reveal Himself to sinful men.[5]

But when Luther spoke of hiddenness in *The Bondage of the Will* he was not alluding to the coincidence of revelation and concealment, but rather to "God's hiddenness behind and beyond revelation in the mystery which forms the background of His almighty double-willing and double-working of salvation and damnation. 'God Himself' is to be found behind and beyond the word and not in it."[6] Luther also based this distinction between the hidden and revealed God on the verse in II Thessalonians 2:4 where Paul described the Antichrist as the one who sets himself above everything "that is preached and honoured as God".[7] Luther saw a differentiation here between the revealed God who was preached and worshipped, and the hidden God who was altogether invulnerable.[8]

---

[1] BW. 66.   [2] LW. 31. 53.   [3] Althaus, op. cit., p. 277.
[4] LW. 31. 53. Luther also quoted John 14:6.
[5] LW. 26. 29; LW. 31. 52. Cf. Edgar M. Carlson, *The Reinterpretation of Luther* (1948), pp. 146–8; Althaus, op. cit., p. 25.
[6] Althaus, op. cit., p. 277.   [7] BW. 171–2.   [8] Ibid., 172.

What Luther intended to convey was not simply that God was once concealed but is now made manifest. It is rather that the revelation itself is restricted by the divine decree and that God is *Deus Absconditus* even whilst he is *Deus Revelatus*. And this is a matter not merely of parallelism but even of sharp antipathy. It is not that God is in part revealed and in part concealed in his Word, but that behind and beyond the Word itself there stands an incomprehensible mystery. It is this that colours and conditions all that is made known. The known only serves to underline the unknown. Gustaf Aulèn has expounded this theme in a manner which reflects Luther's outlook. "It is important to note in what manner God appears as the Unfathomable. It does not mean simply that there are certain limits to revelation, and that beyond these limits there exists a hidden territory which would grow less and less in the measure that revelation increases. Nor does it mean merely that under these earthly circumstances there always will remain questions which cannot be answered and riddles which cannot be solved: or that the Christian faith cannot become a rational world-view to which the divine government of the world would be transparently clear. It means rather that the nature of divine revelation appears to faith as an impenetrable mystery. Since the very centre of this revelation is divine love which gives itself in order to establish fellowship with sinners, that love itself appears inscrutable and impenetrable. Faith beholds the revealed God as the Unfathomable, the 'hidden' God. In fact, we may even agree to this proposition: the more God reveals Himself, and the deeper faith looks into the mystery of His divine heart, the more He appears as the Unfathomable. Thus the apostle writes, 'Let a man so account of us . . . as stewards of the mysteries of God' (1 Cor. 4:1)."[1]

Luther charged Erasmus with failure to distinguish between "God preached and God hidden".[2] Behind His proffered mercy lies His hidden and fearful will, which "is not to be curiously inquired into, but to be adored with reverence as the most profound secret of His divine majesty, which He reserves to Himself and keeps hidden from us, and that much more religiously than the mention of ten thousand Corycian caverns".[3] Even the Antichrist cannot challenge the unrevealed God. He can only oppose and exalt himself "above all that is God as preached and worshipped": that is, according to Luther, "above the word and worship of God, by which He is known to us and has intercourse with us. But above God not worshipped and preached, that is, as He is in His own nature and majesty, nothing can be exalted, but all things are under His powerful hand".[4] Even if we disagree with Luther's exegesis on the ground that the

---

[1] Gustaf Aulén, *The Faith of the Christian Church* (1954), p. 47.
[2] BW. 172.
[3] Ibid., 171. The Corycian cave in Mount Parnassus derived its name from a nymph who by Apollo became the mother of Lyconus (Pausanius, 10. 6. 2; 10. 32. 2).
[4] BW. 172; cf. 2 Thess. 2:4.

verse from II Thessalonians alludes to so-called gods and objects of
worship, as the Revised Standard Version makes clear, the point he
stressed is nevertheless valid apart from its accompanying proof-text.

Now, argued Luther, as Christians we have only to do with God as He
reveals Himself, "as far as He is clothed in and delivered to us by His
Word: for in that He presents Himself to us, and that is His beauty and
glory, in which the Psalmist celebrates Him as being clothed. Wherefore
we say that the righteous God does not 'deplore that death of His people
which He Himself works in them'; but He deplores that death which He
finds in His people, and which He desires to remove from them. For God
preached desires this: that, our sin and death being taken away, we might
be saved. 'He sent forth His word and healed them' (Ps. 107:20). But God
hidden in majesty neither deplores nor takes away death, but works life and
death in all things; nor has He, in this character, defined himself in His
Word, but has reserved to Himself a free power over all things."[1] Elsewhere Luther further distinguished between God's presence everywhere
though concealed, and His presence "for us".[2] In this careful manner
Luther related divine revelation to divine volition and upheld the irre
fragable sovereignty of God.

In a passage which Conrad Bergendorff commends as containing "as
profound words as Luther ever wrote", which "carry us into the very heart
of his theology", Luther took Erasmus to task for overlooking this crucial
factor.[3] "God does many things which He does not make known to us in
His Word: He also wills many things which He does not in His Word
make known to us that He wills. Thus, He does not 'will the death of a
sinner', that is in His Word; but He wills it by that will inscrutable. But in
the present case we are to consider His Word only, and to leave that will
inscrutable; seeing that it is by His Word, and not by that will inscrutable
that we are to be guided; for who can direct himself according to a will
inscrutable and incomprehensible? It is enough to know only that there is
in God a certain will inscrutable: but what, why and how far that will
wills it is not lawful to inquire, to wish to know, to be concerned about, or
to reach unto – it is only to be feared and adored!"[4]

Despite the impression created by current misconceptions of his teaching, Luther quite certainly recognized a twofold knowledge of God:
general and particular. The first is the natural possession of all men as
God's creatures: the second is the spiritual possession of believers as God's
children. "It is hardly too much to say," wrote Philip Watson, "that the
problem of reconciling the contents of these two kinds of knowledge sets

[1] BW. 172; cf. 2 Cor. 2:16.
[2] Cf. WA. 39. i. 245.
[3] Conrad Bergendorff, "The Revelation and the Ministry of Grace", *World Lutheranism Today: A Tribute to Anders Nygren* (1950), p. 24.
[4] BW. 173.

its mark, in one way or another, on the whole of Luther's thought."[1] Although there are apparent contradictions and even occasional inconsistencies in Luther's numerous allusions to this dual knowledge, it is nevertheless sufficiently clear that he regarded the one as at best partial and imperfect – and indeed positively misleading if not allowed to introduce the other, which for him is final and determinative. "All men have the general knowledge," he explained (expounding Galatians 4:8), "namely, that God is, that He has created heaven and earth, that He is just, that He punishes the wicked, etc. But what God thinks of us, what He wants to give and to do to deliver us from sin and death and to save us – which is the particular and the true knowledge of God – this men do not know."[2] And then Luther introduced a most effective simile: "The same can happen that someone's face may be familiar to me, but I do not really know him, because I do not know what he has in his mind. So it is that men know naturally that there is a God, but they do now know what He wants and what He does not want. For it is written (Rom. 3:11), 'No one understands God'; and elsewhere (Jn. 1:18), 'No one has ever seen God,' that is, no one knows what the will of God is. Now what good does it do you to know that God exists if you do not know what His will is toward you?"[3] Such natural knowledge of God, if it is not permitted to bring man to the proper knowledge in Christ, will instead lead him into superstition and idolatry.

Luther insisted that this general knowledge of God is a revelation to man and not a discovery by him. It is not something he attains by reaching up towards God: it is something given from above. Here Luther parted company from Thomas Aquinas and the Schoolmen who spoke of an ascent by the light of reason through created things to the knowledge of God, and regarded the special revelation only as a downward movement from God. There was for Luther no unmediated relationship between God and man.[4] He maintained the scriptural principle that man cannot see God in His transcendence and live.[5] In all His dealing with men, God assumes a mask (*larva*) or veil (*involucrum*). This is true even of His special revelation to believers, so that Luther could speak of Christ Himself in such terms.[6] To the natural man, the created world is the appointed medium through which God addresses him, that he may be without excuse. This conception extends beyond the animal kingdom to include the several orders of men. "The magistrate, the emperor, the king, the

---

[1] Watson, op. cit., p. 73. Watson's treatment of the subject in his chapter on "The Revelation of God" is most enlightening, pp. 73–96.
[2] LW. 26. 399. [3] Ibid., 399–400.
[4] Watson, op. cit., p. 78. [5] LW. 26. 29.
[6] LW. 2. 49. "The Incarnate Son of God is, therefore, the covering in which the Divine Majesty presents Himself to us with all His gifts, and does so in such a manner that there is no sinner too wretched to be able to approach Him with the firm assurance of obtaining pardon. This is the one and only view of the Divinity that is available and possible in this life."

prince, the consul, the teacher, the preacher, the pupil, the father, the mother, the children, the master, the servant" – all are God's instruments and outward veils of Himself.[1]

But in Luther's view, revelation proper is confined to that particular redemptive knowledge of Himself in Christ which God conveys to the believer or awakened inquirer. As Watson points out, "it is not opposed to general knowledge in itself, but to what men have falsely made of it; and it furnishes the necessary principle for its correct interpretation."[2] It is in this specific revelation in Christ that Luther saw "a most manifest distinction" between Christianity and all other religions of the world – including the medieval misrepresentation of the gospel.[3] This is the saving knowledge of God which alone can rescue man from ignorance and sin. He is an one incomplete and can only find fulfilment in God.

Where is this special revelation to be found? Luther recognized it nowhere save in the Word, in which God "has revealed His will and His divine nature".[4] "If you want to encounter God, you must first see Him under the mask, in the Word. Then one day you can behold Him also in His majesty. For now God will not present you with anything special apart from and contrary to His command contained in His Word."[5] Until the ultimate revelation of God's glory at the end of the age, there is still no unmediated disclosure of Himself: not even in Christ.[6] Luther insisted on a *theologia crucis* as over against the Schoolmen who attempted to climb up into the majesty of God. The Word itself is another *involucrum*: that is no more than a medium of revelation, even though it exactly expresses what God desires to declare with no shadow of inaccuracy. The substance, however, is nothing less than God himself. And yet so realistic is the impact that we may borrow John Baillie's apposite phrase and characterize it as a "mediated immediacy".[7] The incarnate Christ, according to Luther, is not only a veil, but also a glass or mirror in which we behold the face of God by reflection.[8]

By the Word, then, Luther did not invariably mean Holy Writ, as we have noted. He used the term sometimes with reference to Scripture, sometimes with reference to Christ himself, and sometimes with reference to the content or act of preaching. Yet there was no final cleavage or contradiction in his mind, since for him the Bible was always a living message with Christ at its heart. "Ultimately, then, there was only one 'Word of God', which came in different forms," concludes Jaroslav

[1] LW. 26. 95.   [2] Watson, op. cit., p. 93.
[3] SW. I. 179.   [4] LW. 22. 17.   [5] LW. 24. 69.
[6] LW. 2. 49. "But on the Last Day those who have died in this faith will be so enlightened by heavenly power that they will see even the Divine Majesty itself. Meanwhile we must come to the Father by that was which is Christ Himself; He will lead us safely, and we shall not be deceived."
[7] John Baillie, *Our Knowledge of God* (1939), pp. 178–80, 196.
[8] LW. 26. 396.

Pelikan.[1] Written Word and Living Word are almost inseparably con-joined, since for Luther Christ is the core of Scripture. He could even suggest that the Bible is Christ's spiritual body by which He is here and now available to believers.[2] It is "God's Word written, presented in letters, as Christ is the eternal Word presented in human nature".[3] Thus, when Luther spoke of particular revelation as confined to the Word of God, he meant that it is conveyed through Scripture and expressed in Christ. And this is proclaimed in preaching, which is basically a setting forth of Christ from Scripture.

Luther's conception of the place occupied by Scripture in revelation was allied to his unremitting emphasis on what he called its perspicuity. He held that the Bible is luminously clear in its meaning as befits the chosen medium of God's own self-disclosure. He rebuked Erasmus for inclining to "that impudent and blasphemous saying, 'the Scriptures are obscure'".[4] "They who deny the all-clearness and all-plainness of the Scriptures, leave us nothing else but darkness," he complained. "Moreover I declare against you concerning the whole of the Scripture that I will have no one part of it called obscure," he continued; "and to support me stands that which I have brought forth out of Peter, that the Word of God is to us a "lamp shining in a dark place" (II Peter 1:19). But if any part of this lamp does not shine, it is rather a part of the dark place than the lamp itself. For Christ has not so illuminated us, as to wish that any part of His Word should remain obscure, even while He commands us to attend to it: for if it be not shining plain, His commanding us to attend to it is in vain."[5]

Furthermore, it was Luther's tireless accusation against the papal hierarchy that they clouded the inherent radiance of the Word and kept the people from its unambiguous truth. He objected that they "take from the Scripture its single, simple and stable meaning; they blind our eyes, so that we stagger about and retain no reliable interpretation. We are like men bewitched or tricked while they play with us as gamblers with their dice."[6] After citing some instances of this malpractice, Luther added: "This is the way human reason works when, without divine illumination, it interferes with God's Word and works and tries to calculate and measure them according to its own power."[7] It was because the Word is the lucid revelation of God's essential truth that Luther was prepared to take his stand on it in the face of all opponents. "You must plant yourself upon the clear, transparent, strong statements of the Scriptures, by which you will then be enabled to hold your ground."[8]

When Luther thus spoke of Scripture as the medium of revelation, he included its totality. He allowed no licence to select or reject. To dispute

[1] LW. Companion Volume, 70.   [2] LW. 32. 11.
[3] WA. 48. 31.   [4] BW. 109.   [5] Ibid., 109–10.
[6] LW. 32. 26.   [7] Ibid., 27.   [8] EA. 28. 223.

any one item is to impugn the whole. "My friend, God's Word is God's Word – this point does not require much haggling! When one blasphemously gives the lie to God in a single word, or says it is a minor matter if God is blasphemed or called a liar, one blasphemes the entire God and makes light of blasphemy. There is only one God who does not permit Himself to be divided, praised at one place and chided at another, glorified in one word and scorned in another. The Jews believe in the Old Testament but because they do not believe Christ, it does them no good. You see, the circumcision of Abraham (Gen. 17:10 ff.) is now an old dead thing and no longer necessary or useful. But if I were to say that God did not command it in its time, it would do me no good even if I believed the gospel. So St. James asserts, 'Whoever offends in one part is guilty in all respects.' He probably heard the apostles say that all the words of God must be believed or none, although he applies their interpretation to the works of the law. Why is it any wonder, then, if fickle fanatics juggle and play and clown with the word of the Supper (the quotation is from Luther's treatise *This is My Body*) according to their fancy, since at this point they are convicted of belittling God's words and concerns and making them secondary human lore? Just as if God must yield to men, and let the authority of the Word depend on whether men are at one or at odds over it."[1]

This clarity of revelation, however, is confined to believers. It is not apparent to unaided reason: it commends itself only to faith. The gospel is hidden from those who are lost, in whose case "the god of this world has blinded the minds of the unbelievers, to keep them from seeing the light of the gospel of the glory of Christ, who is the likeness of God" (II Cor. 4:4). "God's Word has to be the most marvellous thing in heaven and on earth," declared Luther in his *Exhortation to the Knights of the Teutonic Order* (1523). "That is why it must at one and the same time do two opposite things, namely, give perfect light and glory to those who believe it, and bring utter blindness and shame upon those who believe it not. To the former it must be the most certain and best known of all things; to the latter it must be the most unknown and obscure of all things. The former must extol and praise it above all things; the latter must blaspheme and slander it above all things. So does it operate to perfection and achieve in the hearts of men no insignificant works, but strange and terrible works. As St. Paul says in II Corinthians 4(:3), 'even if our gospel is veiled, it is veiled only to those who are perishing.'"[2]

We have noticed how Luther virtually identified the Word with Christ Himself. He recognized a similarly intimate association with the Holy Spirit. For him Word and Spirit belonged together in the sphere of revelation. The Romanists wanted the Word without the Spirit – the

---

[1] LW. 37. 26-7.   [2] LW. 45, 156.

Word, as Reid explains, "perverted and exanimated by the influence of canonical law."[1] The Anabaptists and Enthusiasts, on the other hand, wanted the Spirit without the Word. Luther held the two together in vital tension. As the Holy Spirit is the divine author of Scripture, so also He is the divine interpreter. The Bible is the Holy Spirit's Book.[2] He who inspired its pages in the first place now makes it live again. It is by His operation that the written Word is recreated as a living Word. If God does not bestow the help of His Spirit, the Word will not be "for us".[3] Just as Luther described the Scripture as Christ's spiritual body, so he regarded it as the incarnation of the Holy Ghost. He said that it corresponds to the Spirit as the voice to breathing or the rays of the sun to its heat.[4]

Regin Prenter resolves the paradox involved in this double emphasis on Word and Spirit by reference to Luther's Christological presuppositions. "Only in the moment when the Spirit by the outward Word makes Christ truly present are the Word and the Spirit directly one."[5] Hence "only when the Holy Spirit makes Christ present in the Word does it become God's own living Word. If this does not happen the Word is only a letter, a law, a description of Christ. From the opposite point of view it is true that the Spirit, when it (sic) undertakes to make Christ present, is not able to work independently of the Word. For Christ is indeed the incarnate Logos in the person who appeared in history, Jesus of Nazareth, who by the Old and New Testament writings is proclaimed as the Christ. It is therefore only by the Word depending on Scripture that the Spirit can make Jesus present. A spirit who could work independently of this definite outward Word about the incarnate Logos would not be the Spirit of Jesus Christ. We are always referred to this definite Word. But we are not referred to it as our guaranteed possession, but as the place where we expect the Spirit to make Jesus present for us. Without the work of the Spirit the Word may continue to be the Word which speaks of Jesus Christ, but it is not the Word which bestows Christ on us."[6]

This definitive status of the written Word forbade Luther to envisage any further revelation. The Spirit "makes men wise *up to* what is written, but not beyond it", as Joseph Angus observed.[7] "Now that the apostles have preached the Word and have given their writings, and nothing more than what they have written remains to be revealed," concluded Luther, "no new and special revelation or miracle is necessary."[8] It is enough now that the Holy Spirit himself is present in the revelation of the Word. Any

[1] John K. S. Reid, *The Authority of Scripture: A Study of the Reformation and Post-Reformation Understanding of the Bible* (1957), pp. 60–61.
[2] SL. 9. 1775.
[3] Cf. WA. 3. 250, 255–6, 261–2, 347–8.
[4] WA. 4. 189; 10. ii. 92; 57. 143.
[5] Prenter, *Spiritus Creator*, p. 106.
[6] Ibid., pp. 106–7.
[7] Joseph Angus, *The Bible Hand-Book; An Introduction to the Study of Sacred Scripture*, ed. Samuel G. Green (n.d.), p. 179.
[8] LW. 24. 367.

teaching which does not square with the Scriptures is to be rejected "even if it snows miracles every day".[1] Christians are not to hanker after new signs and disclosures and manifestations. Rather, urged Luther, "let us faithfully adhere to this revelation or proclamation of the Holy Spirit. He alone must tell us what we are to know."[2] Revelation has been finalized in Christ. The Spirit's function is to evoke from the Word what is already there. There must be no addition to the Book, any more than there should be subtraction from it (Rev. 22:18, 19).

[1] Ibid., 371.   [2] Ibid.

CHAPTER XIII

LUTHER AND THE INSPIRATION OF SCRIPTURE

FOR LUTHER, THE SUPREMACY OF THE BIBLICAL revelation arose from its supernatural origin, and this in turn was bound up with the fact of inspiration. Only by a unique work of the Holy Spirit could divine truth be accurately conveyed to men through the medium of writers and writing. All that Luther taught about the authority of the Bible and the nature of revelation found its climax and corollary in his doctrine of inspiration. Seeberg has stressed the connexion.[1] Luther's view of Scripture was all of a piece. We cannot isolate one part from another. Since it is derived from the Word itself, it displays the same coherency as is to be observed in the whole of revelation.

Although the inspiration of the Scriptures was a commonly held belief in Luther's time, on the basis of the Church's own teaching, in practice it tended to be modified so as to accommodate and safeguard the role of the Church as the interpreter. In his *Dictata super Psalterium* (1513–15) Luther himself made concessions to this generally accepted adjustment. God did not put his Spirit into the letters of Scripture, he could affirm, but into the ecclesiastical office-holders to whom was entrusted the task of interpretation.[2] To them can be applied the injunction of Deuteronomy 32:7 – "Ask . . . your elders, and they will tell you." But this was an immature conception which Luther soon left behind, as he grew in understanding. It is his developed attitude to inspiration that we must now examine.

The supernatural origin of the Word was a fact which demanded a theory to explain it. "The Holy Scriptures did not grow on earth," Luther declared.[3] All other books are purely of human derivation. The Bible is an exception.[4] Although composed by men and set down in writing, it nevertheless stands out from all other literature as being from God. In Luther's eyes, only by means of inspiration could a book become the channel of revelation in this way. A miracle of the Spirit was required. Luther often saw a parallel between the written Word and the incarnate Word. Just as the fulness of the Godhead was expressed in the humanity of Jesus, so in Scripture the truth of God was disclosed in the words of men. It was by the intervention of the Holy Spirit in the Virgin Birth that the

[1] Seeberg, op. cit., Bd. III, p. 414.
[2] WA. 3. 579.
[3] SL. 7. 2095.
[4] LW. 24. 228.

incarnation was made possible. It was equally by the intervention of the Holy Spirit that the Scriptures were produced.

Luther employed a number of designations for the Bible, all of which were used interchangeably with the title "God's Word". It is true that he did not always equate the Word of God with Scripture: sometimes it meant the message as preached. But, as Rupert Davies admits, even in his mature thought Luther was still liable to speak and write as if he identified the text of the Bible with the Word of God.[1] The distinction between God's Word written and God's Word preached, or between God's Word as the text of Scripture and God's Word as the basic message of Scripture, was not consistently made. For the most part Luther adhered to his original practice of using "God's Word" as an equivalent for the Bible. He referred regularly to "Sacred Scripture" or "Holy Writ", each of which he brackets with "God's Word".[2] He spoke of "Divine Scripture" or "God's Scripture", which again he associated with "God's Word".[3] He often called the Bible Simply "God's Book".[4] It is the sanctuary in which God dwells.[5] It is man's meeting place with his Maker.

In the Scriptures God Himself addresses us. The articles of faith are therein "handed over and shown to us by the Divinity, without our discovery".[6] "When you read the words of Holy Scripture, you must realize that God is speaking in them."[7] To hear the Scriptures is nothing else than to hear God Himself.[8] It is God who confronts us and lays His command on us. "You are so to deal with the Scriptures that you bear in mind that God Himself is saying this."[9] "Holy Scripture says" and "God says" are used alternately as signifying the same thing. Scripture is God's testimony to Himself.[10] Belief in God and belief in His Word are one. "When His Word is changed, He Himself is changed: for He Himself is in His Word."[11]

The Bible is God's Book. It is also Christ's Book. As we shall be noting in our final chapter, for Luther Christ is the centre of Scripture. It is all about Him. He is its heart and He alone is the key to understanding it. In the gospel the Master is present: it is Christ Himself speaking.[12] We are compelled to ask what kind of a book this is which stands in so unique a relationship to the Son of God and the coming Messiah.

[1] Rupert E. Davies, *The Problem of Authority in the Continental Reformers: A Study in Luther, Zwingli and Calvin* (1946), p. 36.
[2] LW. 26. 46; LW. 24. 293; LW. 27. 156; LW. 24. 54.
[3] LW. 27. 154, 386; LW. 36. 337. LW. 27. 155, 308; LW. 24. 37.
[4] LW. 3. 297; SL. 9. 1071. Cf. LW. 34. 227, "God's Scriptures"; SL. 1. 1055, "God's Epistle".
[5] LW. 14. 250.
[6] LW. 12. 53. The article under consideration here in Luther's exposition of Ps. 2:7 is the Virgin Birth.
[7] SL. 3. 21.
[8] WA. 3. 1. 4; cf. WA. 4. 318.
[9] SL. 3. 21.
[10] LW. 24. 173; LW. 34. 227.
[11] LW. 9. 22.
[12] WA. 4. 535.

Luther also alluded to the Bible as "the book of the Holy Spirit".[1] It was written through Him.[2] "The entire Scriptures are assigned to the Holy Spirit."[3] "The Holy Scriptures have been spoken by the Holy Spirit."[4] The words were "not born in our house, but are brought down from heaven by the Holy Spirit."[5] It is indeed only this miraculous work of the Holy Spirit which accounts for the unique character of Scripture. A book which is so different from all others can only be explained in terms of inspiration. For Luther, inspiration was at once a truth revealed in Scripture itself, and the only reasonable hypothesis by which to account for the evidence presented by the phenomenon of God's Book.

Luther could refer to "the sayings of the Holy Spirit" or "the writings of the Holy Spirit".[6] "The Holy Spirit says" was a frequent expression with him.[7] He could interpret "Scripture" in Galatians 3 : 8 as "the Spirit in Scripture".[8] He could even talk about "the rhetoric of the Holy Spirit".[9] "The Holy Spirit speaks" was a recurring formula.[10] Within this context, Luther resorted to a multiplicity of variations. Within a few pages of his exposition of the Second Psalm, he runs almost through the whole gamut. In Scripture, the Holy Spirit teaches, consoles, mentions, omits, forewarns, explains, advises, reassures, admonishes, comforts, designates, considers, sees, calls, demands, adds and forbids.[11] These instances not only indicate Luther's firm convictions about the inspiration of Scripture, but also reflect his awareness of the Spirit's personality.

The promises of Scripture are "proposed by the Holy Spirit".[12] Scripture is "the Holy Spirit's proclamation".[13] It is "the vehicle of the Spirit".[14] Its contents are "written by the Spirit", or "recorded by the Spirit".[15] So close is the connexion between the actual words of the Bible and the instrumentality of the Spirit that it must be concluded that Luther believed not only in inspiration, but in verbal inspiration. It is noticeable that recent scholarship is recognizing afresh that this element in Luther's attitude to Scripture cannot be ignored. In an able study, Brian A. Gerrish of Chicago agrees that Luther never really questioned the traditional theory of inerrant Scripture, and speaks of his "strict view of verbal inspiration".[16]

Luther stated unambiguously that Scripture consists of "divine words without whose authority nothing must be asserted".[17] We must "honour the Holy Spirit by believing His words and accepting them as the divine

[1] SL. 9. 1775.   [2] LW. 3. 342.   [3] SL. 3. 1890.
[4] Ibid., 1895.   [5] LW. 12. 124.   [6] LW. 26. 169; LW. 8. 74.
[7] LW. 12. 76, 278; LW. 14. 8.   [8] LW. 27. 253.   [9] LW. 3. 34.
[10] LW. 12. 340; LW. 26. 266, 270; LW. 37. 310.
[11] LW. 12. 10, 14, 18, 20, 23, 32, 36, 43, 68–69, 77, 89–92.
[12] WA. 13. 100.   [13] LW. 22. 286.   [14] LW. 30, 321.
[15] LW. 3. 316; LW. 12. 255; LW. 8. 74.
[16] Brian A. Gerrish, "Biblical Authority and the Reformation", *Scottish Journal of Theology*, Vol. X (1957), p. 344.
[17] LW. 32. 315.

truth".[1] There is no differentiation between the inspiration of the message and the inspiration of the terms in which that message is conveyed. Indeed the one depends on the other. We cannot be sure that we are in possession of God's revelation unless we can be satisfied that it has been brought to us in the very language He intended. If only some of it comes from Him and some of it is no more than what man has said, by what means can we distinguish between the two? Luther would not be content with anything less than plenary inspiration.

The Holy Spirit was concerned not merely with the inspiration of the writers or of their message. He descended to details and was responsible for the words and even the letters. "All the words of God are weighed, counted, and measured," Luther declared.[2] Every word of Scripture is precious since it comes from the mouth of God, is written down and preserved for us and will be proclaimed until the end of the age.[3] The prophets are those "into whose mouth the Holy Spirit has given the words".[4] "When you read the words of Holy Scripture, you must realize that God is speaking them."[5] We have already quoted that injunction of Luther in order to show that he regarded Scripture as a book in which God spoke. We repeat it so as to draw attention to the fact that it is in the actual words of Scripture that God speaks, in Luther's view. The Holy Spirit writes, "pen in hand, and presses the letters into the heart."[6] In all the Bible there is not a superfluous letter.[7]

In a moving passage in his commentary on Genesis, Luther wrote: "Concerning the letters of princes it is stated in a proverb that they should be read three times; but surely the letters of God – for this is what Gregory calls Scripture – should be read seven times three, yes, seventy times seven, or, to say even more, countless times. For they are divine wisdom, which cannot be grasped immediately at the first glance. If someone reads them superficially like familiar and easy material, he deceives himself."[8] Later in the same series of lectures, Luther repeated the analogy. "It is correct to say that the letters of princes should be read three times and that the letters of God should be read far more frequently. There is a difference between the thoughts and opinions of princes and those of private individuals. All the concerns of princes are grand, but those of private persons are small

[1] LW. 22. 10.   [2] WA. 3. 64.   [3] WA. 4. 535.
[4] WA. 3. 172.   [5] SL. 3. 21.
[6] LW. 22. 473. Luther believed that the Holy Spirit was not only at work when the Scriptures were originally indited, but also whenever they were read or preached.
[7] LW. 26. 227.
[8] LW. 3. 114. Luther elsewhere quoted the proverb about the letters of princes, cf. LW. 3. 126; WATR. 3. 383. No. 3537. For Gregory the Great on "the letters of God" cf. Epistolae 5. 46: "The Emperor of heaven, the Lord of men and of angels, has sent you His epistles for your life's advantage – and yet you neglect to read them eagerly. Study them, I beg of you, and meditate daily on the words of your Creator. Learn the heart of God in the words of God. . . ." Augustine similarly spoke of the Bible as "a letter from our Fatherland" (Enarrationes in Psalmos Ps. 64).

and insignificant. Therefore if princes either write or say something, it must be carefully pondered. But with how much greater propriety we do this in those matters which divine wisdom prescribes and commands!"[1] There follows immediately an allusion to "God's own words" as recorded in Scripture.[2]

Luther claimed that inspiration covered not only vocabulary, but construction as well. The letters of God are altogether in the language of God. "Not only the words but also the expressions used by the Holy Spirit and Scripture are divine."[3] Inspiration extends to "phraseology and diction".[4] As he dealt with the text of Scripture, Luther analysed the way in which the Spirit had done His distinctive work. For example, in expounding Psalm 51:10, Luther was at pains to point out how carefully each phrase was shaped as David prayed: "Create in me a clean heart, O God, and put a new and right spirit within me." The ability to acquire a clean heart does not rest in man's nature. It comes by divine creation. Only God can give it. "This is why the Spirit wanted to use the term 'create' here," explained Luther, "for those are vain dreams that the Scholastics foolishly thought up about the cleansing of the heart."[5] Passing on to the second part of the clause, Luther dilated upon "the adjective which the Spirit adds here" – namely, "right". He showed that it meant "stable, solid, full, firm, certain, indubitable", and was thus a fitting description of the human spirit when steadied by the Spirit of God.[6] It is all the more remarkable that Luther should discern the Spirit's supervision in a passage like this, containing as it does a recorded prayer. It looks as if he saw a double inspiration: first in David as he prayed, and then in the transcription. Even the more extreme literalists today would hardly go so far as Luther. They would probably find it sufficient to be assured that David's prayer was faithfully preserved, without committing themselves to the further belief that it was verbally inspired when first uttered.

Without attempting to defend Luther's doctrine of inspiration to the last detail, it cannot be denied, surely, that in principle it expressed a profound and necessary conviction. It is significant that one of the younger contemporary Scandinavian Luther scholars, Per Lönning, has conceded this. "Even the doctrine of verbal inspiration may be said to contain a not unimportant element of truth. The different biblical books are something far more than what the authors understood and planned. The full Bible, which none of its authors ever knew they were contributing to, was planned and produced by the Holy Spirit."[7] This is so in the sense "that the totality of Scripture given to us is a message from God, to which the

[1] LW. 3. 126–7.   [2] Ibid., 127.   [3] WA. 40. iii. 254.
[4] LW. 22. 119.   [5] LW. 12. 379.   [6] Ibid.
[7] Per Lönning, The Dilemma of Contemporary Theology, Prefigured in Luther, Pascal, Kierkegaard, Nietsche (1962), p. 139.

authors have contributed far beyond what they personally understood. Our time has to break the bounds of historical exegesis and march back to truly theological exegesis. We must proceed from the question, What does the author intend to say? – although this may be significant enough – to another question, What does God intend to say? And this question can only be answered when the single verse or chapter or book is considered within the fulness of the Scripture, that is, when interpreted *to* and *in* and *by* Christ the Word Himself."[1]

It has already been made apparent that Luther's doctrine of inspiration is inseparably linked with that of inerrancy. Because the Word of God was given by the Spirit of God it was inconceivable that it should be subject to human fallibility. To receive it as indeed from God was *ipso facto* to treat it as in every way reliable. The God of truth could not authenticate a book which contaired even the slightest element of falsehood. Such was Luther's argument. "The Scriptures have never erred," he claimed categorically.[2] The Bible is the only book in the world in which inaccuracies do not occur.[3] It is not man's word which could lie and be wrong.[4] It is God's Word which must be true.[5] Even when we might think we have detected a loophole, Luther is quick to correct himself. "If Scripture is true here," he says of Galatians 3:12; but he hastens to add: "as it must be." "The Scriptures cannot lie," he insisted.[6]

Such unequivocal assertions are to be found even when the text under review is problematical. In handling Genesis 11:11, Luther tackled the chronological technicalities involved in the birth of Arpachshad, Shem's third son. Some exegetes supplied one answer, some another, Luther admitted.[7] He proceeded to venture his own explanation. But he did not think that any great harm would result if there were no information available about such things.[8] "Our faith is not endangered if we should lack knowledge about these matters. This much is sure: Scripture does not lie. Therefore answers that are given in support of the trustworthiness of Scripture serve a purpose, even though they may not be altogether reliable."[9] That was Luther's unshakeable position. He never doubted the trustworthiness of the Bible. Just because he himself could not find a foolproof resolution of some of its difficulties, he was not tempted to imagine that one did not exist and that therefore Scripture itself was discredited. He preferred to retain his faith in the inerrancy of Scripture, and to await further light on some of its apparent discrepancies. He clung to the premise that "the Word of God is perfect: it is precious and pure: it is truth itself. There is no falsehood in it".[10] God's Word "is such perfect

[1] Lönning, op. cit., pp. 139–40.
[2] LW. 32. 11.   [3] SL. 14. 491.   [4] LW. 23. 95.
[5] LW. 14. 18; LW. 23. 390.   [6] LW. 27. 258.   [7] LW. 2. 232.
[8] Ibid.   [9] Ibid., 233.   [10] LW. 23. 236.

truth and righteousness that it needs no patching or repair; in its course it makes a perfectly straight line, without any bends in any direction".[1]

"One letter, even a single tittle of Scripture means more to us than heaven and earth," Luther announced. "Therefore we cannot permit even the most minute change."[2] There is no deception in the Scriptures – not even in one word. "Consequently, we must remain content with them and cling to them as the perfectly clear, certain, sure words of God, which can never deceive us or allow us to err."[3] Luther's complaint against the Enthusiasts was that they did not really believe that the Scriptures enshrined the very words of God Himself. With reference to the dominical institution of the Lord's Supper in Matthew 26:26, Luther said of the fanatics: "If they believed that these were God's words, they would not call them 'poor, miserable words', but would prize a single tittle and letter more highly than the whole world, and would fear and tremble before them as before God himself. For he who despises a single word of God certainly prizes none at all."[4]

Luther wrote similarly in a later treatise on the Holy Sacrament in 1544. "Is it not certain that he who does not or will not believe one article correctly (after he has been taught and admonished) does not believe any sincerely and with the right faith? And whoever is so bold that he ventures to accuse God of fraud and deception in a single word and does so wilfully again and again after he has been warned and instructed once or twice will likewise certainly venture to accuse God of fraud and deception in all of His words. Therefore it is true, absolutely and without exception, that everything is believed or nothing is believed. The Holy Spirit does not suffer Himself to be separated and divided so that He should teach and cause to be believed one doctrine rightly and another falsely."[5]

Luther's recognition of biblical inerrancy was confined to the original autographs, and was not tied to the transmitted text. This gave him the freedom to query the accuracy of the existing readings and on occasion to offer emendations of his own. Reu listed a number of relevant instances of Luther's uninhibited treatment of the text in translation.[6] At times he would alter the conventional verse divisions, which were by no means sacrosanct, and in any case were a comparatively recent innovation.[7] He did not accept all the superscriptions to the Psalms as authentic.[8] He deviated from the traditional pointing of the Hebrew text in numerous passages, and even urged the Christian Hebrew scholars to produce a new

[1] LW. 13. 268.
[2] WA. 40. ii. 52; cf. LW. 27. 41, for a variant translation.
[3] LW. 47. 308.   [4] LW. 37. 308.   [5] WA. 54. 158.
[6] Reu, *Luther and the Scriptures*, pp. 103–8. The examples are derived from the protocols of the commission for the revision of Luther's Bible translation published in WADB. 3. 167–577.
[7] WADB. 3. 121. 127. Ps. 25:6, 7; 102:25.
[8] WADB. 3. 117. Ps. 92 was regarded as correct, but the assumption is that others were not so.

Hebrew Bible which would no longer perpetuate the distortions of the Jews.[1] Luther also took liberties with the *textus receptus* and in places reconstructed it, usually in conformity with the Septuagint and the Vulgate.[1] He was not afraid to indicate where the traditional text was simply an error in copying.[2]

But it must be emphasized that Luther allowed himself this freedom only within the limits already prescribed – namely, that infallibility attaches solely to the original autographs of Scripture. He had no thought of doubting the reliability of the underlying text. His aim was to reach it – if necessary by conjecture, if no clear evidence was forthcoming. It was within the same sanctions that Luther was able to sit loose to matters of what we now call higher criticism, where the testimony of Scripture itself was not impugned thereby. He was reported by Mathesius as saying that in his opinion "Genesis was not by Moses, for there were books before his time and books are cited – for example, the Book of the Wars of the Lord and the Book of Jasher".[3] "I believe that Adam wrote for several generations," he added, "and after him Noah and the rest, to describe what happened to them. For the Jews were writers in very ancient times."[4] Afterwards, Moses took this material and organized it. He may have borrowed some items from the tradition and practice of the fathers and even from the records and customs of neighbouring nations, yet nevertheless the law is rightly named after him and, whether he actually wrote it all or not, the Pentateuch belongs to him.[5] It was at God's command that Moses acted, and the Holy Spirit arranged the narrative and caused it to be recorded for our instruction.[6]

Concerning some of the prophetic books of the Old Testament, Luther expressed views which strikingly anticipate the discoveries of more recent research. Hosea is a case in point. Luther suggested that this prophecy "was not fully and entirely written, but that pieces and sayings were taken out of his preaching and brought together into a book".[7] The utterances of Isaiah were collected and committed to writing by others and it is uncertain as to whether Isaiah himself or his amanuenses arranged his material.[8] The Psalter was compiled by a number of contributors.[9]

In dealing with the New Testament, Luther not only showed himself aware of problems relating to authorship, as in the case of Hebrews which

[1] WA. 53. 646. Is. 9:6.
[2] WADB. 3. 459, 502, 514. 2 Chron. 18:29; Job 33:17; 40:21.
[3] WADB. 3. 377, 402, 415, 419. 1 Sam. 13:1; 2 Sam. 14:26; 23:8; 1 Kgs. 5:19; WA. 40. iii. 664; Ps. 54:5. Cf. Bornkamm, *Luther und das Alte Testament*, pp. 162–5.
[4] LW. 54. 373. No. 4964.   [4] Ibid.
[5] LW. 3. 250; WATR. 3. 23. No. 2844a.
[6] WATR. 1. 21. No. 291; 174. No. 402; LW. 5. 67, 290; LW. 8. 6–7.
[7] LW. 35. 317.
[8] Ibid., 277. For similar theories about Jeremiah, *vide* pp. 280–1.
[9] Ibid., 253–4. Luther did not deny that the Holy Spirit was the ultimate compiler.

he regarded as non-Pauline, but also of the difficulties involved in harmon-
izing the Gospel narratives.[1] In the *Lenten Postil* of 1525 he discussed the
temptations of Christ and came to the conclusion that their order cannot
be determined with absolute assurance since the evangelists do not appear
to agree.[2] What Matthew places in the middle, Luke places at the end, and
what Luke places in the middle, Matthew places at the end. He wondered
whether these were not three successive temptations, but three recurring
temptations which came now in one order and now in another. Again, in
expounding the opening chapters of John's Gospel, Luther frankly faced
the fact that the cleansing of the temple was there placed at the outset of
our Lord's ministry, whereas in Matthew it is said to have occurred at the
end. He advanced one or two hypotheses, but he did not pretend that they
were altogether convincing.[3] "These are problems and will remain problems. I shall not venture to settle them. Nor are they essential. It is only
that there are so many sharp and shrewd people who are fond of bringing
up all sorts of subtle questions and demanding definite and precise answers.
But if we understand Scripture properly and have the genuine articles of
our faith – that Jesus Christ, God's Son, suffered and died for us – then our
inability to answer all such questions will be of little consequence. . . . If
one account in Holy Writ is at variance with another and it is impossible
to solve the difficulty, just dismiss it from your mind."[4] Luther's attitude
might well be dismissed as obscurantist today, but in his own age he
would hardly be regarded as such. Without for one moment querying the
inspiration and inerrancy of Scripture, Luther kept an open mind as to
how the dilemmas might be resolved. But his inability to light on an
immediate explanation did not lead him in the direction of doubt. Instead,
he clung the more tenaciously to the vast proportion of Scripture which
he could quite clearly understand, and trusted that one day the few rough
places would be made plain.

In closing this discussion of Luther's view of inspiration, it needs to be
stated that he was not committed to any stereotyped theory of dictation
which overlooked the co-operation of the human authors of Scripture.
"They are not, in his opinion, mechanical instruments and dead machines,
mere amanuenses who set down on paper only what was dictated to them
by the Spirit of God," affirmed Reu. "He regarded them rather as independent instruments of the Spirit who spoke *their* faith, *their* heart,
their thoughts; who put their entire will and feeling into the words to
such an extent that from what Luther reads in each case he draws conclusions concerning the character and temperament of the authors."[5]
Joel, for example, is "a kindly and gentle man" who "does not denounce

[1] For Hebrews, *vide*, p. 394.   [2] WA. 17. ii. 196.
[3] LW. 22. 218.   [4] Ibid., 218-19.
[5] Reu, *Luther and the Scriptures*, p. 109. He cited the examples which follow.

and rebuke as do the other prophets, but pleads and laments".[1] Amos, on the contrary, is violent, "and denounces the people of Israel throughout almost the entire book until the end of the last chapter. . . . No prophet, I think, has so little in the way of promises and so much in the way of denunciations and threats. He can well be called Amos, that is, 'a burden', one who is hard to get along with and irritating."[2] Jeremiah was a "sad and troubled prophet who lived in miserably evil days" and had "a peculiarly difficult ministry".[3] He shrank from the harshness of the message God gave him to deliver, and for this reason Luther likened him to Melanchthon. Paul was sometimes given to excess of fervour and near incoherence, which led him on occasion to infringe the rules of grammar.[4]

Reu has shown how careful Luther was to eschew the terminology of dictation.[5] In medieval writers and nouns *calamus* and *secretarius* and the verb *dictare* are frequently found in connexion with the inspiration of Scripture. Only once, it appears, did Luther refer to a biblical writer as the pen of the Spirit, and this was in one of his earliest writings.[6] It was left to some of Luther's contemporaries and the later dogmaticians to formulate a more rigidly mechanical theory of inspiration.[7] He himself refused to be tied down by any such doctrinaire account of the Spirit's operation. He knew that He is the Spirit of liberty, and that He works in as well as through man to achieve His purpose. Luther was content to recognize the results of the Spirit's inspiration without attempting to provide an analysis of the methods involved. Both in what he affirmed and in what he refrained from affirming, his only aim was to reflect the attitude of Scripture itself.

[1] LW. 35. 318.   [2] Ibid., 320.
[3] Ibid., 280.   [4] LW. 26. 93.
[5] Reu, *Luther and the Scriptures*, p. 114.
[6] In his *Dictata super Psalterium* (1513–1515), WA. 3. 256.
[7] The theory of the dogmaticians was not in all cases so hidebound as has sometimes been supposed, cf. Robert Preus, *The Inspiration of Scripture. A Study of the Theology of the Seventeenth Century Lutheran Dogmaticians* (1955), pp. 66–73.

CHAPTER XIV

LUTHER AND THE UNITY OF SCRIPTURE

"A FUNDAMENTAL ASSUMPTION OF LUTHER'S CRITI-
cism and of his exegetical work generally . . . is the unity of the Bible."[1]
Such is the judgment of Pelikan. A scrutiny of Luther's writings, particularly those which are of an expository nature, amply vindicates the
statement. Luther's approach to Scripture was never atomistic. He treated
the Bible as a homogeneous whole. For him it was not simply a set of unrelated books, but a divine library, selected by the Holy Spirit himself, in
which no part was superfluous and all parts were interlaced. In thus
recognizing the intrinsic integration of Scripture, Luther anticipated the
findings of much more recent inquiry. Biblical theologians pay due regard
to this factor today. Whereas the nineteenth century critics ignored the
underlying oneness of the revealed Word to a serious extent, the tendency
of late has been to reinstate it.

Luther appealed again and again to "the constant and unanimous judgement of Scripture".[2] It was this awareness of unity in the Bible which not
only distinguished him from some of his predecessors, but also from the
rationalistic critics of more recent times, as Pelikan points out.[3] This is
most marked in the case of the Old Testament. But after driving a wedge
between the Old and the New Testaments, and virtually advocating a
resuscitated Marcionism, the pioneers of modern criticism proceeded to
insert similar wedges in the New Testament itself – between Jesus and
Paul, between the Synoptics and John, and eventually between Paul and
pseudo-Paul. "Partly because they often found the origins of New
Testament thought and language elsewhere than in the Old Testament,
scholars who practised such interpretation of the New Testament sought
to explain the divergences within New Testament speech by reference to
extra-biblical sources; and so they frequently ignored the possibility that
differences of language and of emphasis between one writer of the New
Testament and another could be part of a unity underlying and preceding
the whole. For Luther, as for most of the theologians that preceded him,
that was more than a possibility; it was one of the most consistent devices
he employed in interpreting the New Testament. Sometimes he looked for
synonyms or equivalent expressions by which one New Testament writer

---

[1] LW. 21. xiii. Introduction by Jaroslav Pelikan.
[2] LW. 3. 210.   [3] LW. 21. xiii.

said what another writer had said in some other way. Sometimes he proceeded on the assumption that the same term was used in the same way by different writers, although he was quick to notice the differing shades of meaning in various biblical books. The New Testament formed a unit with the Old Testament, and it was also a unit within itself."[1]

Luther's recurring reference was to "all Scripture" – a phrase which appears regularly throughout his works.[2] At other times he used the alternatives "all Holy Writ", "all of Holy Writ", and "the entire Bible".[3] His employment of the expression "the Word of God" – which was often though not always resorted to as an equivalent for the Scriptures – also implied the wholeness of the written revelation. Luther insisted that because of this inherent unity, the Bible must always be treated as being of a piece, and that it is impermissible to accept one portion of it and discard another. The Holy Spirit is in every verse of it, and, although not all is equally edifying, yet nothing is to be dismissed as negligible. Unless all is believed, nothing is believed.[4]

It is the heretics who refuse to respect the oneness of Scripture. It is because of their fragmented conception that they fall into error, failing to balance one area of biblical teaching with another. "At first they deny only one article, but afterwards all must be denied. It is as with a ring; if it has only one defect, it can no longer be used. And if a bell cracks in only one place it does not sound any longer and is useless."[5] And again, from Luther's sermon on "The Christian Armour": "When the devil has succeeded in bringing matters so far that we surrender one article to him, he is victorious, and it is just as bad as though all of them and Christ Himself were already lost. Afterwards he can unsettle and withdraw others because they are all intertwined and bound together like a golden chain, so that if one link be broken, the whole chain is broken, and it pulls apart. And there is no article that cannot be overthrown if it once comes to pass that reason intrudes and tries to speculate and learns to turn and twist the Scripture so that it agrees with its conclusions. That penetrates like a sweet poison."[6] For Luther, of course, the articles of faith were drawn from Scripture.

In his lectures on Romans, Luther had occasion to refer to Matthew 4:4 – "It is written, Man shall not live by bread alone, but by every word that proceeds from the mouth of God." "But why the phrase 'by every word'? Because by disbelieving one single word you no longer live by the Word of God. For the whole Christ is in every word, and He is wholly in all single words. When, therefore, one denies in one word Him who is in

[1] Ibid.
[2] LW. 7. 344; LW. 8. 472; LW. 14. 75, 99, 168, 305; LW. 26. 341, 397, 418; LW. 27. 15, 212; LW. 30. 165, 307.
[3] LW. 23. 42, 483; 16, 27; 17.   [4] WA. 54. 158.
[5] Ibid.; cf. WA. 31. i. 208.   [6] W. 9. 950.

all words, one denies Him in His totality."[1] In our final chapter we shall be considering the Christocentricity of Scripture. For Luther the oneness of the written Word was related to the oneness of the living Word. As Christ is one so also is the Scripture. That is why it cannot be broken without impairing the whole.

Luther's conception of biblical unity was also associated with the completeness of faith. "Faith consists of something indivisible: it is either a whole faith and believes all there is to believe, or it is no faith at all if it does not believe one part of what there is to believe. This is why our Lord likens it to one single pearl and one single mustard seed, etc. (cf. Matt. 13:45, 46; 31, 32). For Christ is not divided; therefore, one either denies Him in His totality when one denies Him with respect to one point or affirms Him in His totality. But one cannot at the same time deny and confess Him now in this, and then in that, word."[2] It will be realized that for Luther the oneness of Scripture is bound up with the oneness of Christ and the oneness of faith.

The unity of Scripture is such that there is no possible contradiction between one part of it and another. What seem to be discrepancies are capable of resolution. If we do not know the answer now, we will eventually. "I see that Scripture is consonant in all and through all and agrees with itself in such a measure that it is impossible to doubt the truth and certainty of such a weighty matter in any detail."[3] This perfect inner harmony of Scripture was a basic principle with Luther. "Scripture is not against itself," he strongly affirmed.[4] "Holy Scripture is in excellent agreement with itself and is uniformly consistent everywhere."[5] It is not to be supposed that this was the conclusion of one who had failed to face the difficulties involved in a reconciliation of intransigent passages. That would be to charge Luther with a naiveté which was quite foreign to his nature. Over a period of thirty-four years he was a professional exegete. Few men in his age had given more attention to these matters than he had. It was with eyes wide open, not tight shut as some would have us imagine, that Luther maintained his convictions about the unanimity of Scripture. It was his opponents who denied it. "I let you cry in your hostility that Scripture contradicts itself, ascribing righteousness now to faith and then to works. It is impossible that Scripture should contradict itself; it only seems so to foolish, coarse, and hardened hypocrites."[6] That may sound severe and unsympathetic language, but Luther had suffered too much at the hands of those who played ducks and drakes with the holy Word of God.

The nub of Luther's recognition of biblical unity lies in the relationship between the New Testament and the Old. This is still a crucial issue today.

[1] LCC. 15. 105.   [2] Ibid., 102.   [3] WA. 40. iii. 652.
[4] WA. 9. 450.   [5] LW. 3. 247.   [6] WA. 40. i. 420.

Luther declared that it is characterized both by unity and diversity. Such a realistic appraisal of the situation is typical of him. His stress on the oneness of Scripture did not lead him to ignore its obvious divergences. However, for Luther the decisive distinction in the Bible was not that between the two Testaments. It was that between law and gospel. These distinctions are not coincidental. That is to say, the differentiation between law and gospel is not a refinement of the differentiation between the old covenant and the new. The law-gospel dichotomy runs through both Testaments, as Althaus brings out.[1]

The gospel is to be found in the Old Testament in terms of the promises, and the law is to be found in the New Testament, as for instance in our Lord's reinterpretation in the Sermon on the Mount. "Thus the books of Moses and the prophets are also gospel, since they proclaimed and described in advance what the apostles preached and wrote."[2] On the other hand, "what the gospel or the preaching of Christ brings is not a new doctrine to undo or change the law, but, as St. Paul says (Rom. 1:2), the very same thing that was 'promised beforehand through the prophets in Scripture'."[3] As McDonough has cogently argued, this law-gospel interrelation lay at the heart of Luther's theology.[4] It arose from his biblical presuppositions.

Luther did concede, however, that the Old Testament contained more law and the New Testament contains more gospel. In his Preface to the Old Testament, he explained that it is primarily "a book of laws, which teaches what men are to do and not to do – and in addition gives examples and stories of how these laws are kept or broken – just as the New Testament is gospel or book of grace, and teaches where one is to get the power to fulfil the law".[5] After pointing out that in the New Testament there are also given, along with the teaching about grace, many other commandments for the control of the flesh, and that in the Old Testament there are besides the law certain promises and words of grace by which the patriarchs and prophets were kept in the faith of Christ, Luther added: "Nevertheless just as the chief teaching of the New Testament is really the proclamation of grace and peace through the forgiveness of sins in Christ, so the chief teaching of the Old Testament is really the teaching of laws, the showing up of sin, and the demanding of good."[6] Thus the Old Testament may correctly be described as a law-book and the New Testament as a gospel.[7]

"This is the first way in which they are different from each other," explains Althaus, "and indicates that a tension exists between them. In so far as the Old Testament also contains the gospel, there is a basic unity

---

[1] Althaus, op. cit., p. 87.   [2] LW. 30. 19.   [3] LW. 21. 69.
[4] McDonough, op. cit., p. 146.
[5] LW. 35. 236.   [6] Ibid., 237.   [7] WA. 10. i. 159.

between both parts of the Bible; the only difference is that the Old Testament promises Christ and salvation while the New Testament bears witness that His promise is fulfilled. The two Testaments are therefore related to each other as promise and fulfilment."[1] "The ground and proof of the New Testament is surely not to be despised," argued Luther, "and therefore the Old Testament is to be highly regarded. And what is the New Testament but a public preaching and proclamation of Christ, set forth through the sayings of the Old Testament and fulfilled through Christ?"[2]

A further distinction recognized by Luther was that between Scripture and preaching. Unlike the law-gospel classification, this does coincide with the division between the Testaments. At times Luther spoke of Scripture as the New Testament itself necessarily does, that is, as referring to the Old Testament. The New Testament he preferred to regard as preaching. This differentiation between *Schrift* and *Predigt* could lead Luther to speak about "the authority of Scripture" and "the testimony of the New Testament" as separate witnesses.[3] The gospel, or the New Testament, Luther believed, "should really not be written but should be expressed with the living voice which resounds and is heard throughout the world."[4] He could even suggest that "the fact that it is also written is superfluous".[5] The Old Testament alone has been put in writing when the apostles were compiling the documents which were eventually to be incorporated into the New Testament. So they call it Scripture. It pointed to Christ who was to come – Luther was commenting in this passage on I Peter 1:10–12. "But the gospel is a living sermon on the Christ who has come."[6]

To the extent that both Testaments contain the gospel, Luther's understanding of their relationship may be expressed in two theses, according to Althaus.[7] In the first place, the entire truth of the gospel is already implicit in the Old Testament, and thus the New Testament is based on the Old. In the second place, although this truth is present, it is nevertheless hidden and must therefore be made known and revealed, and this takes place through the word of the New Testament. It was within the orbit of these twin considerations that Luther's elucidation of intertestamental relationships moved. It is essential to hold both aspects of it in tension.

With regard to the first, Luther went out of his way to make it clear that he valued the Old Testament, not only as adumbrating the gospel, but as actually providing the basis of it in embryo. He dismissed those neo-Marcionites of his day who played down the significance of the Old Testament and tossed it aside as "a book that was given to the Jewish people only and is now out of date, containing only stories of past times."[8]

[1] Althaus, op. cit., p. 87.   [2] LW. 35. 236.   [3] LW. 3. 297.
[4] LW. 30. 19.   [5] Ibid.   [6] Ibid.
[7] Althaus, op. cit., p. 87.   [8] LW. 35. 235; cf. LW. 9. 6.

Luther quoted the testimony of Christ Himself, and of the New Testament writers, in order to confute such an erroneous view. The Old Testament is not to be despised but diligently read.[1] The New Testament cannot be understood apart from the Old, Luther insisted – and current scholarship is re-echoing his insight. He could speak of Moses as "a well of all wisdom and understanding, out of which has sprung all that the prophets knew and said. Moreover even the New Testament flows out of it and is grounded in it."[2] And again: "The apostles have drawn everything which they taught and wrote out of the Old Testament; for it proclaims everything which Christ would do and preach in the future. It is for this reason that they base all their sermons on the Old Testament and that there is no statement in the New Testament that does not refer back to the Old Testament in which it was previously proclaimed."[3] Luther could even declare that the "first chapter of Genesis contains the whole Scripture in itself."[4] Similarly, Luther found the whole gospel in the promise attached to the first commandment – "I am the Lord your God."[5]

This dependence of the New Testament on the Old meant that only in the light of the Old could the New be made plain. In this axiom of interpretation Luther had laid hands on the key to a fresh approach to Scripture. It was largely by means of it that he managed to shake off the grip of medieval hermeneutics. "By rooting his interpretation of the New Testament in his understanding of the Old Testament, Luther thus helped to break the exegetical habits of many centuries," wrote Pelikan. "He read the New Testament as the early Church had apparently intended it, as an addition to the Scriptures which the Church already possessed in the Old Testament. Far from being a Marcionite, as he has sometimes been portrayed, Luther did precisely what Marcion seems to have criticized. He read the Old Testament as Christian Scripture, and he read the New Testament on the basis of the Old."[6]

Coming to the second thesis distilled by Althaus from Luther's comments, the evangelical significance of the Old Testament, being concealed, can only be brought to the surface by the New.[7] Luther could even claim that basically the New Testament has no other function than to open up the Old Testament so as to reveal the gospel hidden in it.[8] If the New Testament is preaching, it is preaching on the text of the Old Testament with a view to interpreting its meaning in the light of Christ. Thus, when the New Testament is "understood well, the entire Scripture of the Old Testament is clear".[9] Paul's aim in writing Romans was to "sum up briefly the whole Christian and evangelical doctrine and to prepare an introduction to the entire Old Testament. For, without doubt, whoever has this

[1] LW. 35. 236.
[2] Ibid., 247.
[3] WA. 10. i. 181.
[4] WATR. 3. 155. No. 3043a.
[5] LW. 9. 112.
[6] LW. 21. xi.
[7] Althaus, op. cit., p. 88.
[8] WA. 10. i. 181.
[9] LW. 3. 73.

epistle well in his heart, has within him the light and power of the Old
Testament."[1] Hence "the New Testament is nothing more than a revelation of the Old".[2] "In the New Testament the Old Testament is quoted
and used everywhere; by God's mercy and His revelation this leads to a
clear understanding of faith, no matter how dark and obscure it remains
for the unbelievers. We reach into the dark, black forest and become snow-
white. We observe that all the apostles appeal to the Old Testament, citing
clear and lucid passages from it in substantiation of the faith. And prior to
that, the Jews had quoted these same passages daily, and yet they remained
obscure and dark to them. For the שׁרִי, the Distributor and Nourisher,
who spreads the wings of the cherubim and the doves, had not been given
at the time. First Christ had to die and to bring Him. Is it still surprising to
hear that black becomes white and darkness light? That is the miraculous
work of God."[3]

We cannot adequately discuss Luther's conception of biblical unity
without dealing with his attitude to the canon. It is at this point that he has
come in for considerable criticism on the grounds of alleged inconsistency.
His strictures on the Letter of James have been repeated *ad nauseam*. Every
theological student knows that Luther dismissed it as an epistle of straw.
What is not so generally realized is that Luther wrote differently on other
occasions about James, and that if the actual context of the offending
reference is consulted a rather different construction is placed upon his
observation.[4] It occurs at the close of his Preface to the New Testament –
although not in any editions after 1537, or in any copy of the complete
Bible.[5] Luther has been asking and answering the question: "Which are
the true and noblest books of the New Testament?"[6] From what he had
already written it has become clear that "John's Gospel and St. Paul's
epistles, especially that to Romans, and St. Peter's first epistle are the true
kernel and marrow of all the books".[7] These are the foremost books to set
forth the essence of the Christian faith, and a new convert should turn to
them first.[8] They teach all that is necessary for salvation, and therefore,
Luther adds, "St. James's epistle is really an epistle of straw, compared to
these others, for it has nothing of the nature of the gospel about it."[9]

It will be realized that the operative clause is "compared to these others"
(*gegen sie*). Luther was merely making a comparative estimate. In the
preface to the Letter itself, Luther said that he praised James and held it
to be a good book.[10] But he was compelled by candour to add that he
personally did not regard it as apostolic. "Therefore I cannot include him
among the chief books, though I would not thereby prevent anyone from

[1] LW. 35. 380.   [2] WA. 10. i. 181.   [3] LW. 13. 17.
[4] LW. 35. 362.   [5] Ibid., 358 n. 5.   [6] Ibid., 361.
[7] Ibid., 361-2.   [8] Ibid., 362.   [9] Ibid.
[10] Ibid., 395.

including him or extolling him as he pleases."[1] From this point of view James may be an epistle of straw, but, as Philip Watson pertinently observes, "even straw is not an entirely valueless commodity."[2]

This familiar instance, however, raises the whole question of Luther's approach to the canon, and to that of the New Testament in particular. Not only did he hesitate about James. He was not disposed to deny that Jude was an extract or copy of Second Peter, in view of the similarity of its contents.[3] Moreover, the author "speaks of the apostles like a disciple who comes long after them (v.17) and cites sayings and incidents that are found nowhere else in Scripture (vv. 9, 14)".[4] It was for this reason that the ancient fathers excluded it from the main body the Scriptures. "Therefore, although I value the book," Luther concluded, "it is an epistle that need not be counted among the chief books which are supposed to lay the foundations of the faith."[5] As with James, Luther did not reject it outright, but relegated it to the second division, as it were.

We have seen that he questioned the Pauline authorship of Hebrews. He took it that the language of Hebrews 2:3 sets the author at a remove from the apostles themselves – "it was declared at first by the Lord, and it was attested to us by those who heard Him."[6] It was "the work of an able and learned man", but "who wrote it is not known, and will probably not be known for a while: it makes no difference".[7] But Luther felt he could not classify it with "the true and certain chief books of the New Testament".[8] The same reservation was expressed in the case of the Apocalypse. Luther left everyone free to form their own opinions, but for his part he could not accept it as either apostolic or prophetic.[9] He could "in no way detect that the Holy Spirit produced it".[10]

In the catalogue of New Testament books immediately following his overall preface, Luther included these four – James, Jude, Hebrews and Revelation – at the bottom and in a group apart.[11] The other twenty-three were all numbered, but these were not. The intertestamental books of the Apocrypha were listed in the same way.[12] Erasmus was suspicious of these four writings, and his viewpoint would be familiar to Luther from his *Annotationes* to his Greek New Testament of 1516.[13] The same outlook was

---

[1] Ibid., 397. Editions before 1530 read: "Therefore I will not have him in my Bible to be numbered among the true chief books, though I would not thereby prevent anyone from including or extolling him as he pleases." Luther added: "One man is no man in worldly things (a reference to the proverb, *Einer est keiner*); how, then, should this single man alone avail against Paul and all the rest of Scripture?" (Ibid., n. 55; cf. WADV. 7. 386 nn.17–21).

[2] Philip S. Watson, "Texts and Contexts", *Expository Times*, Vol. LII (1941), p. 313.

[3] LW. 35. 397.   [4] Ibid., 397–8.   [5] Ibid., 398.

[6] Ibid., 394.   [7] Ibid., 395.   [8] Ibid., 394.

[9] Ibid., 399.   [10] Ibid., 398.   [11] WADB. 6. 13.

[12] WADB. 8. 34.

[13] Cf. Brooke Foss Westcott, *A General Survey of the History of the Canon of the New Testament* (1855), pp. 439–41.

shared by Cajetan and Sixtus Senensis.[1] Did Luther's devaluation of these four books imply that he was unready to allow the full inspiration and unity of Scripture? Are we justified in regarding him as a progenitor of radical criticism?

To do this is to prove guilty of trying to squeeze Luther into a modern mould. Although in many ways he was a man ahead of his time, it would be quite incongruous in this instance to hail him as the precursor of eighteenth or nineteenth century radical liberalism.[2] Luther's attitude to the New Testament canon was not so much a foreshadowing of the future as a recreation of the past. He himself appealed in this matter to the tradition of the early Church and noted that the authenticity of these four books had been queried by some of the fathers. In particular, he adduced the example of Eusebius of Caesarea, the pioneer ecclesiastical historian, as witnessing to a primitive distinction between recognized writings (*homologoumena*) and those that were disputed (*antilegomena*).[3] At the opening of Book III in his extensive survey, Eusebius wrote: "But as my history advances I shall deem it profitable to indicate, along with the successions, what Church writers in each period have made use of which of the disputed (books), and what they have said about the canonical and acknowledged writings, and anything that they have said about those that are not such."[4] From this and other passages in his *Ecclesiastical History* we learn that Eusebius grouped five of the seven catholic epistles under the heading of *antilegomena* – namely, James, Jude, II Peter, II and III John. The Book of the Revelation he classed with the *homologoumena*, although with a query. Eusebius accepted the Pauline authorship of Hebrews, and thus included it amongst the fourteen epistles of Paul which are "manifest and clear" as regards their genuineness.[5] But he was aware that others doubted the apostolic provenance of Hebrews, and elsewhere he mentioned it amongst the disputed books.[6]

The appeal to Eusebius, therefore, establishes the precedent for distinguishing between *homologoumena* and *antilegomena*, without suggesting that the components of these categories were fixed. Luther availed himself of the breathing-space provided by such a convenient differentiation without at all abusing it. As Walther contended, for Luther the extent of the

[1] Reu, *Luther's German Bible*, pp. 175-6. Sixtus Senensis, i.e. of Siena, was a leading biblical scholar of the sixteenth century. His *Bibliotheca Sacra* appeared in 1566. Based on scientific principles, it is considered the first of the modern introductions. He distinguished between protocanonical and deuterocanonical books (NCE. 13. 275a).
[2] Althaus considers that Luther's sporadic excursions into the field of textual, canonical and historical criticism scarcely qualify him to be regarded as a harbinger of modern developments (op. cit., p. 82).
[3] LW. 35. 400. Later writers referred to protocanonical and deuterocanonical books.
[4] Eusebius, *The Ecclesiastical History and the Martyrs of Palestine*, ed. H. J. Lawlor and J. E. L. Oulton (1927). Vol. I, Bk. III. 3. 3., p. 66.
[5] Ibid., Bk. III, 3. 5, p. 66. [6] Ibid., Bk. VI, 13. 6, p. 188.

canon was an open question, but the books that were unchallenged remained absolutely authoritative for him as the inspired Word of God.[1] In a more recent assessment, Carl F. H. Henry has reached the same conclusion: "Whatever Luther's questions may have been about the canonicity of certain books . . . he had no question whatever about the authority and inerrancy of the books viewed as canonical."[2]

When Luther spoke about "all Scripture" he intended therefore to indicate all canonical Scripture. He had his own opinions about the four books of the New Testament mentioned above, but he did not quarrel with others who accepted them. To this degree it might be admitted that his conception of biblical unity was impaired. But he would doubtless have defended himself by denying that the disputed books contain anything necessary to salvation which is not also to be found in those that are universally acknowledged. "All the genuine books agree in this," he wrote "that all of them preach and inculcate Christ. And that is the true test by which to judge all books, when we see whether or not they inculcate Christ."[3] It is in Christ that the real unity of Scripture is to be sought.

[1] Wilhelm Walther, *Das Erbe der Reformation in Kampfe der Gegenwart*, Bd. I, *Der Glaube an das Wort Gottes* (1903), p. 42; cf. Francis Pieper, *Christian Dogmatics*, Vol. I (1924), p. 292.
[2] Carl F. H. Henry, *The Protestant Dilemma* (1949), Appendix. Note B, p. 251.
[3] LW. 35. 396. He added: "Whatever does not teach Christ is not yet apostolic."

CHAPTER XV

LUTHER AND THE INTERPRETATION OF SCRIPTURE

"THE REFORMATION INTERPRETATION OF THE BIBLE ... was given classical expression by Martin Luther," writes Robert M. Grant. "His contribution has permanent value. . . . Today the reviving theological interpretation of the Bible must look back to him."[1] That judgment by a distinguished contemporary scholar carries considerable conviction. Its implications are being increasingly recognized. If the current dialogue about Scripture focuses on the question of its interpretation – and it does – then Luther's hermeneutical approach has something to tell us still. Once the broader concept of revelation has been dealt with, those who seek to reassess the value of the Bible today are confronted with the problem of its interpretation. Even if its authority, inspiration and unity are recognized, how is it to be treated? That is a burning issue for us, as it was for Luther in his time.

He began by laying it down as axiomatic that the Scriptures are not to be pushed around at the whim of the commentator. He would have none of such cavalier methods. He repudiated the role of reason as the sole interpreter of God's Word. The truths of revelation cannot be comprehended intellectually – that is to say, they cannot be arrived at by any ratiocinative process. This is not to imply that once the truth of Scripture has been disclosed that it is not intellectually satisfying. Luther's strictures on "the devil's bride, reason" must be understood in these terms.[2] They were directed against the abuse of reason in opposing, distorting and rejecting the Word, not against its proper use as it submits in faith to receive that Word. The right apprehension of Scripture, declared Luther, "does not arise from the human heart or mind," since it is "a teaching revealed from heaven".[3] Nor can it be grasped by the self-opinionated. The man who seeks to impose his own will on Scripture will find it closed and barred to him. "He will never smell or taste a spark or a tittle of the true meaning of a passage or a word of Scripture. He may make much noise and even imagine that he is improving on Holy Scripture, but he will never succeed."[4]

[1] Robert M. Grant, *The Bible in the Church: A Short History of Interpretation* (1954), pp. 116–17.
[2] LW. 51. 374. Luther also described reason as "Frau Hulda" – a capricious elfin creature in Germanic mythology – and as "the lovely whore" or "the devil's prostitute" (LW. 40. 174; LW. 51. 374; WA. 51. 126).
[3] LW. 12. 87.　　　　[4] LW. 23. 230.

On this ground, Luther set aside the right of the pope or his priests, the Church or the councils, to interpret the Word of God.[1] His complaint was that too often they had been guilty of wilful misrepresentation. Luther's favourite phrase to describe such maltreatment roundly accused them of pulling it about "like a nose of wax".[2] "When some ascribe to the Scriptures the flexibility of a waxen nose, and say that it is like bending a reed, this is due to the work of those who misuse the Holy Word of God for their incompetent and unstable opinions and glosses. They reach the point where the Word of God, which is fitting for everything, fits nothing."[3] Luther, however, did not propose to succumb to them. "But we will be masters over these wiseacres, so that they cannot twist the nose of Holy Writ as they please; and if they do, it will be on their own head."[4]

The interpretation of Scripture is the prerogative of God and not of man. "If God does not open and explain Holy Writ, no one can understand it; it will remain a closed book, enveloped in darkness."[5] As Joseph realized, "interpretations belong to God" (Gen. 40:8). God gives His Word and the interpretation too.[6] This He does through the Holy Spirit. Jesus spoke about the gatekeeper who opens the door (John 10:3): He is none other than the Interpreter Spirit.[7] Without Him there is no revelation nor any interpretation either.[8] "The Holy Spirit must be the Teacher and Guide."[9] It was "the work of the Holy Spirit alone" to illuminate the heart of Joseph so as to be able to explain Pharaoh's dreams: it is His function to expound the Scriptures.[10] The disclosures of God "require the Holy Spirit as an interpreter".[11] The "divine and heavenly doctrines" of "repentance, sin, grace, justification, worship to God" to be found in Scripture, cannot enter the heart of man "unless they be taught by the great Spirit".[12] The articles of faith are statements of such things as "no eye has seen, nor ear heard, nor the heart of man conceived" (I Cor. 2:9). "They can be taught and understood only by the Word and the Holy Spirit. It is characteristic of all the articles of faith that reason abhors them, as we see in the case of the heathen and the Jews. They cannot be understood without the Holy Spirit, for they are abysses of divine wisdom in which the reason is completely submerged and lost."[13]

"Proper understanding" of Scripture comes only through the Holy Spirit.[14] It is not enough to possess the revelation of the Word: it is also necessary to have the enlightenment of the Holy Spirit so as to know its meaning.[15] Concerning the doctrine of the Logos in John 1, Luther stressed that "it is foreign and strange to reason, and particularly to the worldly-

---

[1] Ibid.; cf. 105.   [2] PE. 1. 367.   [3] LW. 14. 338.
[4] LW. 24. 96.   [5] LW. 13. 17.   [6] LW. 7. 151.
[7] LW. 13. 16.   [8] LW. 7. 112.
[9] LW. 13. 87; cf. LW. 30. 230; WA. 13. 303.
[10] LW. 7. 150.   [11] Ibid., 149.   [12] LW. 12. 203.
[13] Ibid., 284-5.   [14] LW. 24. 367.   [15] Ibid.

wise. No man can accept it unless his heart has been touched and opened
by the Holy Spirit. It is as impossible of comprehension by reason as it is
inaccessible to the touch of the hand."[1] He concluded that "in the end only
the Holy Spirit from heaven above can create listeners and pupils who
accept this doctrine and believe that the Word is God, that God's Son is
the Word, and that the Word became flesh, that He is also the Light who
can illumine all men who come into the world, and that without this
Light all is darkness."[2]

Luther inquired into the process involved as the Spirit acts as Interpreter. The Word of God in Scripture being spiritual, "excels reason and
rises higher than reason can rise."[3] Hence "understanding of these words
that I hear must be wrought in me by the Holy Spirit. He makes me
spiritual too. The Word is spiritual and I also become spiritual: for He
inscribes it in my heart, and then, in brief, all is spirit."[4] The Holy Spirit,
Luther insisted, works only through the Word. "The Spirit is given to no
one without and outside the Word; He is given only through the Word."[5]
Without the Word, "the Holy Spirit does not operate."[6] The Spirit who
originally spoke the Word and inspired the writers who recorded it,
remains united with the Word, and when He interprets it to us today He
recreates it to become once again a living, an oral Word.[7] As the divine
interpreter, then, the Spirit without appeals to the Spirit within the sacred
writings. Luther laid particular stress on this factor when he argued
against the charismatic radicals, some of whom tended to dissociate the
Spirit from the Word.

A further elaboration of the Spirit's hermeneutical role is to be found in
Luther's axiom that Scripture is its own interpreter.[8] "One passage of
Scripture must be clarified by other passages," was a rule which he often
reiterated.[9] It was only another way of saying that the Holy Spirit is the
true interpreter. To interpret Scripture by Scripture is simply to let the
Holy Spirit do His own work. It is "better to read Scripture according to
what is inside", Luther claimed, as over against the rabbinical exegetes
who adhered to the maxim that "Holy Scripture cannot be understood
without what is above and what is below", i.e., the upper and lower
vowel points.[10] After shedding light on Deuteronomy 1:20 by reference
to Numbers 13:2, Luther added: "Such is the way of the whole Scripture:

---

[1] LW. 22. 8.   [2] Ibid.   [3] LW. 23. 175.
[4] Ibid.   [5] EA. 58. 163; cf. SL. 11. 1073.   [6] EA. 58. 164.
[7] Ibid. Cf. Pieper, op. cit., Vol. I., p. 315.
[8] *Scriptura sui ipsius interpres* (WA. 7. 97). On this axiom in Luther, cf. Gerhard Ebeling,
"Word of God and Hermeneutic", *New Frontiers in Theology*, Vol. II, *The New Hermeneutic*
ed. James M. Robinson and John B. Cobb, Jr. (1964), pp. 77–80.
[9] LW. 37. 177.
[10] LW. 8. 142. "He who does not pay attention to what is written both above and below in
books perverts the words of the living God" – a rabbinical dictum quoted by Sebastian Münster
cf. Ibid., 141. n. 47.

F

it wants to be interpreted by a comparison of passages from everywhere, and understood under its own direction. The safest of all methods for discerning the meaning of Scripture is to work for it by drawing together and scrutinizing passages."[1] "That is the true method of interpretation," he declared elsewhere, "which puts Scripture alongside of Scripture in a right and proper way."[2] This comparative technique had been recommended by some of the fathers, including Origen, Jerome and Augustine.[3] Luther acknowledged his indebtedness to the past when he wrote: "The holy fathers explained Scripture by taking the clear, lucid passages and with them shed light on obscure and doubtful passages."[4] "In this manner," he declared, "Scripture is its own light. It is a fine thing when Scripture explains itself."[5] This self-interpreting factor in Scripture was related in Luther's mind to the basic perspicuity of the Word, of which mention was made in dealing with his view of revelation.[6]

In establishing the principle that one passage must be explained by another, Luther made his meaning explicit: "namely, a doubtful and obscure passage must be explained by a clear and certain passage."[7] Obviously, the clear passage needs no explanation, although, of course, it may be corroborated by other Scriptures. In his controversy with the *Schwärmer*, Luther had occasion to object to their habit of obscuring what was already sufficiently plain by further comparisons. Behind their spurious exegesis of John 6, for instance, there lay the misconception that even what is clear must be further elaborated. Luther repudiated such a work of exegetical supererogation. "The result of this method will be that no passage in Scripture will remain certain and clear, and the comparison of one passage with another will never end. . . . To demand that clear and certain passages be explained by drawing in other passages amounts to an iniquitous deriding of the truth and injection of fog into the light. If one set out to explain all passages by first comparing them with other passages, he would be reducing the whole of Scripture to a vast and uncertain chaos."[8]

But whilst it is unnecessary to pull in parallel passages to supplement what is amply clear and plain, yet it is advantageous to take note of complementary truths lest an imbalance should creep in. "Well known is the stupidity of the ostrich, which thinks it is totally covered when its head is covered with some branch. Thus a godless teacher seizes upon one particular saying of Scripture and thinks his notion is fine, not noticing

---

[1] LW. 9. 21.   [2] PE. 3. 334.
[3] Origen, *De Principiis*, 4; Jerome, *Epistolae*, 53. 6. 7; Augustine, *De Doctrina*, 2. ix. 14.
[4] SL. 20. 856.   [5] SL. 11. 2335.   [6] Above, p. 135.
[7] SL. 5. 335. In this and some subsequent paragraphs I am reproducing a certain amount of material which first appeared in my Tyndale Lecture, *Luther's Principles of Biblical Interpretation*, pp. 21–33, with the kind permission of the publishers.
[8] SL. 20. 325.

that he is maintaining his position as one who is bare and unarmed on every side."[1] It is such failure to envisage the wholeness of Scripture which leads to unbalanced presentation. On the other hand, it is equally dangerous to range over the biblical terrain in a comprehensive manner without paying due attention to context. All that can be produced by such a procedure is an unassorted pot-pourri of excerpts. "If it were fair to take a word or two out of context and to ignore what precedes or follows, or what Scripture says elsewhere, then I, too, could interpret and twist all Holy Writ . . . as I chose."[2]

The formula of Scripture as its own interpreter was closely linked by Luther with another: that all exposition should be in agreement with the analogy of faith. Everything must be "weighed according to the analogy of faith and the rule of Scripture".[3] The use of this term by Luther and the reformers generally was in fact a misapplication of its original occurrence in Romans 12:6. It proved useful nevertheless to delineate Luther's own attitude to Scripture. For him the *analogia fidei* was the Scripture itself. No extraneous canon was invoked. He found his sufficient criterion within the Word of God. Creeds and confessions were of value only in so far as they embodied the rule of Scripture – as Luther believed the great historical affirmations to do. He demanded, however, that reference should be made to the Scripture as a whole and not merely to selected parts of it.[4] The "abominable sophists . . . support themselves with Scripture, because they would look laughable if they tried to force only their own dreams on men; but they do not quote Scripture in its entirety. They always snatch up what appears to favour them; but what is against them they either cleverly conceal or corrupt with their cunning glosses."[5] That is why Luther could call the Bible a heresy book, because the mere citation of texts, without recourse to the rule of faith, may be so manipulated as to give the impression of vindicating the most extreme heterodoxy. What Luther means by *analogia fidei* is neatly expressed by James Wood when he said that "the interpretation has to be congruent with the general norm of the Word of God".[6]

This is something radically different, however, from Schleiermacher's *das Schriftganze* by which he claimed that the Christian articles of faith must not be drawn from those Scriptures which treat of separate doctrines, but only from the general scope and tenor of the Bible. He contended that "it is a most precarious procedure to quote Scripture passages in dogmatic treatises, and besides, in itself, quite inadequate".[7] Luther was equally

[1] LW. 9. 135.   [2] LW. 24. 104.   [3] LW. 3. 168.
[4] OL. 3. 185.   [5] LW. 1. 107.
[6] James D. Wood, *The Interpretation of the Bible: A Historical Introduction* (1958), p. 89.
[7] Friedrich D. E. Schleiermacher, *Die Christliche Glaube den Grundsätzen der evangelischen Kirche*, Bd. I (2nd edn. 1830), para. 30; Pieper, op. cit., Vol I, p. 201. *Das Schriftganze* – the general scope of Scripture.

conscious of the peril involved. He disapproved the indiscriminate concatenation of Bible verses without due respect to their meaning and context, as we have seen. "Heretofore I have held that where something was to be proved by the Scriptures, the Scripture quoted must really refer to the point at issue. I learn now that it is enough to throw many passages together helter-skelter whether they fit or not. If this is to be the way, then I can easily prove from the Scriptures that beer is better than wine."[1] But, as Mueller brings out, Schleiermacher's application of *das Schriftganze* was only a pretext to excuse his thoroughly unscriptural method of deriving theological truths from reason or the pious self-consciousness.[2] Theodor Kliefoth was surely justified in dismissing this alleged disparity between the part and the whole in Scripture, as represented in Schleiermacher (and in Hofmann and Ihmels after him), as an "inconceivable concept".[3]

This brings us to what is perhaps the most valuable of Luther's hermeneutical principles, namely, his insistence on the primacy of the literal or grammatico-historical sense. He resolutely set aside the verbal legerdemain involved in the multiple exegesis of the Schoolmen, and firmly took his stand on the plain and obvious meaning of the Word. It was through this that he came to his own illumination, and he made it the main plank in his interpretative platform. "The Christian reader should make it his first task to seek out the literal sense, as they call it. For it alone is the whole substance of faith and Christian theology; it alone holds its ground in trouble and trial."[4] And again: "If we want to treat Holy Scripture skilfully, our effort must be concentrated on arriving at one simple, pertinent, and sure literal sense."[5] Those who are occupied with the exposition of Holy Writ "should take pains to have one definite and simple understanding of Scripture and not to be a wanderer and vagabond, like the rabbis, the Scholastic theologians, and the professors of law, who are always toiling with ambiguities".[6] It is with "the true and actual meaning" that commentators should be concerned.[7]

As we shall show later, Luther did not altogether set aside spiritual interpretation, but he emphatically urged the priority and superiority of the literal sense. For a thousand years the Church had buttressed its theological edifice by means of an authoritative exegesis which depended on allegory as its chief medium of interpretation. Luther struck a mortal blow at this vulnerable spot. From his own experience in the monastery he knew the futility of allegorization – and stigmatized it as "mere jugglery", "a

[1] WA. 6. 301.
[2] J. Theodore Mueller, *Christian Dogmatics: A Handbook of Doctrinal Theology* (1934), p. 94.
[3] Theodore Kliefoth, *Der Schriftbeweis des Dr. J. C. K. von Hofmann* (1860), p. 32; J. C. K. von Hofmann, *Der Schriftbeweis: Ein theologicther Untersuchung*, Bd. I (1852), pp. 671–3; Ludwig Ihmels. *Zentralfragen der Dogmatik in der Gecenwart* (1911), pp. 88–89.
[4] LW. 9. 24.   [5] LW. 3. 27.
[6] LW. 8. 209.   [7] Ibid.

merry chase", "monkey tricks", "looney talk".[1] He had suffered much
from that sort of pseudo-exposition of which John Lowe speaks so
trenchantly, where "anything can mean anything".[2] "When I was a
monk," Luther frankly acknowledged, "I was an adept at allegory. I
allegorized everything. But after lecturing on the Epistle to the Romans,
I came to have some knowledge of Christ. For therein I saw that Christ
is no allegory, and learned to know what Christ was."[3] His emancipation was only gradual, for there are occasions, especially in his *Operationes in Psalmos* (1518–21), when we catch him relapsing into his former
style. "It was very difficult for me to break away from my habitual
zeal for allegory," he confided. "And yet I was aware that allegories
were empty speculations and the froth, as it were, of the Holy Scriptures. It is the historical sense alone which supplies the true and sound
doctrine."[4]

Luther did not altogether abandon allegory, for in the passage quoted
above (which is from his late lectures on Genesis) he added: "After this
(i.e., the literal sense) has been treated and correctly understood, the one
may employ allegories as an adornment and flowers to embellish or
illuminate the account. The bare allegories, which stand in no relation to
the account, and do not illuminate it, should simply be disapproved as
empty dreams. ... Therefore let those who want to make use of allegories
base them on the historical account itself. The historical account is like
logic in that it teaches what is certainly true; the allegory, on the other
hand, is like rhetoric in that it ought to illustrate the historical account but
has no value at all for giving proof."[5] Commenting on a different chapter
in Genesis, Luther wrote: "But now that the foundation has been laid on
the basis of other sure and clear passages of Scripture, what is there to
prevent the additional use of an allegory, not only for the sake of adorning
but also for the sake of teaching, in order that the subject may become
clearer?"[6]

Luther's chief objection to the heavenly prophets at Zwickau was that
they spiritualized away the literal sense of Scripture. "Brother" – so he
addressed Karlstadt – "the natural meaning of the words is queen, tran-
scending all subtle, acute, sophistical fancy. From it we may not deviate
unless compelled by a clear article of the faith. Otherwise the spiritual
jugglers would not have a single letter in Scripture. Therefore, interpretations of God's Word must be lucid and definite, having a firm, sure,

---

[1] PE. 3. 334; LW. 9. 7; cf. Frederic W. Farrar, *History of Interpretation* (1886), p. 328.
[2] John Lowe, in *The Interpretation of the Bible*, ed. Clifford Dugmore (1944), p. 121.
[3] WA. 1. 136.   [4] LW. 1. 283.
[5] LW. 3. 192; cf. LW. 9. 24–25 – "Not as though the allegorical meaning proved or
supported the statement of doctrine; but it is proved and supported by the statement just as a
house does not hold up the foundation but is held up by the foundation."
[6] LW. 3. 192; cf. LW. 8. 269; LW. 9. 8, where Luther speaks of "a proper allegory".

and true foundation on which one may confidently rely."[1] Erasmus was rebuked for the same tendency. "When then shall we ever have any plain and pure text, without tropes and conclusions, either for or against free will? Has the Scripture no such texts anywhere? And shall the cause of free will remain for ever in doubt, like a reed shaken with the wind, as being that which can be supported by no certain text, but which stands upon conclusions and tropes only, introduced by men mutually disagreeing with each other? But let our sentiment rather be this: that neither conclusion nor trope is to be admitted into the Scriptures, unless the evident state of the particulars, or the absurdity of any particular as militating against an article of faith, require it: but, that the simple, pure and natural meaning of the words is to be adhered to, which is according to the rules of grammar and to that common use of speech which God has given to men. For if everyone be allowed, according to his own desire, to invent conclusions and tropes in the Scriptures, what will the whole Scripture together be, but a reed shaken with the wind, or a kind of Vertumnus?"[2] This too was the offence of the Romanists who, according to Luther, tossed the words of God to and fro, as gamblers throw their dice, and took "from the Scripture its single, simple and stable meaning".[3]

Luther apparently preferred to speak of the grammatical and historical rather than the literal sense, although it is evident that the three are intimately related. "No violence is to be done to the words of God, whether by man or angel. They are to be retained in their simplest meaning as far as possible. Unless the context manifestly compels it, they are not to be understood apart from their grammatical and proper sense, lest we give our adversaries occasion to make a mockery of all the Scriptures."[4] This is "not well named the literal sense", for by the letter the Bible means something quite different, as Augustine recognized.[5] "They do much better who call it the grammatical, historical sense. It would be well to call it the speaking or language sense, as St. Paul does in I Corinthians 14, because it is understood by everybody in the sense of the spoken language."[6]

According to Pelikan, the basic hermeneutical principle which Luther sought to defend might be expressed thus: "A text of the Scriptures had to be taken as it stood unless there were compelling reasons for taking it otherwise."[7] Anyone who took it upon himself to interpret the words in any other sense than as read had the obligation to prove that such a departure was justifiable.[8] It seems that Luther allowed for three possible

---

[1] LW. 40. 190.
[2] BW. 205. Vertumnus was a god who changed or metamorphosed himself. The Romans connected him with the change of seasons, the ebb and flow of tides, and the purchase and sale of goods or land. (Propertius, 4. 2. 6; Ovid, *Metamorphoses*, 14. 642.)
[3] LW. 32. 26.   [4] LW. 36. 30.   [5] PE. 3. 352.
[6] Ibid., 352-3.   [7] LW. Companion Volume, 126.
[8] LW. 37. 34; cf. 174, 177.

grounds: the statement of the text itself that it was not to be interpreted literally, the evidence of another passage Scripture to this same effect, and the application of the *analogia fidei*.[1] It has to be admitted that in practice this axiom involved the expositor in something of a difficulty. Who was to decide the relative weight of the evidence, and which text was to interpret which? Luther's own exegesis at times reflected this dilemma.

Even though Luther, then, placed unusual emphasis on the literal sense, he did not refuse to permit any other. It can hardly be said that to *sola Scriptura* he allied the further principle *sola historica sententia*, as Gerrish claims.[2] Indeed, the latter went on to admit that Luther even allowed a legitimate use of allegory. In effect, as Kurt Aland brings out, Luther did concede a dual meaning in Scripture – or at least two aspects of the same meaning.[3] There is the outward meaning obtained by the help of the Word, and another which lies in the knowledge of the heart. That is why Luther talked so much about the understanding of Scripture by faith. To read without faith is to walk in darkness.[4] Nothing but faith can comprehend the truth.[5] Through faith we have all we need to grasp the Word of God.[6] We must moreover feel the words of Scripture in the heart if we are to arrive at their deepest meaning. "Experience is necessary for the understanding of the Word. It is not merely to be repeated or known, but to be lived and felt."[7] Thus, although Luther was staunchly opposed to unbridled allegorization, he nevertheless admitted a significance in Scripture which went beyond the strictly literal.[8]

The Lutheran dogmaticians elaborated this unsystematized insight into a distinction between the external and internal *forma* of Scripture. The external *forma* is the idiom and style of writing. The internal *forma* is its inspired meaning, "the thoughts of the divine mind concerning divine mysteries, thoughts which were conceived in eternity for our salvation, revealed in time and communicated to us in Scripture," so Robert Preus explains.[9] The internal *forma*, then, is that which makes the Scripture what it is, and distinguishes the Bible from any other book. Quenstedt defined it thus: "We must distinguish between the grammatical and outer meaning of the divine Word and the spiritual, inner and divine meaning of the divine Word. The first is the *forma* of the Word of God in so far as it is a word, the latter is its *forma* in so far as it is a divine Word. The first can be grasped even by any unregenerate man, the latter, however, cannot be

---

[1] LW. Companion Volume, 126–7; LW. 37. 186, 262; LW. 40. 157.
[2] Gerrish, "Biblical Authority and the Reformation", *Scottish Journal of Theology*, Vol. X (1957), p. 346.
[3] Kurt Aland, "Luther as Exegete", *Expository Times*, Vol. LXIX (1957), p. 46.
[4] LW. 8. 287.   [5] LW. 22. 8.
[6] LW. 30. 69.   [7] WA. 42. 195.
[8] Cf. A. Skevington Wood, *The Principles of Biblical Interpretation*, pp. 80–81.
[9] R. Preus, op. cit., p. 14.

received except by a mind which has been enlightened."[1] As we shall be demonstrating in the next chapter, this tension is only resolved when the outer and inner meaning of Scripture are seen to cohere in Christ.[2]

One of the features of current hermeneutical discussion is the interest being shown in what is identified as the plenary sense of Scripture. One of its outstanding advocates is Joseph Coppens of Louvain.[3] He defines it as the deeper sense intended by the Holy Spirit which is included along with the literal meaning. It may go beyond what the writer himself originally had in mind. This *sensus plenior* is "related to, homogenous with, and derived from, the literal sense".[4] It becomes explicit through the text itself, through the rest of Scripture, and through the illumination of the Spirit. Another Roman Catholic scholar, Reginald Fuller, thinks that, though "the concept of the plenary sense is still in the process of elucidation and is far from being universally accepted", it is nevertheless "surely very reasonable".[5] Now, without hailing Luther as the progenitor of modern theories which he might well have repudiated, it would appear that it was along such lines that his fertile mind was working. What a strange circumstance it is that this interpretational clue should be nowadays attracting the attention primarily of Roman exegetes!

---

[1] Johannes Andreas Quenstedt, *Theologia Didactico-Polemica* (3rd. edn., 1696), Vol. I, p. 56.
[2] Below, pp. 176–180.
[3] Cf. Joseph Coppens, *The Old Testament and the Critics* (E.T. 1942) and *Von Christlichen Verständnis des Alten Testaments* (1952). Also Raymond E. Brown, *The Sensus Plenior of Sacred Scripture* (1964).
[4] J. D. Wood, op. cit., p. 163.
[5] *A Catholic Commentary on Holy Scripture,* ed. Bernard Orchard, Edmund F. Sutcliffe, Reginald C. Fuller, Ralph Russell (1953), p. 55 39k.

CHAPTER XVI

LUTHER AND THE CHRIST-CENTREDNESS
OF SCRIPTURE

IT IS BEING RECOGNIZED TODAY THAT WHAT HAS been described as Luther's Copernican revolution in theology involved a revision of traditional views about Christ as well as those about salvation. Indeed, the one depended upon the other. This was the pattern of Luther's own experience. It was only as he came to know Christ as a gracious redeemer, and not just as a "judge sitting on a rainbow", that he entered into the liberation which none but those who are right with God can enjoy.[1] For him, justification by faith did not occur in a vacuum as it were. It had its source and centre in Christ. It is he who is the believer's righteousness, as well as wisdom, sanctification and redemption (1 Cor. 1:30).

This realization that Luther's new approach to the Church's doctrine had as its basis a rediscovery of Christology was expressed by Robert L. Ottley in his major work on *The Doctrine of the Incarnation.* "Luther did indeed restore to Christendom the sovereign significance of the historical person of Christ," he declared, "obscured as it actually was in the popular mind by an immense formal system of mediation. He recalled men's minds from a false to a true conception of faith; from blind and mechanical reliance on a complex system to simple trust in a living person, the Divine Christ."[2] As a result of this Christological reorientation, the whole of Luther's theology found its focus in our Lord. Wilhelm Herrmann was hardly exaggerating when he claimed that "the attitude towards Jesus which Luther consciously held marks a step forward in the development of the Christian religion."[3]

We may trace the genesis of this awareness on Luther's part to the influence of Johann Staupitz, the vicar-general of his order. It was he who had told Luther: "One must keep one's eyes fixed on that man who is called Christ"; and who had on another occasion affirmed: "In Christ all treasures are hidden: apart from Him they are closed to us."[4] Luther followed the clue to its logical conclusion. Hence his theology was thoroughly Christocentric. Even his pivotal article of justification by faith alone found its ultimate reference in the person of our Lord. It was only

---

[1] *Dok.,* 346, 358, 381. LW. 24. 24.
[2] Robert L. Ottley, *The Doctrine of the Incarnation* (1896), p. 537.
[3] Wilhelm Herrmann, *The Communion of the Christian with God* (2nd edn. E.T. 1906), p. 148.
[4] LW. 54. 97. No. 526; WATR 2. 582. No. 2654a.

because Christ was no less than Son of God and Saviour of the world, that He could thus save to the uttermost those who came to the Father by Him. For Luther, according to Cave, "the Divinity of Christ was not just a doctrine of the Church. It was the one guarantee of men's salvation."[1]

In expounding the Apostles' Creed in his *Larger Catechism*, Luther drew out the soteriological significance of Christ's Lordship. "I believe that Jesus Christ, the true Son of God, has become my Lord. And what do the words 'to become thy Lord' mean? They mean that He has redeemed me from sin, from the devil, from death and all misfortunes. . . . So the main point of this article is that the little word Lord, taken in its simplest sense, means as much as Redeemer; that is, He who led us back from the devil to God, from death to life, from sin to righteousness, and holds us safe."[2] The Christian's assertion of belief, in the words of the *Credo*, implies that Christ is regarded both as Son of God and Saviour. The two belong together. If Christ is indeed the Son of God, then He will save; and only because He is divine is He able to save. "If Christ is divested of His deity," Luther stated, "there remains no help against God's wrath and no rescue from His judgment."[3] "If I saw in Christ only a man crucified and dying for me, then I would be lost."[4] But Luther had no hesitation about proclaiming the deity of our Lord.[5] His own testimony substantiated what he had learned from the Scriptures. "I have had so many experiences of Christ's divinity, that I must say: either there is no God, or He is God."[6]

The humanity of Jesus was nevertheless fully recognized. Indeed, Luther found that the biblical account starts here, and only gradually builds up to a disclosure of our Lord's Messiahship and deity. "The Scriptures begin very gently, and lead us on to Christ as to a man, and then to one who is Lord over all creatures, and after that to one who is God. So do I enter delightfully and learn to know God. But the philosophers and doctors have insisted on beginning from above. We must begin from below, and after that come upwards."[7] Unless we do as the Bible does, we shall fail to set our feet on Christ the Ladder let down by the Father to bring us up to himself.[8] It is through the man Christ Jesus that we come to acknowledge the Saviour and the Son. "If you can humble yourself, hold to the word with your heart and hold to Christ's humanity – then the divinity will indeed become manifest."[9] Luther realized that the true manhood of our Lord is essential to salvation. If Christ is not "a real and natural man, born of Mary, then He is not of our flesh and blood. Then He has nothing in common with us; then we can derive no comfort from Him."[10]

[1] Cave, op. cit., p. 139. [2] PW. 99, 100.
[3] LW. 22. 22. [4] EA. 7. 185.
[5] Heinrich H. Schultz, *Die Lehre von der Gottheit Christi: Communicatio Idiomata* (1881), pp. 207–8.
[6] WATR. I. 269. No. 583. [7] EA. 12. 412. [8] WA. 40. iii. 656.
[9] LW. 23. 102; cf., 103. [10] LW. 22. 23.

In considering the relationship between the divine and human natures of our Lord, Luther adhered strictly to the Chalcedonian formula. But he supplemented it with an explanatory theory of the *communicatio idiomatum* or transference of attributes. He firmly rejected Zwingli's conception of *alloeosis*, by which the interchange of qualities between the natures was reduced simply to a figure of speech.[1] Luther traced back this error to Nestorius.[2] He declared that he knew no God except the child at Mary's breast and the man nailed to the cross.[3] He insisted that the Saviour suffered for us in His divine as well as in His human nature. As Harnack discerned, no teacher of the Church since Cyril of Alexandria had laid such stress on the mystery of Christ's two natures, or drawn such consolation from it.[4] This must be borne in mind, for we shall shortly see that Luther's Christology at this point has an important bearing on his view of Scripture.

It is not surprising that, since for Luther "Christ fills the whole sphere of God", as Lindsay expressed it, he should regard the Bible as first and foremost a book about the Saviour.[5] The entire Scripture is "concerned only with Christ when you see its inner meaning, even though it may look and sound differently on the outside."[6] A favourite illustration is that of the *punctus mathematicus*: Christ is the "central point of the circle", around which everything else in the Bible revolves.[7] "This is the new element in Luther's doctrine of Scripture, the reformatory turn of his biblical theology," claims Kooiman. "To place the Bible in a central position had been done by the theologians of earlier centuries. To place Christ in the centre of the Bible, as totally as Luther did, was previously unheard of. With great monotony he hammered consistently upon this single anvil."[8] The Christ-centredness of Scripture was his most distinctive insight.

It was developed very early in his career as a biblical exegete.[9] Even so soon as in the *Dictata super Psalterium* (1513–15), he could announce: "I see nothing in Scripture except Christ and Him crucified."[10] In a sermon preached in November 1515, a fragment of which has been preserved, Luther said: "He who would read the Bible must simply take heed that he does not err, for the Scripture may permit itself to be stretched and led, but let no one lead it according to his own inclinations but let him lead it

[1] SL. 20. 1310; cf. Huldreich Zwingli, *Opera* (1581), 3. 523.

[2] LW. 23. 101 n. 80. Nestorius of Constantinople was a fifth-century heretic who held that there were two separate persons in the incarnate Christ, as against the orthodox doctrine that there was a single person with two natures. Nestorius denied the title θεοτόκος to Mary and rejected the *communicatio idiomatum*. It was only in His humanity that Christ was born, suffered and died. "I cannot worship a God who was born, put to death, and buried," he declared.

[3] WA. 39. ii. 280.
[5] DCG. 2. 862.
[7] WATR. 439. No. 2383.
[9] Reu, *Luther and the Scriptures*, pp. 46–48.

[4] Harnack, op. cit., Bd. III, p. 695.
[6] WA. 56. 414.
[8] Kooiman, op. cit., pp. 207–8.
[10] WA. 4. 153; cf. WA. 3. 597.

to the source, that is the cross of Christ. Then he will surely strike the centre."[1] And in his exposition of the *Seven Penitential Psalms* (1517), Luther wound up like this: "As for me, I confess: Whenever I found less in the Scriptures than Christ, I was never satisfied; but whenever I found more than Christ, I never became poorer. Therefore it seems to me to be true that God the Holy Spirit does not know and does not want to know anything besides Jesus Christ, as He says of Him, 'He will glorify me' (John 16:14)."[2]

Erasmus had already anticipated Luther in stressing this. "Nothing is to be sought in Scripture but Christ," he had demanded.[3] But, as Reu brought out, there is a difference in viewpoint between Erasmus and Luther. "For Erasmus Christ was the centre of the Scriptures because He is the best model of the moral life; for Luther, because He is the crucified and risen One who brought about forgiveness, righteousness, and life, and gives it to us, as he continues in his exposition to the Psalms (1517): 'Christ is God's grace, mercy, righteousness, truth, wisdom, power, comfort, and salvation, given us of God without any merit.'"[4] This quest for Christ in Scripture is not to be confined to the New Testament. It applies equally to the Old. The whole Bible treats of Christ. Readers are not to imagine that the Old Testament is incapable of conveying such a revelation. In the memorable words of his preface to the Old Testament, Luther warned against such a superficial conclusion. "I beg and really caution every pious Christian not to be offended by the simplicity of the language and stories frequently encountered there, but fully realize that, however simple they may seem, these are the very words, works, judgments and deeds of the majesty, power, and wisdom of the most high God. For these are the Scriptures which make fools of all the wise and understanding, and are open only to the small and simple, as Christ says in Matthew 11(:25). Therefore dismiss your own opinions and feelings, and think of the Scriptures as the loftiest and noblest of holy things, as the richest of mines which can never be sufficiently explored, in order that you may find that divine wisdom which God here lays before you in such simple guise as to quench all pride. Here you will find the swaddling clothes and the manger in which Christ lies, and to which the angel points the shepherds (Luke 2:12). Simple and lowly are these swaddling clothes, but dear is the treasure, Christ, who lies in them."[5]

Luther employed a variety of metaphors to express the centrality of Christ in Scripture. We have noted his allusion to the mid-point of the circle. Another favourite expression of his was to speak about Christ as

[1] WA. 1. 52.   [2] LW. 14. 204.
[3] Oecolampadius acknowledged that he had learned this from Erasmus (Otto Scheel, *Luthers Stellung zur Heiligen Schrift* (1902), p. 10; Reu, *Luther and the Scriptures*, p. 148, n. 92.
[4] Reu. *Luther and the Scriptures*, p. 47; WA. 1. 219; LW. 14. 204.
[5] LW. 35. 236.

"the sun and truth in Scripture".[1] Everything else, even within the Bible itself, is not to be compared with Christ as a source of illumination. Indeed, it is only as He sheds his light on the rest that it becomes intelligible to us. When the sun rises, it supersedes the moon and stars. Their light – so bright in the darkness of night – fades away when the sun comes up. "The same thing is true of Christ. The prophets are the stars and the moon, but Christ is the sun. Wherever Christ appears, speaks, and shines, His words have a validity that invalidates and stifles all others and renders them of no account, even though the moon and the stars also glitter and glisten beautifully. Thus Moses, the Law, and the prophets are a good and learned message, but compared with the message of Christ they are as nothing; for they are like a wax candle that is lighted during the day to compare it with the brilliance of the sun. The candle's gleam pales and fades before the sun's rays and light. Thus Moses and the prophets also pale into insignificance before Christ. For Christ alone must prevail."[2] And again: "All Holy Writ points to the fact that Moses must proclaim the law, but that Christ will abolish and obscure the message of the law, just as the sun dims the light of the moon and the stars. You can see that the stars are not shining during the day, though they are fixed in the heavens before your very eyes. The sun deprives them of their light. But when the sun sets, we again behold the glittering stars. When the big light vanishes, the lesser lights begin to shine and gleam. *But if Christ, the Sun, should go down, then may God help us!*"[3] Hence Christ "should be acknowledged as the sun, and His Word as such a light of grace that men forget everything else".[4]

All Scripture has been given for the sake of Christ, in order that He might be made known and glorified. In Him alone does it find its meaning. Because of this, everything is to be understood with reference to Him. Christ is "the substance of Scripture" and "if He is known, everything else becomes plain and perspicuous".[5] Christian doctrine as set out in Scripture is "one eternal and round golden circle, in which there is no crack".[6] It has to do only with Christ. Commenting on Romans 10:4 – "For Christ is the end of the law, that everyone who has faith may be justified" – Luther explained that this meant "every word in the Bible points to Christ".[7] The question in Deuteronomy 30:12 – "Who will go up for us to heaven?" – seems to have nothing at all to do with Christ, but in Romans 10:5–9 Paul shows that it has. It was as if the apostle "wanted to give us an impressive proof of the fact that the whole Scripture, if one contemplates it inwardly, deals everywhere with Christ, even though in so far as it is a sign and a shadow, it may outwardly sound differently".[8]

Thus Luther can conclude that "in the whole Scripture there is nothing

[1] WA. 3. 26.   [2] LW. 23. 279–80.   [3] Ibid., 281.
[4] Ibid.   [5] LW. 7. 285.   [6] LW. 27. 38.
[7] LCC. 15. 288.   [8] Ibid.

but Christ, either in plain words or involved words".[1] "Take Christ out of the Scriptures," he asked Erasmus, "and what will you find remaining in them?"[2] Scripture contains "nothing but Christ and the Christian faith."[3] It is this Christocentric approach to the Bible which transforms it for the reader, as Luther had discovered for himself. In particular, the Old Testament when interpreted in this way takes on a totally fresh significance "Everything becomes new in this Christ, even the prayers of the dear patriarchs, because they called upon this very same Christ, who has now come and has fulfilled what they believed and looked for. Now Scripture and the Psalms ring just as new on our lips, if we believe in Christ, as they did when David first sang them. In brief, from now on Christ wants all variation and disparity removed and everything unified, so that, as St. Paul declares, there will henceforth be but one God, one church, one faith, one prayer and worship, one Christ (Eph. 4 : 4–6), 'the same yesterday and today and forever' (Heb. 13:8). To sumarize, God will hear and acknowledge only what is presented in the name of Christ."[4]

It is in terms of this recognition that all Scripture relates to Christ that Luther's oft-quoted statement in his Preface to James must be understood. There he claimed that "all the genuine sacred books agree in this, that all of them preach and inculcate (*treiben*) Christ. And that is the true test by which to judge all books when we see whether or not they inculcate Christ."[5] Attempts have been made to raise this to the level of a discriminating criterion within Scripture itself, as if Luther was prepared by such a yardstick to pick and choose from the whole range of God's Word that which was ultimately authoritative for the Christian. But this, of course, was far from his mind. He believed that all the canonical books inculcated Christ, and for this reason he accepted them in their entirety. His query about James was concerned with its canonicity. He did not hesitate to announce in the following sentence in the Preface that "all the Scriptures show us Christ".[6] In view of this, everything in Scripture is to be seen in the light of Christ. "If you would interpret well and confidently, set Christ before you," Luther wrote in his introduction to the Old Testament, "for He is the man to whom it all applies, every bit of it."[7] This was his "brief suggestion for seeking Christ and the Gospel in the Old Testament".[8] And again, in his lectures on Romans: "There a great stride has been made towards the right interpretation of Scripture, by understanding it all as bearing on Christ."[9] It in this context that we realize the shrewdness of Kramm's comment that for Luther the rule, "what inculcates Christ," is a principle of interpretation within Scripture, not a principle of selection.[10]

[1] WA. II. 223.   [2] BW. 26.   [3] WA. 8. 236.
[4] LW. 24. 397.   [5] LW. 35. 396.   [6] Ibid.
[7] Ibid., 247.   [8] Ibid., 248.   [9] WA. 56. 4.
[10] Hans Herbert Walther Kramm, *The Theology of Martin Luther* (1947), p. 114.

Luther's Christocentric approach to Scripture provides the clue to the paradox involved in his insistence on the primacy of the literal sense, whilst conceding that there is a further, inner, spiritual meaning.[1] Luther took his stand on the literal sense. That for him was fundamental. But he recognized that there is an inward meaning of the Word to which the eyes of faith must penetrate. It is not supplementary to the literal sense, but communicated by it. Luther's major contribution to biblical interpretation lay in the fusion of the literal and spiritual in a new and dynamic relationship. His view treated the Scriptures dialectically. It resolved the tension between the literal and the spiritual sense. It took into account the interaction between the historical elements of the Bible. It transcended the normal categories of internal and external significance and achieved a vital synthesis between the letter and the spirit.

This *rapprochement* was made possible because, as Blackman hints, for Luther Christ is both the literal and the spiritual sense of Scripture, and these two are one in Him.[2] It is He who reconciles the apparently incompatible. The acknowledgement of Christ as Lord of Scripture supplied the context in which the holy alliance of letter and spirit may be effected.[3] In the first flush of his own discovery of this hermeneutical key, Luther could declare: "Christ is the head of all the saints, the origin of all, the source of all streams. . . . Therefore the words of Scripture concerning Christ at the same time share life with Him. And in this way all the four senses of Scripture flow into one."[4] Eventually he discarded the *quadriga* altogether because of its misuse by Roman propagandists. But his Christocentric exegesis nevertheless ensured that ample justice should be done to every intrinsic shade of biblical meaning.

That introduces us lastly to Luther's Christological conception of Scripture, which was determinative for his whole outlook. His Christocentric perspective led him to affirm that, since Christ is the only revealer of God, He is the essential content of Scripture. But if the question is raised as to the mode of our Lord's manifestation in the Word, Luther offered a profoundly constructive solution. As the divinity and power of God are embedded in the vessel of Christ's incarnate body, so the same divinity and power of God are embedded in Scripture, a vessel made of letters, composed of paper and printer's ink.[5] In order to grasp the biblical revelation in its fulness it is necessary to conceive of Scripture in terms of the divine-human nature of Christ.[6]

[1] Cf. A. Skevington Wood, *Luther's Principles of Biblical Interpretation*, p. 34. Some material in the remainder of the chapter first appeared in this Tyndale Lecture in Historical Theology which I was privileged to deliver at Cambridge in 1959.
[2] Blackman, op. cit., p. 120.
[3] Hubert Cunliffe-Jones, *The Authority of the Biblical Revelation* (1946), p. 102.
[4] *Luther Today*, 74.   [5] WA. 3. 515.
[6] WA. 3. 403–4. Cf. Erich Roth, "Martin Luther and the Continental Reformation" *Church Quarterly Review*, Vol CLIII(1952), p. 173.

Luther's recognition of this incarnational factor in the doctrine of Scripture was one of his most relevant insights. The clue to his biblical interpretation is the Christological method of Scripture itself. The very categories Luther employed were Christological rather than scientific, philosophical, or even narrowly theological. For him the basic problem was the reconciliation of the divine and human elements in Scripture. The Bible is God's Book. Its writers were God-inspired men. Through it God still speaks. But the writers were also human, and what they wrote has been recorded in the normal fashion. Luther realized that the issue raised is Christological at the core. His argument stemmed from the statement that "sacred Scripture is God incarnate".[1] He drew a deliberate analogy between Scripture and the person of Christ, between the Word written and the Word made flesh. "And the Word," he said, "is just like the Son of God."[2]

As in the doctrine of the incarnation the Church announces that our Lord was at once fully God and fully man, so Luther would have us maintain the full divinity and full humanity, as it were, of Holy Scripture. Orthodox theology enjoins us to hold in tension the humanity and divinity of our Lord. We have to confess that He was both fully man and yet fully God. It is a heresy to deny either. Docetism erred in overlooking His humanity: Psilanthropism erred in rejecting His divinity.[3] The same sort of problem confronts us in the Bible: namely, the reconciliation of the divine and human elements in the Word. Luther believed that the Chalcedonian formula concerning the two natures of Christ should also be applied to the Bible. As we are required to recognize the two natures of our Lord, "without confusion, without mutation, without division, without separation," so too we ought to recognize the dual nature of Scripture and hold both to its full humanity and its full divinity.[4] Moreover, Luther related his concept of *communicatio idiomatum* to the Scriptures, as well as to the person of Christ and the sacraments, thus safeguarding the unity of the Bible from arbitrary fragmentation.[5] What is predicated of one element pertains to the other: there is a sort of interpenetration. The relevance of Luther's Christology, as summarized at the beginning of this chapter, will be appreciated.

Luther's Christological approach to Scripture retains its value today, and has something to teach us as once again the issue of its divine-human composition has been raised in the forefront of discussion. "The Church must develop its doctrine of the Scriptures," suggested Emil Brunner, "on

[1] Cf. SL. 3. 21.   [2] *Luther Today*, p. 84.
[3] Cf. A. Skevington Wood, *The Principles of Biblical Interpretation*, p. 83.
[4] ἀσυγχύτως, ἀτρέπτως, ἀδιαρέτως, ἀχωρίστως. *Symbole der Alten Kirche ausgewählt von Hans Lietzmann* (1931), pp. 35–36.
[5] Cf. Yngve Brilioth, *Eucharistic Faith and Practice* (E.T. 1930), p. 105; Seeberg, op. cit., Bd. IV, pp. 382–3.

the same lines as the doctrine of the two natures. The Bible shares in the glory of the divinity of Christ and in the lowliness of his humanity."[1] Luther would have concurred. But he would hardly have drawn the unconvincing 'conclusion that Brunner did from his assertion, when he wrote elsewhere: "Naturally the Scripture is an historical document written by men and, to that extent, also participating in the frailty of all that is human, in the relativity of all that is historical. Men must first have forgotten what to come in the flesh, to become historical, meant, to be able to set up a doctrine of an infallible book."[2] As Paul K. Jewett, who has submitted Brunner's concept of revelation and inspiration to critically searching analysis, points out with compelling pertinency: "What Brunner nowhere makes clear is why this dualism, which renders impossible an infallible written revelation, is no barrier to an infallible personal revelation in Christ."[3] Luther, on the other hand, pressed the analogy between the incarnation and the nature of Scripture to its logical limit in his Christological approach. The human element of Scripture for him was no more liable to error than was the human nature of Christ.

In conceding that Scripture was both human and divine, Luther did not thereby open the door to the suggestion of fallibility. He scrupulously avoided the charge of what we might describe as biblical Nestorianism. "Luther . . . was well acquainted with the 'human side' of Scripture," wrote Francis Pieper, "but only in the sense that God caused His Word to be written by men in the human tongue. Luther is horrified at people who dare to claim that Scripture is not entirely and in all its parts the Word of God because the writers, such as Peter and Paul, after all were men."[4] Commenting on I Peter 3:15, Luther advised his readers how to meet the objections of those who argue: "You preach that one should not hold to the teaching of men, even though Peter and Paul, yes, even Christ, were men too."[5] It was sufficient, Luther counselled, for Christians to base their proof on Scripture. If others refused to believe it, they should not argue. They were under no obligation to compel unbelievers to regard Scripture as something more than merely the human words of Peter and Paul, but as the Book of God. "If you hear people who are so completely blinded and hardened that they deny that this is God's Word or are in doubt about it, just keep silence, do not say a word to them, and let them go their way. Just say: 'I will give you enough proof from Scripture. If you want to believe it, this is good; if not, I will give you nothing else.'"[6] Thus firmly

---

[1] Emil Brunner, *Revelation and Reason* (E.T. 1947), p. 272.
[2] Emil Brunner, "Christliche Glaube nach reformierter Lehre", *Der Protestantismus der Gegenwart* (1926), p. 254; cf. *Inspiration and Interpretation*, ed. John F. Walvoord (1957), p. 230.
[3] Paul King Jewett, "Emil Brunner's Doctrine of Scripture", *Inspiration and Interpretation*, p. 230. Cf. Armin Moellering, "Brunner and Luther on Scriptural Authority", *Concordia Theological Monthly*, Vol XXI (1950), pp. 801–18.
[4] Pieper, op. cit., p. 278.   [5] LW. 30. 107.   [6] Ibid.

did Luther, in his Christological account of Scripture, hold to its absolute
divine authority, despite the fact that it was mediated through men.

Kooiman is therefore justified in claiming that Luther's view of the
Bible has closer bonds with his doctrine of the incarnation than with any
theory of inspiration.[1] "Behind his concept of Scripture stands his doctrine
of the descent of God in the flesh. Christ is both God and man – a miracle
at which the reformer never ceased to be astonished. So also the Scripture
is divine and human, at the same time. God's Word, clad in human words,
is really present among us."[2] "The Holy Scripture is God's Word, written,
and so to say, 'in-lettered,'" according to Luther, "just as Christ is the
eternal Word of God incarnate in the garment of His humanity. And just
as it is with Christ in the world, as He is viewed and dealt with, so it is also
with the written Word of God. It is a worm and no book, compared with
other books."[3] Like the Son of Man, the Scripture possesses neither form
nor comeliness. There is no outward attraction. It is not esteemed by
unbelieving men, any more than the Saviour is. Yet within this "simple
basket of reeds, patched with clay, pitch, and such things . . . there lies . . .
a beautiful living boy, like Moses."[4] "Christ lies in the crib, wrapped in
swaddling clothes."[5] It is He who makes the Book unique to faith.

[1] Kooiman, op. cit., p. 237.   [2] Ibid.   [3] WA. 48. 31.
   WA. 16. 82.   [5] WA. 10. i. 15.

ABBREVIATIONS

BW.   *The Bondage of the Will, by Martin Luther,* ed. Henry Cole. Revised Henry Atherton (London, 1930).

CC.   *Corpus Catholicorum. Werke katholischer Schriftseller im Zeitalter der Glaubenspaltung* (Münster, 1919 ff.).

CE.   *Catholic Encyclopedia,* ed. Charles G. Herbermann, *et al.* (New York, 1907–14).

CHB.   *The Cambridge History of the Bible: The West from the Reformation to the Present Day,* ed. S. L. Greenslade (Cambridge, 1963).

CL.   *Luthers Werke in Auswahl,* ed. Otto Clemen (Bonn, 1912–33; Berlin, 1950–56).

CR.   *Corpus Reformatorum,* ed. C. G. Bretschneider and H. E. Bindseil (Halle-Salle, 1834–60).

Cole   *Martin Luther's Complete Commentary on the first Twenty-Two Psalms,* ed. Henry Cole (London, 1823).

DCG.   *Dictionary of Christ and the Gospels,* ed. James Hastings (Edinburgh, 1906–8).

DTC.   *Dictionnaire de Théologie Catholique,* ed. A. Vacant, E. Mangenot, and É. Amann (Paris, 1903–50).

Dok.   *Dokumente zu Luthers Entwicklung bis 1519,* ed. Otto Scheel (2nd edn. Tübingen, 1929).

EA.   *D. Martin Luthers sämtliche Werke,* ed. J. G. Plachmann and J. K. Irmischer (Erlangen, 1826–57).

ERE.   *Encyclopaedia of Religion and Ethics,* ed. James Hastings (Edinburgh, 1908–26).

End.   *D. Martin Luthers Briefwechsel,* ed. Ernst Ludwig Enders and Georg Kawerau (Stuttgart and Leipzig, 1884–1932).

LC.   *Luther's Correspondence and Other Contemporary Letters,* ed. Preserved Smith and Charles M. Jacobs (Philadelphia, 1913–18).

LCC.   *The Library of Christian Classics,* ed. John T. McNeill and Henry P. van Dusen (London, 1953–).

LML.   *The Letters of Martin Luther,* ed. Margaret A. Currie (London, 1908).

LW.   *Luther's Works,* ed. Jaroslav J. Pelikan and Helmut T. Lehmann (Philadelphia and St. Louis, 1955–).

NCE.   *The New Catholic Encyclopedia* (San Francisco, 1967).

NCMH. *The New Cambridge Modern History,* I. ed. G. R. Potter (Cambridge, 1961); II. ed. G. R. Elton (Cambridge, 1958).

NSH.   *New Schaff-Herzog Encyclopaedia of Religious Knowledge,* ed. S. M. Jackson *et al.* (New York, 1908–12).

ODCC. *Oxford Dictionary of the Christian Church,* ed. F. L. Cross (Oxford, 1957).

OL.   *D. Martini Lutheri Opera Latina,* ed. H. Schmidt (Frankfurt and Erlangen, 1865–83).

PE.   *Works of Martin Luther,* ed. Henry E. Jacobs (Philadelphia, 1915–32).

PL.   *Patrologia Latina*, ed. J. P. Migne (Paris, 1844–64).

PW.   *Luther's Primary Works*, ed. Henry Wace and Charles A. Bucheim (London, 1896).

SL.   *D. Martin Luthers sämtliche Schriften*, ed. Johann Georg Walch (Revised, St. Louis, 1880–1910).

SW.   *Select Works of Martin Luther*, ed. Henry Cole (London, 1826).

SVR.   *Schriften des Vereins für Reformationsgeschichte*.

W.   *D. Martin Luthers sämtliche Schriften*, ed. Johann Georg Walch (Halle, 1739–53).

WA.   *D. Martin Luthers Werke, kritische Gesamtausgabe*, ed. J. F. K. Knaake *et al.* (Weimar, 1883–).

WAB.   *D. Martin Luthers Briefwechsel*, ed. Konrad Burdach *et al.* (Weimar, 1930–48).

WADB. *Die Deutsche Bibel*, ed. Karl Drescher *et al.* (Weimar, 1906–61).

WATR. *Tischreden*, ed. Karl Drescher (Weimar, 1912–21).

SELECT BIBLIOGRAPHY

PRIMARY SOURCES
LUTHER'S WORKS:

D. Martin Luthers Werke, kritische Gesamtausgabe, ed. J. F. K. Knaake, *et al.* 57 vols. (Weimar, 1883-).

Die Deutsche Bibel, D. Martin Luthers Werke, kritische Gesamtausgabe, ed. Kar Drescher *et al.*, 9 vols. (Weimar, 1906-61).

D. Martin Luthers Briefwechsel, D. Martin Luthers Werke, kritische Gesamtausgabe, ed. Konrad Burdach *et al.*, 11 vols. (Weimar, 1930-48).

Tischreden, D. Martin Luthers Werke, kritische Gesamtausgabe, ed. Karl Drescher, 6 vols. (Weimar, 1912-21).

D. Martin Luthers sämtliche Schriften, ed. Johann Georg Walch, 24 vols. (Halle, 1739-53). Revised (St. Louis, 1880-1910).

D. Martin Luthers sämtliche Werke, ed. J. G. Plachmann and J. K. Irmischer, 67 vols. (Erlangen, 1826-57).

D. Martini Lutheri Opera Latina, ed. H. Schmidt, 7 vols. (Frankfurt and Erlangen, 1865-83).

Martin Luther, Ausgewählte Werke, ed. Hans Heinrich Borcherdt, 8 vols. (Munich, 1922-).

Luthers Werke in Auswahl, ed. Otto Clemen, 8 vols. (Bonn 1912-33, Berlin 1955-6).

Martin Luthers Ausgewählte Werke, ed. Hans Heinrich Borcherdt and Georg Merz, 5 vols. (Munich, 1934-. 3rd edn. 1948-).

Die Werke Martin Luthers in neuer Auswahl für die Gegenwart, ed. Kurt Aland, 9 vols. (Berlin, 1948-).

D. Martin Luthers Evangelien-Auslegung, ed. Erwin Mülhaupt (Göttingen, 1939).

Luthers Vorlesung über den Römerbrief 1515-1516, ed. Johannes Ficker, 2 vols. (Liepzig, 1908).

Luthers Vorlesung über den Hebräerbrief, ed. Emanuel Hirsch and Hans Rückert (Berlin, 1929).

Luthers Hebräerbrief Vorlesung 1517-1518. Deutsche Übersetzung, ed. Erich Vogelsang (Berlin, 1930).

Luthers Vorlesung über den Galaterbrief 1516-1517, ed. Hans von Schubert (Heidelberg, 1918).

D. Martin Luthers Tischreden oder Colloquia . . . nach Aurifabers erste Ausgabe, ed. Karl Eduard Förstemann and Heinrich Ernst Bindseil, 4 vols. (Berlin, 1844-8).

Martin Luthers Tischreden, ed. Hans Heinrich Borcherdt and Wilhelm Rehm (Munich, n.d.).

Martin Luthers Briefe, ed. Wilhelm Martin Leberecht de Wette, 5 vols. (Berlin, 1825-38).

D. Martin Luthers Briefwechsel, ed. Ernst Ludwig Enders and Georg Kawerau, 19 vols. (Stuttgart and Leipzig, 1884-1932).

Hans von Campenhausen, *Martin Luther: Die Hauptschriften* (Berlin, 1939).

Kurt Aland, *Die Hauptschriften* (Berlin, 1951).
Dokumente zu Luthers Entwicklung bis 1519, ed. Otto Scheel, 2nd edn. (Tübingen, 1929).
Kurt Aland, *Hilsbuch zum Lutherstudium* (Gütersloh, 1956).
Josef Benzig, *Lutherbibliographie verzeichnis der gedruckten Schriften Martin Luthers bis zu dessen Tod*, Bibliotheca Bibliographica Aureliana, X, XVI, XIX, (Baden-Baden, 1966).

TRANSLATIONS:

Luther's Works, ed. Jaroslav J. Pelikan and Helmut T. Lehmann, 55 vols. (Philadelphia and St. Louis, 1955–).
Select Works of Martin Luther, ed. Henry Cole, 4 vols. (London, 1826).
Luther's Primary Works, ed. Henry Wace and Charles A. Bucheim. (London, 1896).
The Precious and Sacred Writings of Martin Luther, ed. John Nicholas Lenker, 14 vols (Minneapolis, 1903–10).
Works of Martin Luther, ed. Henry E. Jacobs, 6 vols. (Philadelphia, 1915–32).
Reformation Writings of Martin Luther, ed. Bertram Lee Woolf. Vol I, *The Basis of the Protestant Reformation* (London, 1952) Vol. II, *The Spirit of Reformation* (London 1956).
Martin Luther: Selections from His Writings, ed. John Dillenberger (New York, 1961).
A Compend of Luther's Theology, ed. Hugh Thompson Kerr (Philadelphia, 1943).
Martin Luther's Complete Commentary on the first Twenty-Two Psalms, ed. Henry Cole, 2 vols. (London, 1826).
A Commentary on the Psalms called Psalms of Degrees by Martin Luther, ed. Henry Cole (London, 1823).
A Commentary on St. Paul's Epistle to the Galatians by Martin Luther, ed. Erasmus Middleton (London, 1807). Revised, ed. Philip S. Watson (London, 1956).
Martin Luther, *Lectures on Romans*, ed. Wilhelm Pauck, Library of Christian Classics, Vol. XV (London, 1961).
Luther: Early Theological Works, ed. James Atkinson, Library of Christian Classics, Vol. XVI (London, 1962).
The Bondage of the Will, by Martin Luther, ed. Henry Cole. Revised Henry Atherton (London, 1930).
Martin Luther, *The Bondage of the Will*, ed. James I. Packer and O. R. Johnston (London, 1957).
Special and Chosen Sermons of D. Martin Luther, ed. William Gace (London, 1649).
The Table Talk of Martin Luther, ed. William Hazlitt (London, 1848).
Conversations with Luther, ed. Preserved Smith and Herbert P. Gallinger (Boston, 1915).
The Letters of Martin Luther, ed. Margaret A. Currie (London, 1908).
Luther's Correspondence and Other Contemporary Letters, ed. Preserved Smith and Charles M. Jacobs, 2 vols. (Philadelphia, 1913–18).
Luther: Letters of Spiritual Counsel, ed. Theodore Tappert, Library of Christian Classics, Vol. XVIII (London, 1955).

SECONDARY SOURCES
LUTHER'S LIFE AND WORK:

Bainton, Roland H., *Here I Stand: A Life of Martin Luther* (New York, 1950).

Beard, Charles, *Martin Luther and the Reformation in Germany* (London, 1889).

Boehmer, Heinrich, *Road to Reformation* (E.T. Philadelphia, 1946).

Boehmer, Heinrich, *Luther and the Reformation in the Light of Modern Research* (E.T. London, 1930).

Dickens, A. G., *Martin Luther and the Reformation* (London, 1967).

Farner, Oskar, *Martin Luther* (Zurich, 1946).

Febvre, Lucien, *Martin Luther: A Destiny* (E.T. London, 1930).

Fife, Robert H., *Young Luther: The Intellectual and Religious Development of Martin Luther to 1518* (New York, 1928).

Fife, Robert H., *The Revolt of Martin Luther* (New York, 1957).

Green, Vivian H. H., *Luther and the Reformation* (London, 1964).

Hausrath, Adolf, *Luthers Leben*, 2 vols. (Berlin, 1904).

Hyma, Albert, *Luther's Historical Development from Erfurt to Augsburg* (New York, 1928).

Kooiman, Willem Jan, *By Faith Alone* (E.T. London, 1954).

Köstlin, Julius and Kawerau, Georg, *Martin Luther*, 2 vols. (Berlin, 1903).

Kuhn, Félix, *Luther: sa vie et son oeuvre*, 3 vols. (Paris, 1883-4).

Lau, Franz, *Luther* (E.T. London, 1963).

Mackinnon, James, *Martin Luther and the Reformation*, 4 vols. (London, 1925-30).

Meissinger, Karl A., *Der Katholische Luther* (Munich, 1952).

Ritter, Gerhard, *Luther: His Life and Work* (E.T. London, 1963).

Rupp, E. Gordon, *Luther's Progress to the Diet of Worms* (London, 1951).

Scheel, Otto, *Martin Luther, Vom Katholizismus zur Reformation*, 2 vols. (Tübingen, 1917).

Schwiebert, Ernest G., *Luther and His Times: The Reformation from a New Perspective* (St. Louis, 1950).

Strohl, Henri, *L'Évolution religieuse de Luther jusqu'en 1515* (Strasbourg, 1922).

Strohl, Henri, *L'Épanouissement de la pensée religeuse de Luther jusqu'en 1520* (Strasbourg, 1924).

Thiel, Rudolf, *Luther* (E.T. Philadelphia, 1955).

LUTHER'S THEOLOGY:

Althaus, Paul, *The Theology of Martin Luther* (E.T. Philadelphia, 1966).

Bornkamm, Heinrich, *Luther's World of Thought* (E.T. St. Louis, 1958).

Carlson, Edgar M., *The Reinterpretation of Luther* (Philadelphia, 1948).

Grass, Hans, *Die Abendmahlslehre bei Luther und Calvin* (Gütersloh, 1954).

Gyllenkrok, F. K. A., *Rechfertigung und Heiligung in der frühen evangelischen Theologie Luthers* (Uppsala, 1952).

Harnack, Theodosius, *Luthers Theologie*, 2 vols., revised W. F. Schmidt (Munich, 1926-7).

Holl, Karl, *Gesammelte Aufsätze zur Kirchengeschichte*, Vol. I, *Luther* (Tübingen, 1921).

LUTHER AND THE BIBLE

Jundt, André, *Le développement de la pensée religieuse de Luther jusqu'en 1517* (Paris, 1905).
Köstlin, Julius, *The Theology of Luther*, 2 vols (E.T. Philadelphia, 1897).
Kramm, H. H. W., *The Theology of Martin Luther* (London, 1947).
Loewenich, Walther von, *Luther's Theologia Crucis* (Munich, 1919).
Pinomaa, Lennart B., *Faith Victorious: An Introduction to Luther's Theology* (E.T. Philadelphia, 1965).
Prenter, Regin, *Spiritus Creator* (E.T. Philadelphia, 1953).
Rupp, E. Gordon, *The Righteousness of God: Luther Studies* (London, 1953).
Saarnivaara, Uuras, *Luther Discovers the Gospel* (St. Louis, 1951).
Seeberg, Erich, *Luthers Theologie in ihren Grundzügen* (Stuttgart, 1950).
Stange, Karl, *Studien zur Theologie Luthers* (Gütersloh, 1928).
Strohl, Henri, *La substance de l'évangile selon Luther* (Paris, 1934).
Vajta, Vilmos, *Luther on Worship: An Interpretation* (E.T. Philadelphia, 1958).
Watson, Philip S., *Let God be God! An Interpretation of the Theology of Martin Luther* (London, 1947).

LUTHER AND THE BIBLE

Bluhm, Heinz, *Martin Luther: Creative Translator* (St. Louis, 1965).
Boehmer, Heinrich, *Luthers erste Vorlesung* (Leipzig, 1924).
Bornkamm, Heinrich, *Luther und das Alte Testament* (Tübingen, 1948).
Bring, Ragnar, *Luthers Anschauung von der Bibel* (Berlin, 1951).
Davies, Rupert E., *The Problem of Authority in the Continental Reformers: A Study in Luther, Zwingli and Calvin* (London, 1946).
Ebeling, Gerhard, *Evangelische Evangelien-Auslegung: Eine Untersuchung zu Luthers Hermeneutik* (Munich, 1942).
Geroldet, K. T., *Luther considéré comme exégète* (Strasbourg, 1866).
Hirsch, Emanuel, *Luthers Deutsche Bibel* (Munich, 1928).
Kooiman, Willem Jan, *Luther and the Bible* (E.T. Philadelphia, 1961).
Koerner, E., *Luther und die Schrift* (Chicago, 1926).
Loewenich, Walther von, *Luther als Ausleger der Synoptiker* (Munich, 1954).
Meissinger, Karl A., *Luthers Exegese in der Frühzeit* (Leipzig, 1911).
Mueller, J. Theodore, "Luther and the Bible", *Inspiration and Interpretation*, ed. John F. Walvoord (Grand Rapids, 1957).
Noltensmeier, Hermann, *Reformatorische Einheit: Das Schriftverständnis bei Luther und Calvin* (Graz-Cologne, 1953).
Pelikan, Jaroslav J., *Luther the Expositor: Introduction to the Reformer's Exegetical Writings*, Luther's Works Companion Volume (St. Louis, 1959).
Preuss, Hans, *Die Entwicklung des Schriftprinzips bei Luther bis zur Leipziger Disputation* (Leipzig, 1901).
Reichert, Otto, *D. Martin Luthers Deutsche Bibel* (Berlin, 1910).
Reu, J. Michael, *Luther's German Bible* (Columbus, 1934).
Reu, J. Michael, *Luther and the Scriptures* (Columbus, 1944).
Romberg, Ernst, *Die Lehre Luthers von der Heiligen Schrift* (Wittenberg, 1868).
Stange, Karl, *Luther und das Evangelium* (Berlin, 1953).

Scheel, Otto, *Luthers Stellung zur Heiligen Schrift* (Tübingen, 1902).
Schempp, Paul, *Luthers Stellung zur Heiligen Schrift* (Munich, 1929).
Sittler, Joseph, *The Doctrine of the Word in the Structure of Lutheran Theology* (Philadelphia, 1948).
Thimme, Karl, *Luthers Stellung zur Heiligen Schrift* (Gütersloh, 1903).
Undritz, Otto, *Die Entwicklung des Schriftprinzips bei Luther in der Anfangsjahren der Reformation*, Leipzig, 1897.
Walther, Wilhelm, *Luthers Deutsche Bibel* (Berlin, 1917).
Wood, A. Skevington, *Luther's Principles of Biblical Interpretation* (London, 1960).

GENERAL (A) THE REFORMATION

Atkinson, James, *The Great Light: Luther and Reformation* (Exeter, 1968).
Bainton, Roland H., *The Reformation of the Sixteenth Century* (London, 1953).
Bainton, Roland H., *Studies on the Reformation* (London, 1964).
Bainton, Roland H., *Bibliography of the Continental Reformation* (Chicago, 1935).
Beard, Charles, *The Reformation of the Sixteenth Century* (London, 1885).
Brandi, Karl, *Die Deutsche Reformation* (Leipzig, 1927).
Brandi, Karl, *Gegenreformation und Religionskriege* (Leipzig, 1930).
Chadwick, Owen, *The Reformation*. Pelican History of the Church, Vol. III (London, 1964).
Dickens, A. G., *Reformation and Society in Sixteenth Century Europe* (London, 1966).
Elton, Geoffrey R., *Reformation Europe 1517–1559* (London, 1963).
Green, Vivian H. H., *Renaissance and Reformation: A Survey of European History between 1450 and 1660* (London, 1952).
Grimm, Harold J., *The Reformation Era 1500–1560* (New York, 1954).
Hagenbach, Karl R., *History of the Reformation in Germany and Switzerland Chiefly*, 2 vols. (E.T. Edinburgh, 1878–9).
Holborn, Hajo, *A History of Modern Germany. The Reformation* (E.T. New York, 1959).
Hyma, Albert, *The Christian Renaissance* (New York, 1925).
Joachimsen, P., *Die Reformation als Epoche der deutschen Geschichte* (Munich, 1951).
Léonard, Émile G., *Histoire générale du Protestantisme*, Vol. I, *La Réformation* (Paris, 1961).
Lindsay, Thomas M., *A History of the Reformation*, 2 vols. (Edinburgh, 1907–8).
Lortz, Joseph, *Die Reformation in Deutschland*, 2 vols. (Freiburg, 1941).
Mackinnon, James, *The Origins of the Reformation* (Edinburgh, 1939).
Moreau, E. de; Jourda, Pierre; and Janelle, Pierre, *La crise religieuse du XVIᵉ siècle. Historie de l'Église*, ed. Augustin Fliche and Victor Martin, Vol XVI (Paris, 1950).
Pauck, Wilhelm, *The Heritage of the Reformation* (Boston, 1950).
Payne, Ernest A., *The Anabaptists of the Sixteenth Century and their Influence in the Modern World* (London, 1949).
Pelikan, Jaroslav J., *Obedient Rebels: Catholic Substance and Protestant Principle in Luther's Reformation* (London, 1964).
Ranke, Leopold von, *History of the Reformation in Germany* (E.T. London, 1905).

Schaff, Philip, *History of the Christian Church. Modern Christianity: The German Reformation 1517–1530*, 2 vols. (E.T. Edinburgh, 1888).

Schmidt, K. D., *Grundriss der Kirchengeschichte*, Vol. III, *Geschichte der Kirche im Zeitalter der Reformation und der Gegenreformation* (Göttingen, 1952).

Smith, Preserved, *The Age of the Reformation* (London, 1920).

Tour, Pierre Imbart de la, *Les origines de la réforme*, 3 vols. (Paris, 1905–14).

Verduin, Leonard, *The Reformers and their Stepchildren* (Exeter, 1966).

Wace, Henry, *Principles of the Reformation Practical and Historical* (London, 1910).

Whitney, J. P., *The Reformation* (London, 1907).

Whitney, J. P., *Reformation Essays* (London, 1959).

Williams, George Hunston, *The Radical Reformation* (London, 1962).

GENERAL (B) THE BIBLE IN HISTORY:

Bainton, Roland H., "The Bible in the Reformation", *The Cambridge History of the Bible*, ed. S. L. Greenslade (Cambridge, 1963).

Berger, Samuel, *La Bible au Seizième Siècle* (Paris, 1879).

Blackman, Edwin C., *Biblical Interpretation: The Old Difficulties and the New Opportunity* (London, 1957).

Braaten, Carl E., *History and Hermeneutics, New Directions in Theology Today*, ed. William Hordern, Vol. II (London, 1968).

Elliott-Binns, Leonard E., *The Reformers and the Bible* (Cambridge, 1923).

Farrar, Frederic W., *History of Interpretation* (London, 1886).

Grant, Robert M., *The Bible in the Church: A Short History of Interpretation* (New York, 1954).

Hall, Basil, "Biblical Scholarship: Editions and Commentaries", *The Cambridge History of the Bible*, ed. S. L. Greenslade (Cambridge, 1963).

Harbison, E. Harris, *The Christian Scholar in the Age of Reformation* (New York, 1956).

Holzhey, Karl, *Die Inspiration der Heiligen Schrift in der Anschauung des Mittelalters* (Munich, 1895).

Kropatscheck, Friedrich, *Das Schriftprinzip der lutherischen Kirche* (Leipzig, 1904).

Preus, Robert, *The Inspiration of Scripture: A Study of the Theology of the Seventeenth Century Lutheran Dogmaticians* (Edinburgh, 1955).

Ramm, Bernard, *Protestant Biblical Interpretation* (Boston, 1950).

Ried, John K. S., *The Authority of Scripture: A Study of the Reformation and Post-Reformation Understanding of the Bible* (London, 1957).

Rohnert, Wilhelm, *Die Inspiration der Heiligen Schrift und ihre Bestreiter* (Leipzig, 1889).

Schwarz, Werner, *Principles and Problems of Biblical Translation: Some Reformation Controversies and their Background* (Cambridge, 1955).

Smalley, Beryl, *The Study of the Bible in the Middle Ages* (Oxford, 1952).

Spicq, C., *Esquisse d'une histoire de l'exégèse latine au moyen age* (Paris, 1944).

Wood, A. Skevington, *The Principles of Biblical Interpretation: as enunciated by Irenaeus, Origen, Augustine, Luther and Calvin* (Grand Rapids, 1967).

Wood, James D., *The Interpretation of the Bible: A Historical Introduction* (London, 1958).

INDEX

NAMES

Abelard, Peter, 38
Abraham, 136
Adam, 146
Adolf, Bishop of Merseberg, 108
Agricola, Johann, 78
Aland, Kurt, 167
Albert the Great, 79
Albrecht of Brandenberg, 62
Aldus Manutius, 102
Aleander, Girolamo, 70–1
Alsager, Thomas, 11
Althaus, Paul, 128, 130, 152–4
Alveld, Augustine von, 108, 110
Ambrose of Milan, 32, 45
Amos, 78, 148
Amsdorf, Nicholas von, 100
Angus, Joseph, 137
Anne, St., 23
Anselm of Canterbury, 38
Anselm of Laon, 82
Aquinas, Thomas, 37–8, 42, 79, 133
Aristotle, 38, 44, 67, 93
Arius, 31, 127
Arnoldi, Bartholomeus, 34, 44
Arpachsad, 144
Atkinson, James, 60
Augustine of Hippo, 32, 36, 38–40, 45 ,50, 52–3, 58, 83, 98, 103, 125–6, 162, 166
Aulèn, Gustaf, 131
Aurifaber, Johannes, 14, 89
Aurogallus, Matthäus, 102
Autolycus, 63

Bachmann, Theodor, 109, 115
Baillie, John, 134
Bainton, Roland H., 21, 48, 55–6, 72
Barnim, Duke of Pomerania, 99
Basil of Caesarea, 36
Bayne, Peter, 92
Beard, Charles, 13
Beier, Leonhard, 66
Bergendorff, Conrad, 112, 132
Berthold, Archbishop of Mainz, 96–7
Biel, Gabriel, 34, 36–7
Blackman, Edwin C., 79, 175
Bluhm, Heinz, 94, 98–9, 103
Boehmer, Heinrich, 14, 23–4, 30, 35, 37, 45, 51, 56, 65

Bonhoeffer, Dietrich, 64
Bornkamm, Heinrich, 64, 75, 98, 101
Braun, Johann, 18
Brenz, Johann, 78
Brunner, Emil, 176–7
Buber, Martin, 90
Bucer, Martin, 67, 87, 112
Buchwald, Georg, 86
Bugenhagen, Johann, 86–7
Butterfield, Sir Herbert, 7

Cadier, Jean, 38
Caiaphas, 127
Cajetan, Thomas de Vio, 67–8, 126, 157
Calvin, John, 42, 58, 75, 85
Capito, Wolfgang, 112
Cardinal, Hugo, 32
Carlyle, Thomas, 40
Cassian, John, 79
Cave, Sydney, 42, 170
Chadwick, Owen, 69–70
Chapman, George, 11
Chrysostom, John, 32, 45, 81
Clarke, Charles Cowden, 11
Clement VI, 68
Coppens, Joseph, 168
Cordatus, Conrad, 53–4
Cruciger, Kaspar, 89
Cyprian of Carthage, 32
Cyril of Alexandria, 171

D'Ailly, Pierre, 34, 36–7
Dammerman, Bernhard, 103
David, 143, 174
Davies, Rupert E., 140
Decker, Johann, 46, 81
Denifle, Heinrich, 25
Dickens, A. G., 109–10, 112
Diedenhofen, Winand von, 25, 29
Dietrich, Viet, 14–5, 17, 89
Doberstein, John W., 86, 91
Dolsch, Johann, 78

Ebeling, Gerhard, 78, 85
Eberhard, Count, 36
Eck, Johann (Meier) of Ingoldstadt, 70–1, 108, 110, 126

187

SUBJECTS

SCRIPTURE REFERENCES